# The Inner World of Teaching:
## Exploring assumptions which promote change and development

David Tuohy

UK     Falmer Press, 1 Gunpowder Square, London, EC4A 3DE
USA    Falmer Press, Taylor & Francis Inc., 325 Chestnut Street, 8th Floor,
       Philadelphia, PA 19106

First published in 1999

**A catalogue record for this book is available from the British Library**

ISBN 0 7507 0921 9 cased
ISBN 0 7507 0920 0 paper

**Library of Congress Cataloging-in-Publication Data are available
on request**

Jacket design by Caroline Archer
Figures 1.1, 2.1, 6.3 and 8.1 by Matthew Whitton

Typeset in 10/12 pt Times by
Graphicraft Limited, Hong Kong

*Printed in Great Britain by Biddles Ltd., Guildford and King's Lynn on
paper which has a specified pH value on final paper manufacture of not
less than 7.5 and is therefore 'acid free'.*

# Contents

# List of Figures

# Acknowledgments

Many people have contributed to the development of this book. A special word of thanks to all the students in University College Galway, in St. Joseph's University Philadelphia and more recently in the National University of Ireland, Dublin, on whom this material was first tried, and who played such a major role in refining it. My thanks also to the many teachers and principals in Ireland, England, Zambia, Kenya and in Australia, who have shared their stories and helped me appreciate the work of education.

A special word of thanks to Gerry Beggan. His encouragement rekindled an interest I had in this approach to education. He gave me the confidence to examine some of my own assumptions and share them with others. This opportunity gave me the conviction that I had something to say and he helped me put an earlier version of this material together.

A special word of thanks to Nick Rashford for the opportunity to work in St. Joseph's University in Philadelphia over two years. My thanks also to Jim McGloin who helped broaden my own experience when he invited me to work in Zambia and to Sister Pat Murray with whom I worked in Kenya and in Ireland. Pat also read an earlier version of the text and made some very helpful comments. In the summer of 1997, I worked with Patrick Duignan, Denis McLaughlin and Helga Neidhart in the Australian Catholic University, which was also part of my own learning curve. My thanks also to Joe Tetlow, who I met in Texas in 1990 and who shared some of the material you will read in Chapter 2. Suzanne Bailey, Connie Hoffman and Judy Olson-Ness are trainers I met through the Association of Supervision and Curriculum Development. They have had a profound effect on my own approach to teaching and training. Many of the exercises are developments of their work, especially the work on metaphors in Chapter 4.

My special thanks to David Coghlan who read the text and gave valuable advice and shared insights. My thanks also to Pat Riordan, Tom McGrath and Brendan Staunton who have shared insightful seminars and to Dympna Devine and Maureen Killeavy for their patient encouragement at work.

Finally, my thanks to the staff at Falmer Press. Michael Wright was a very thorough and understanding copy-editor. Sarah Daniels and Fiona Drysdale were patient and helpful in the production and editorial phases. Malcolm Clarkson and Anna Clarkson were very encouraging in developing the book and ensuring I kept some focus throughout. Whatever shortcomings remain are my own.

*David Tuohy*
*Dublin*
*May 1998*

# Introduction

There is no shortage of literature on change in education. Recent decades have seen major shifts in our understanding of knowledge and learning which have led to a new focus in curriculum development and teaching strategies (see Brooks and Brooks, 1993). The globalization of world economies and the changing nature of work itself make demands on the type of education that young people receive in preparation for the world of work (see, for example, Handy, 1991, 1994; Naisbitt, 1982; Toffler, 1970, 1981). The changing social fabric of society, evidenced by higher family break-up and single-parent families, has forced schools to take on new roles of giving personal support and building community for students. Pressure on government finances has brought fresh demands for accountability and new definitions of effectiveness for schools (Murgatroyd and Morgan, 1992, Chapter 1). These trends all work to change the expectations of what education should be and how schools should be organized.

Schools are gradually changing to meet these challenges by adapting their structures and curriculum. Frequently, the literature portrays schools and teachers as the victims of such a change process. Government reports condemn education and schools as being ineffective, with no recognition of the systemic effects of previous policies[1]. New initiatives are put in place, often with inadequate preparation and funding. Before these initiatives have time to take root, a new administration takes over and the direction of policy changes. As a result schools experience a lack of coherence in educational policy and a capriciousness in its application and emphasis. In this context, it is not surprising that many teachers react negatively to change initiatives. They look on a new initiative as the current flavour of the month. They wonder how long it will last as the changes seem to address political agendas more than promote educational progress.

Fullan (1993) has reflected on the lessons which can be learnt from the failure of policy reform. He encapsulates the main lesson in the phrase 'What is important, cannot be mandated'[2]. Again and again in my own work with schools and with teachers, I have found this to be true. Teachers in general are positive and idealistic. At times, however, one feels that they strongly resent being changed by others — having the criteria by which their work is evaluated alter dramatically and being told to develop in a very different way. In helping teachers to respond to the demands for change, I have come to appreciate that what is important in planning is developing the strategic capacity to reflect critically and respond creatively to the change forces which impact on their lives. In this context, the implementation of new programmes is relatively simple. To get to this stage, however, teachers need to reflect on their fundamental strategic choices and values, to get in touch with both the mind and the heart of their work in a way which gives direction, meaning and motivation to the process. For Fullan and Hargreaves (1991) successful change involves 'emotional planning'[3], whereby teachers get in touch with the inner world of teaching, with what is important and meaningful, and commit themselves to its implementation.

Senge (1991) has described the five disciplines of the learning organization. One of the key factors which influences learning is what he calls 'mental models'[4], the often subconscious constructs we have on how the world works, which lead us to familiar ways of thinking and acting. He uses the parable of the boiled frog to reflect on ways in which learning can be blocked. When people are faced with totally new circumstances, they react like the frog which is dropped into hot water — it jumps away. However, if the frog is placed in cold water, and the water is slowly heated, the gradual raising of the temperature creates a stupor and inertia in the frog and it does not try to escape. Similarly, circumstances may lull people into a context they would not ordinarily choose for themselves. A key element in developing a learning and responsive school, therefore, is to create positive mental models which allow teachers to be proactive in responding to and creating their own contexts.

Central to the study of mental models is the study of symbols and language. Thomas Carlyle, the nineteenth-century English essayist and philosopher wrote: 'It is in and through symbols that man, consciously or unconsciously, lives, works and has his meaning'[5]. Jung entitled his basic text on psychotherapy *Man and his Symbols*. Our symbols and mental models affect our actions in a profound way, because they affect what we see and how we image the future. One of the ways we communicate our symbols is through language. Language gives us power of expression by which we explore our inner world. However, language can also limit our ability to dream. We frequently need to develop a new language in order to free our images. For Seamus Heaney, the twentieth-century Nobel price-winning poet, the work of the poet is

> ... the discovery of ways to go out of his normal cognitive bounds and raid the inarticulate: a dynamic alertness that mediates between the origin of feeling in memory and experience and the formal ploys that express these in a work of art. (1980, p. 47)

This, I believe, is also the work of personal and school development.

In working with teachers, language and symbols are important aspects of personal growth. But symbols exist and exert control at an organizational level as well. Sarason (1971, 1996) pointed to powerful forces and conservative rhythms and practices in society and in schools. He applies the phrase 'the more things change, the more they stay the same' to reflect on the place of education in society and the way basic images and values of schools and teaching have remained un-affected by the changed external behaviour patterns within schools. His focus on change is that of the total system — the cultural dimension of the school. There is a strong interaction between personal and organizational factors which keeps things the same. To bring about successful change, one therefore needs to focus on the inner world, or culture, of the school and to 'reculture' that world.

Culture is a commodity which gives distinctiveness to a society[6]. It is a social cement that binds individuals together, and defines for them an accepted way of life. Within their own cultures, individuals develop their inner subjective view of the world and its contents — their personal outlooks. This world view embraces both the cognitive and the affective orderings of experience. People learn the 'common sense' of their families and communities — an understanding of how the world is structured and their place in it. They learn a sense of right and wrong, what is acceptable and not acceptable. Stories, myths and legends about their personal family history and their own nation are inherited. Interpersonal bonds are formed within the extended family, between individuals and communities, and the individual develops a sense of emotional belonging and loyalty to people, places and nation. This last loyalty can be seen in the support given to national teams in international competition, in the sense of national pride in the accomplishments of a fellow national, and also in the way that individuals are prepared to sacrifice their lives in a nation's army, if called upon in time of war. Culture, as applied to a society, is a multi-faceted and highly complex commodity, and it is pervasive throughout the life of that society.

The term culture is also applied to large movements within a society. Thus, we speak of a youth culture, built around symbols of pop music and fashion trends, approaches to money and commercialism, attitudes to sexuality, work, family and leisure. This often acts as a counter-culture to the 'establishment'. Similarly, we speak of a working-class, or middle-class culture. The symbols of participation in social class are linked with levels of wealth and types of employment. People are judged on the size of their house, the area they live in, the type of work they do and their salary. These symbols are taken as indicative of deeper values and a complex reality of different lifestyles.

Organizational culture is a comparatively recent concept[7] — mainly the product of cross-cultural investigations into the success of Japanese companies in the United States during the late 1970s and early 1980s. Its study parallels the study of culture in larger systems, with a focus on identity and distinctiveness. The extent to which the culture is shared gives rise to a cohesiveness and social bonding in organizations. Also, subcultures and counter-cultures emerge within large organizations as individuals resist becoming anonymous cogs in the organizational structure, and define a unique identity for themselves.

The focus on culture marked a paradigm shift in organizational research in schools[8]. It heralded a greater concentration on internal value systems, on the meaning which individual members placed on their work and on the artefacts of organizational life, as well as the meaning, values, beliefs shared with other members of the organization. It marked a departure from the study of '*how* things are done around here' to an exploration of '*why* things are done this way around here'. The movement goes beyond the visible symbols and artefacts to an understanding of the assumptions and values that promote particular artefacts.

*forces of our assumptions*
*→ outside*        *"*

When working in schools the pervasiveness of cultural forces is very obvious. Each school is simultaneously the same as all other schools, as some other schools and as no other school. There is much common ground in our experience of schools, yet each school is unique in its configuration of values and assumptions. The process of developmental planning is much enhanced when those involved in the process become aware of the assumptions they bring to the process, as well as the assumptions that impinge on the process from the larger system. This book reflects on some of these forces as experienced in my own work in Ireland, England, the United States and more recently in Africa and Australia. The book is written as an invitation to the reader to become actively involved in the naming, exploration and transformation of symbols. Too often, our engagement with academic models and commentaries is similar to that of a spectator at a football game. We admire the performance of others and we cheer them on as we get caught up in the game. Then we go away, talk about the game with our friends, analyse its high and low points, and wait for the next stimulus when a new game comes along. The invitation of this book, however, is to become a player. As well as offering a commentary to illustrate the theoretical frameworks, exercises are presented which have helped others explore their inner world of meanings, symbols and mental models. The exercises hopefully do not stop at mere description of what exists, but also give hints as to possible developments of the organizational culture, either in the affirmation of the current culture, or in the development of alternative deeper and richer symbols.

The book is primarily for teachers. The images explored refer mainly to those developed by teachers about themselves, their work and their schools. These images have been explored in the workplace of school itself, and also in the classroom where teachers have studied for further degrees. Whatever the engagement of the reader with teachers — as a teacher yourself, or as a consultant, trainer, principal, parent or student — it is hoped that the exercises and reflections here will lead to a deeper awareness of the symbols which operate in schools. As you explore the symbols and the meaning behind them, hopefully you will come to realize the hidden power of your own assumptions about education. In your new self-consciousness you will be able to turn that power to even greater effect in developing your contribution to an educational mission.

The book is written in three parts. Part One deals with theoretical perspectives on organizational culture, and has two main aims. The first is to give a framework which helps understand the nature and pervasiveness of assumptions in organizational culture. The second aim is to develop a framework for intervention in schools and in teacher development. Chapter 1 deals with the identification and pervasiveness of cultural artefacts, values and assumptions in five different areas of school life — the relationship with the environment, the purpose of human activity, the nature of truth and time, human nature and human relationships. Chapter 2 looks to understanding the power of these artefacts, values and assumptions in the life of the school. A six-fold schema (Context–Perspective–Perception–Desire–Choice–Habit) is proposed which helps reflect on the origin and development of aspects of culture, and to look for leverage points in enhancing the culture. Chapter 3 examines ways in which interventions are made in schools. By applying Rashford and Coghlan's

(1994) scheme of four interdependent and interacting levels (individual, team, inter-team coordination and organization) to the work of teachers and schools, we build up an awareness of the systems dynamics that operate in the change process. This helps strategic planning for the future, as well as learning from previous change projects.

Part Two looks at ways of exploring assumptions with individuals and groups. This section of the book uses exercises which you the reader may do for yourself, or which may be presented to various audiences in school settings as a way of uncovering and grounding the assumptions that control school culture. The chapters share some of the reflections developed by teachers and staff groups in my own work with them. Chapter 4 is directed at individuals who wish to examine their inner world of personal attitudes, beliefs and values in education. Three metaphors — the garden, the orchestra and the factory — are used as ways of catching powerful beliefs and hidden assumptions about school and how 'mental models' of school give rise to different assumptions and practices. Chapter 5 uses exercises suited to working with established teams which create a climate or conditions of work for others in the school. Three established typologies of organizations — Blau and Scott, Carlson and Etzioni — are used to explore the way a school community may think of the inner meaning of its work, structures and organization. Chapter 6 looks at system issues in the formation of policy, and can be used with Boards of Management, Governors, etc. in helping them understand the impact of policy on school culture. Three models of schools — as closed or open systems, as value systems and as an economic system — are presented.

Part Three reflects on assumptions around three sets of roles in schools — students and learning; teachers and their development; and leaders and leadership. In the course of the chapters, I present exercises which may reveal some of the hidden assumptions which exist about the three role sets and the way they develop within a school. In Chapter 7, the role of the student as learner is examined. In particular, we reflect on the way organizational culture interacts with three factors in learning — Presage, Process and Product — and the way profiles of motivation to study can develop in a school. The focus of Chapter 8 is on teachers. In particular, we look at assumptions that are made about teacher development, and the way staff development programmes are organized. Chapter 9 looks at leadership, and the opportunities teachers have of redefining their leadership roles within the school context.

The aim of the book is to promote reflection. If you enter into this reflection, hopefully you will be affirmed in much of your own practice. In some instances, you may be encouraged or challenged to develop new paradigms for your work, leading to even more meaningful and rewarding participation in the great project of education.

**Notes**

1 In general, government policy in education implies reform of an inadequate system, which mostly centres on poor teaching. For the United States, this trend is reviewed in Glickman (1993).

2 Fullan (1993) reflects on the process of change, and has developed eight major lessons from the failure of reform movements.

3 This is reflected in the title of their book *What's Worth Fighting For: Working Together for Your School*. Cf. also, Hargreaves (1997).

4 Senge (1991) develops five disciplines which characterize a learning and responsive organization. These are system thinking, personal mastery, mental models, shared vision and team learning. A fuller application of this model to teacher education can be found in Tuohy (1995).

5 A particular development of symbols can be found in a series of essays on heroes and hero-worship, where Carlyle discusses topics such as Hero as Divinity, as Poet, as Priest, as Prophet, as Man of Letters, and as King.

6 For a review of different approaches to culture, see Gallagher (1997), Gray and McGuigan (1993), and Zais (1976).

7 Peters and Waterman (1982), Sackman (1991), Schein (1985), Sergiovanni and Corbally (1986) are examples of this approach.

8 Sarason (1971) is a key example of this development. Bolman and Deal (1991), Deal and Peterson (1994) develop implications for school change. Rutter, Maugham, Mortimore and Ouston (1979) and Mortimore, Sammons, Stoll, Lewis and Ecob (1988) review school culture. Fullan and Hargreaves (1992) review cultural effects on teacher development.

# Part One

## Theoretical Perspectives

*Chapter 1*

# Assumptions of School Culture

**Approaches to Culture**

Culture has a wide variety of meanings. As the root of horticulture and agriculture, it refers to processes of growth and development. Used like this, the term is particularly linked to specialized laboratory conditions which promote and accelerate growth. In this context, the verb *'to culture'* implies a nurturing activity on the part of the cultivator. Teachers readily accept the idea of their work being linked with culture, especially in promoting growth and the climate for development.

Culture also refers to characteristics possessed by individuals. We talk of cultured individuals who have an appreciation of art, music or theatre, who show particular social graces and skill in dealing with others, those who appreciate the finer points of life. There is a sense that this 'high' culture reflects the elite in society and is contrasted with 'popular' or 'low' culture, that shapeless and pervasive milieu in which we live out our lives.

More generally, culture is not something one has, but rather something to which one belongs. The term is applied to national cultures in a way which celebrates distinctive characteristics and engenders a sense of belonging to the nation. Ethnic groups are characterized by their distinctive cultures. The term is also applied to groups within society in the way we speak of middle class, working class, youth, or feminist culture. From this perspective, culture refers to a social condition or a way of life. It encompasses 'the characteristic habits, ideals, attitudes, beliefs and ways of thinking of a particular group of people' (Zais, 1976, p. 157). This is the perspective on the culture of schools and teaching which is explored in this book.

*The Concept of Culture*

Culture is built around a configuration of interlocking beliefs, ideas, values, attitudes, meanings, symbols, rituals and behaviours. None of these individual elements defines a culture, which must be considered as a complex whole. As such, culture is an abstraction used to label a complex reality of many interacting elements. The individual elements take on a variety of appearances, intensities and effects in a group. For instance, the celebration of St Patrick's Day on March 17th is a particular expression of being Irish. One does not become more Irish that day, but the intensity of the identification is different. And this intensity may be different for Irish people living in Ireland and those who live in other countries.

Culture is non-material. Culture is not something a society or a group has, but rather something they are. In this sense, culture refers to the complex, coherent internal reality that is shared by the members. People grow into a culture so that it becomes part of their being, and they gradually become identified with that culture. With time, they become accustomed to what it means to be part of the culture. The meaning of what they see and do is learned from other members and is, in turn, shared with new members. That knowledge is transmitted through the nuances of language, and affirmed and reinforced through symbols, rituals and other socializing experiences.

Participation in culture has dimensions of breadth and depth. The breadth of culture embraces a wide range of disparate elements such as lifestyle, leisure, work, relationships and spirituality. These elements work at different levels of intensity, thus giving the dimension of depth to an individual's experience. Some people are deeply immersed in the culture of the group, while others remain on the fringe. As such, culture is not easy to define. It is not a singular entity, and neither is it static. It evolves through interaction with other cultures, borrowing from them and integrating their wisdom with its own in a dynamic way. Thus, one culture is the same as *all other* cultures, as *some other* cultures and as *no other* culture all at the same time.


*Organizational Culture in Schools*[1]


Schools have interlocking systems of beliefs, ideas, values, attitudes, meanings, symbols, rituals and behaviours. The term organizational culture has been applied to such systems and defined as:

> a pattern of basic assumptions — invented, developed or discovered by a given group in learning to cope with problems of external adaptation and internal integration — that has worked well enough to be considered valid and, therefore, to be taught to new members as the correct way to perceive, think, and feel in relation to those problems. (Schein, 1990, p. 3)

By referring to a pattern of basic assumptions, Schein's definition emphasizes the configurational and non-material nature of organizational culture. It is something which evolves around the meanings shared by a given group arising out of their history and purpose as a group. This pattern of assumptions develops over time and is influenced by two things. Firstly, free choices made by the group from a number of alternatives focus the group's activity and guide its future development. Secondly, the group responds to external forces and circumstances not of its own choosing. These responses are validated in the group's satisfaction with the outcomes. To preserve this level of satisfaction, perceptions are reinforced by habit, and shared with others, especially newcomers as 'the way things are done around

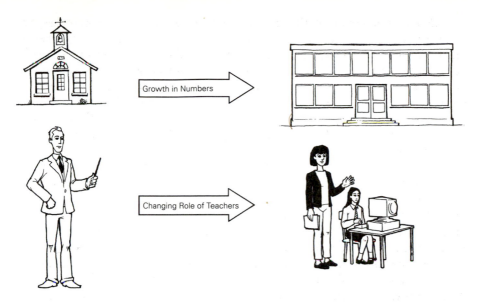

*Figure 1.1    External and internal forces combine to produce a new cultural paradigm*

here'[2]. Thus, assumptions in organizations embrace knowledge, emotions, beliefs and attitudes. The evolution of culture through invention, development and discovery recognizes the dynamic interchange between theoretical and practical knowledge, between the ideal and the possible, between strategic plans and the politics of implementation.

Schools must establish themselves in a wider environment, and are subject to external challenges from competing schools and agencies, changes in the social lives of the students and in the supply of resources such as government funding. These changes require that schools adopt new strategies and self-understanding in order to continue. Internally, schools are challenged to integrate new personnel, or new technology. This reconfigures teaching duties and procedures. The processes of external adaptation and internal integration give rise to new configurations of meaning within the organization. As solutions to challenges are found, they become the new reality (see Figure 1.1).

### The Study of School Culture

Imagine being a tourist in a foreign country. You can study such a country at different levels. You can book yourself on a package holiday and tour the country in a bus. From the relative isolation of the bus, you observe the sights, the buildings, the architecture, the way people go about their business and recreation. You visit art galleries, museums, cathedrals, the theatre, cafes and shops. Your

| LEVEL | CONTENT | STUDY ACTIVITY |
|---|---|---|
| Artefacts | Visible rituals, roles and norms | Observe/describe |
| Values | Images of the desirable | Understand |
| Assumptions | Convictions | Empathize |

*Figure 1.2   Three levels at which culture is studied — the content of these levels and typical activity associated with the study (Based on E.H. Schein, 1985)*

knowledge of the culture remains on the surface, observing the artefacts which make up the culture. A second approach is to take a car and travel around, stopping in different places as the fancy takes you. You talk to the local people, getting their views on different subjects, seeing how they live and learning their attitudes. This is a deeper understanding of culture, moving to the level of understanding the values which operate in that culture. For an even deeper experience, you could decide to go and live in another country, to enter into the way of life there, to become immersed in the language, beliefs and ways of doing things. This involves a deeper level of sharing, where you are caught up in the same assumptions about life and living as the local inhabitants. Each of these levels gives a different insight into the breadth and depth of a culture. A similar approach can be applied to understanding school culture — knowing the artefacts, values and assumptions within a school.

### (i)   Artefacts

Artefacts refer to the visible actions and rituals within an organization. They describe what an organization does. These artefacts appear at different levels:

- *rituals* — what most people expect most people to do most of the time.
- *roles* — formally stated norms which convey rights and impose duties with regard to particular social relationships and activities.
- *norms* — the internalized moral imperatives which are accepted unquestionably and, if broken, severely sanctioned by the group.

Schools have rituals related to timetables, how people greet one another, how success is rewarded and achievements honoured. There are prescribed roles for administrators, teachers, parents and students and there are norms of behaviour internalized by different groups. To step outside these norms results in sanctions, which range from expulsion to social isolation or labelling.

### (ii)   Values

Values can be defined as the images and conceptions of the desirable. They influence the selection of goals and the means available to achieve them. In organizations, values can be implicit or explicit, normative or preferential and central or peripheral. Schools often proclaim very explicit values which they strive to transmit. These co-exist with implicit values which form part of the hidden curriculum of the school. Participation in some values, such as academic diligence, may be seen as normative in the school, whereas other values, such as participation in extra-curricular activities, may be seen as preferential and optional. Another approach to values is to ask how central or peripheral they are in the school by examining their extensiveness (distribution among members), duration (persistence over time), intensity (associated with severity of sanction) and prestige (given to those who represent them). The development of value systems will be dealt with in more detail in Chapter 6.

### (iii)   Assumptions

Assumptions refer to the network of ideas and convictions about the school, its purpose and how it should be organized. These are based on accepted ideas about schooling and education, about the history and prestige of the particular school and popular evaluations of what are appropriate goals for the school and its internal procedures. Each school has its own traditional way of organizing its curriculum, a combination of academic excellence and extra-curricular achievements and a prestige in the local community. Stories are told of past teachers and students, giving them the status of hero or villain, enshrining judgements of value on their activities. These myths and legends reflect the underlying assumptions of the school's organizational culture.

The artefacts of a school are easily observed, however difficult they are to interpret. Values and assumptions belong to individuals and are more difficult to decipher. There is always a problem between the values we espouse and the values which actually govern our behaviour[3]. These latter are often at the level of the unconscious. For example, a student may espouse academic success in examinations and study hard. Yet the student may be driven more by a fear of failure than by a desire for knowledge. Similarly, a teacher may espouse involvement in extra-curricular activities out of a desire to help students more, but may also be driven by a need for status among students. The same thing happens at a school level. The school may espouse a sense of order and quiet because it believes that this atmosphere fosters learning, and yet there is need for control and predictability in the running of the school. The meanings which assumptions give to everyday events in the school are unconscious and taken for granted, and therefore it can be difficult to correctly decipher their effect in a culture. To even identify these assumptions takes commitment, time and hard work, before we then move on to understanding their impact and importance.

## Examples of Assumptions in School Culture

School culture develops around tasks, challenges and issues. As answers are found to particular questions, they become embedded as assumptions about the way things

**CULTURAL ASSUMPTIONS**

1  The School's Relationship to the Environment
2  Human Activity
3  Truth and Time
4  Human Nature
5  Human Relationships.

*Figure 1.3  Five areas in which cultural assumptions operate (Adapted from E.H. Schein, 1985)*

are in the school. Because the assumptions which inform school culture are so pervasive, it is important to have a framework which helps understand and organize the content of these assumptions. We look here at five areas in which assumptions influence the artefacts and value systems of schools. Later in the book we look at ways in which some of these assumptions can be grounded and examined in more detail, with a view to empowering the school to determine and manage its own culture. The treatment of these five areas is not exhaustive, and it is hoped that the reader will be stimulated to reflect on each of the different areas in the light of their own experience.

*Assumptions About the School's Relationship to the Environment*

One of the first questions any group asks is 'Who are we?' and 'Why are we here?'[4]. When teachers answer these questions, the answers identify the relationship a school has with the environment and involve:

(i)    the image the school has of its function in society;
(ii)   its relationship with other institutions; and
(iii)  the way the boundary between the school and others is managed.

The core mission of a school is based on its charter, the original inspiration behind its foundation and establishment. In some schools, the charter is a written document. In others, it is part of an oral tradition. The charter represents the cultural artefact. The sense of purpose which arises from this charter can have a profound effect on the way the school deals with problems and looks for solutions and initiatives.

The charter often contains assumptions about the school's place in the environment and its relationship to other organizations. An example of these assumptions can be seen in the contrast between private and public schools. Private schools are often associated with religious foundations, and have as part of their purpose the socialization of students to a pre-existing value system. Public schools, on the other hand, are part of the general political system, and aim to cater for a pluralism of views. These purposes in turn give rise to assumptions about how decisions are taken, and the criteria used in evaluating these decisions. In private schools, decision-making is often guided by internal criteria such as congruence with traditional practice and the understood value system. In public education, the focus may be more outwards. The criteria used are based on principles of democracy and the satisfaction of demands made by various groups in the environment. In some countries, this democratic involvement extends to curriculum content, as in the historic creation versus evolution debates in some school districts in the United States.

All identity, personal or organizational, is based on an interaction between one's own vision and purpose, and the need to adapt to the demands of others. Some private schools see themselves as self-determining and self-sufficient. Their sense of mission is derived mainly from internal resources which they seek to perpetuate. Basically, the school itself sets the agenda, and external groups are free to accept that agenda or not. As long as there is a demand for what the school has to offer, it does not have to consult these groups. Public schools on the other hand may adopt a philosophy of constant dialogue with the community. The school is seen as an extension of the community, not only in its service to the students, but also in the involvement of the whole community in its decision-making processes. Behind these value systems are assumptions about education and who has the power to guide education.

Individuals and organizations have defence mechanisms which filter the demands from the outside and promote their own desires. This process can be termed boundary management. The artefacts of boundary management in schools are structures such as governance boards, the type of groups and institutions the school relates to and the hierarchy of influence of these institutions in the life of the school. For example, there are different approaches to developing governance structures. Governors may be appointed on the basis of past performance and conformity to tradition. This represents an internal focus. On the other hand, a commitment to an external focus gives rise to democratic election procedures, and with it, a 'risk factor' in how demands for change might develop. Other influential groups may be the alumni/ae or a Parent Association. One can decipher the values and assumptions about these groups by examining their activities. For instance, some parent associations are confined to fundraising activities and do not have a real say in the policy of the school. In other schools, former students have a conservative influence on the school, as preserving tradition is an important part of fundraising in that constituency. Church links, school–industry liaisons, sporting and cultural alliances with other schools, are all artefacts of the boundary management value system. Similarly, an examination of the catchment area of the pupils and the entrance policy of the school will reveal much about the school's prestige and relationship within the local community.

The process of boundary management can be seen as a continuum between two poles; one has an internal focus, with an emphasis on continuity and predictability and the other an external focus, with an emphasis on responsiveness and change. In practice, schools fall somewhere in the middle — the boundaries are semi-permeable, some being more porous than others. The overall balance hints at the value system and the assumptions the school has about its relationship with the environment.

---

**Reflection 1.1**

You might like to explore aspects of your own school's relationship with the environment. How would you respond to the following three questions:
- What contribution would you like your school to be making to your area in 5 years' time?
- What groups are making demands on the school at present? What would they like the school to be doing in 5 years' time?
- What might the school do to ensure that outside groups want the same thing as the school in 5 years' time?

Now, look back over your answers, and observe some of the artefacts and values which are in place. Can you now observe any assumptions that are being made about the nature of the school's relationship with the environment?

---

### *Assumptions about Human Activity*

A school will define what it hopes to achieve with its students. These aspirations involve a perspective on the purpose of human activity. This determines expectations the school has for students, teachers, parents and other participants in its culture. For instance, should humankind be passive and fatalistic in the face of nature and accept things as they come? Or should it be dominant and proactive and strive to make a mark on the world? The answers (conscious or unconscious) to these questions form the basis of cultural norms in a school setting.

When the orientation to human activity is one of passivity and fatalism, then the goal of education becomes one of reproduction and adaptation. Individuals develop a sense of powerlessness, of events being determined by others — be that by nature itself, by God, by fate, or by powerful others. Students are taught to conform to models of learning and to value particular forms of knowledge so that they can get particular types of jobs and take their place in an ordered society. They are not taught to think critically about the structures and values of that society. To do so would be to promote a subversive culture of revolution. Instead, teachers accept their roles of passing on tradition and helping students understand their future role in society. On the other hand, if the expectation of the school is to help students take a proactive stance in the face of nature and to make their mark on the world, then the emphasis is on developing a critical appraisal of one's present state and one's history, of developing a confidence and creativity in devising alternatives for the future, and also developing skills in negotiating and implementing these alternatives. The focus of such activity is on individual leadership skills, or on interpersonal and political skills of working in groups.

Two artefacts which might reveal these orientations to human activity are the teacher–learner relationship in the classroom and the discipline system. In a passive orientation, there is an emphasis on the world as given. The curriculum is seen as exposing the world 'as it is'. Students are encouraged to accept the facts of history, of science and of human experience. Criteria for success and status are the degree to which one knows these facts and can recite them. The relationship between teacher and students is characterized by a level of dependence on the teacher for knowledge and direction. In a proactive orientation, the focus is more on process. The aim is to understand how certain situations arose, and to critically evaluate these processes and learn from them. Criteria for success are based not so much on the amount of knowledge accumulated by students, but rather on the ability of students to apply their understanding of processes to new situations. The relationship of teachers with their students is that of mentors, and there is a dynamic interaction between the knowledge of the teacher and that of the students.

In a discipline code, an orientation to passivity gives rise to expectations of conformity. Rules and procedures are often detailed and comprehensive and persist over time. They are accepted and regarded as having a universal validity. Uniformity and objectivity are hallmarks of the application of the code. In a proactive orientation, there is an expectation of developing and changing personalities. This gives rise to the adaptation of school structures to the developmental stages of the students — to allow greater participation in decision-making together with greater degrees of self-determination and self-regulation. Participation in school governance activities prepares the student for active participation in the political and economic world they will enter after school, and models the possibility of having an active voice in their own future.

In practice, schools are mixtures of both orientations. The organizational culture reflects the balance and tension between these two orientations.

---

**Reflection 1.2**

Looking at artefacts such as the curriculum, evaluation procedures, participation in decision-making, what values about human activity are promoted in your school?

What activities have prominence in the school and its reward system?

What type of student is regarded as a good student or a successful student? What talents do such students have and what behaviours do they typically engage in? What does this tell you about the dominant value system relating to human activity, and the underlying assumptions about passive and proactive human activity?

List the way parents are involved in the school? What assumptions does this reveal about the role of parenting?

## Assumptions about Truth and Time

Schools set criteria by which they judge their work and attribute success. This involves a perspective on the nature of truth and time.

Truth can be viewed in different ways. One view is to see truth as objectively given, something external to the individual, there to be discovered and appreciated. Through learning, the individual comes to appreciate the structure of the world. Knowledge is seen predominantly in rational terms. The truth is determined by intellectual and rational processes which have a universal dimension, abstracting from the concreteness of experience. Feelings, desires and emotions have a secondary place as they are rooted in the present. They must be ordered according to some rational principle. A second view of truth defines it more subjectively. Truth is viewed as having a personal and social construct. It is arrived at by pragmatic test, reliance on wisdom, or by social consensus. From this perspective, truth is that which is validated by the individual for themselves, or by power groups for a society. It may contain both rational and emotive elements and be informed by desire, aspirations, myths and legends.

Different approaches to truth involve different perspectives on time and history. Some people see history moving to some ultimate order — a blueprint of the ideal. Each succeeding generation is seen as part of the evolutionary process, and their function is to add an increment to that order. Human and social development is judged in terms of its conformity to this blueprint. Others view history with no such ultimate goal. They see it developing in a random, but patterned fashion and their function is to appreciate and participate in that pattern. For them, truth is not discovered in linear action–reaction, cause–effect relationships. The relationship between different events is viewed more like the relationship between the numbers drawn in a weekly lottery. Although any single event has the appearance of random chance, a clear pattern emerges over time, where each number appears with equal regularity. From this perspective, reality is viewed in terms of patterns and circles of causation and interaction[5].

Another way of looking at time is the value placed on the past, the present and the future. Schools are charged with the role of passing on the values of past generations, providing a conducive learning environment in the present and preparing students for the future. The value and emphasis that is placed on each of these orientations is linked to a view of truth, and underpins the culture of the school.

Orientation to the past involves the function of passing on the wisdom, heritage and values of previous generations to the next. The past is often valued in a nostalgic and idyllic way. This orientation is reflected in essentialist or idealist philosophies which emphasize moral and spiritual explanations of the world and propose absolute, universal and timeless values. In this perspective, the values which were important to the Ancient Greeks are just as important today, in a changeless way. Thus, the school tries to recreate that sense of timelessness through a classical liberal arts curriculum broken down into distinct disciplines which change little over time. An attempt is made to relive the academic climate

*Value on PAST*

of the ancient academies by reproducing similar timetables and texts, the use of mottoes and uniforms. As well as linking generations through similar artefacts, the school socializes students through participation in activities such as games, rhetorical debate and social mores. This approach frequently gives rise to a general suspicion of the present, and a regret that the 'good old days' seem to have gone forever.

A present orientation focuses on the engagement of the student in the learning process, and on creating a climate which facilitates that engagement. The emphasis is on the clarification and development of present talent, self-esteem and confidence in students. The philosophical foundation is pragmatic and existential, where learning is seen as a transaction between the learner and the environment. The product of education is the ability to cope with change and to reconstruct experience. Teaching involves helping students explore their experience rather than explaining things to them. The methodology is based on dialogue, where teacher and student explore together. The focus of the curriculum is on relevance, on the development of process skills, and the transferability of these skills (e.g. problem solving) to a wide variety of different areas. The curriculum is interdisciplinary and ideally is based on student experience and interest.

A future orientation aims at equipping the student for work and life in an unknown future. The emphasis in education is on defining a self-identity through freeing the person to make choices about themselves and their future. There is a tension between preparing the student for the immediate future, which has relatively predictable skills needs, and preparing them for a long-term future, which, given the rate of social change, is quite unpredictable. The focus on preparing students for employment and the world of work places the school in direct dialogue with the world of politics and economics. From this perspective, education is seen as part of social policy formation. Education provides the wealth and productivity which brings about economic progress by preparing people to be productive in the economic sphere. Education also helps shape policy, in that the wealth that it generates becomes a creative force in resource investment and finding new areas of productivity. It is through education and its application that a new future is envisioned, and it is also education which provides the means to implement that vision. In this way, education is both a means and an end in economic progress.

These three orientations to time of necessity co-exist in a school. All educational systems teach something about history, culture and heritage. They all try to create a positive learning climate by responding in some measure to student needs, and they all aspire to be relevant to the future lifestyles of their students. The emphasis on each of these orientations may change with the age of the child. For instance, the emphasis on socialization to cultural value systems (past) and to child-centred learning (present) may be quite prevalent in primary education, whereas in second-level schools, there is a shift to a curriculum which focuses on preparation for work and for higher education (future). The overriding influence on the organizational culture is the tension between the three orientations, and the possible dominance of one perspective over the others.

---

**Reflection 1.3**

Looking at the curriculum in the school, do some subjects have more prestige than others? What does this say about the nature of knowledge and what is important in it?

Think of what you do when you are correcting examinations. What emphasis do you put on accurate reproduction of detail? What percentage of marks is given for creativity and originality? What assumptions about the nature of truth are revealed in your approach?

Choose some dimension of school life — curriculum, classroom management, discipline, teaching methodology, extra-curricular activities, etc. Identify the artefacts related to the three different orientations of past, present and future. Identify people in the school who typify each of the different orientations.

How do the three orientations relate to one another? Does one orientation dominate over others, and in what circumstances? What challenges the different orientations in your school?

---

### Assumptions about Human Nature

Schools organize around attitudes they have to their pupils — what they believe about them. Views of humankind as basically good, evil or neutral shape one's view of history, of one's self and one's future. Students may be seen in terms of Holden Caulfield in *Catcher in the Rye* — a spirit of innocence to be cultivated — or they can be seen much like the children in *Lord of the Flies* — where evil lay just below the surface and had to be tamed and kept under control. In organizational studies, such assumptions have been termed Theory X (which states that individuals are basically lazy and untrustworthy and need constant supervision if they are not to subvert the goals of the organization) and Theory Y (which states that individuals are positively oriented to work and enjoy responsibility and respond to it by greater commitment and motivation) (McGregor, 1960)[6].

Assumptions about human nature also refer to beliefs about how fixed and unchangeable human nature is and, particularly, whether it is basically flawed but somehow perfectible. One particular manifestation of that in education is our assumption about individual intelligence. The history of intelligence testing covers disputes about the genetic (nature) and the social basis (nurture) of intelligence, and the priority which is to be given to these elements. If intelligence is regarded as inherited and fixed then the measure of current intelligence can be used to predict future performance, to place students in accelerated or remedial programmes, to direct them to particular vocational interests and programmes. On the other hand, if the social context of the individual is given prominence, then different strategies such as providing a stimulating environment, must be used to promote intelligence. In the first view of intelligence, the emphasis in on teaching. The teacher works from an essentialist view of the individual and draws out something which is innate. Reference points of success are, however, external. From the second perspective, the focus is on learning. Students are seen as somehow creating their own knowledge and meaning. Development is judged as appropriate to experience, rather than in relation to fixed external criteria.

We all experience human nature as somewhat flawed. Assumptions about the possible remediation of such flaws play an important part in how a school handles problems of discipline, control and power. Students in schools exhibit a wide range of behaviours. Judgments are made by the school on the tolerance to be given to behaviour at the negative extreme. Schools also decide how to deal with those students who consistently exhibit such behaviour. One approach is to see the behaviour as a manifestation, a symptom, of some flaw in the student's character. The school sees no remedy to curing this flaw and instead deals only with the symptom, and tries to eradicate its appearance through coercive or remunerative behaviour modification strategies. Another approach is to see the behaviour as simply something which is socially learned and to try to help the student realize the consequences of their behaviour, and to develop alternative strategies with more acceptable outcomes. This second approach does not ascribe behaviour to some innate characteristic.

Similar assumptions about human nature can be seen between school administrators and teachers. Differences of opinions and conflicts may be seen as emotive or as substantive issues. When issues are seen in emotive terms, bad motives and conspiratorial intent are often ascribed to those with opposing views. Finding a solution to such issues involves using complex interpersonal and political skills. However, when conflict issues are seen in substantive terms, creative solutions can often be negotiated, as the perspectives of participants are not confused with emotional loyalties. It is clear that underlying assumptions about human nature create a climate and culture in schools which inform structures and behaviours, but particularly, affect the relationships between people in the school.

---

**Reflection 1.4**

Review the text of the school discipline code, the staff handbook, or some other artefact in the school which sets expectations for members of the school. Does the tone of the text suggest a positive or a negative view of students? Of staff members?

Is there a difference in the tone of expectations the school has for students and for teachers? On what is this difference based? What other differences might you detect? For instance, is there a different expectation about males and females — in student activity or among the teaching staff?

How does the school implement its different codes? What practices in the school emerge from a negative expectation of behaviour, and what practices seek to promote positive aspects of human nature? How do these practices balance out? What is the message that is being communicated to students and teachers about themselves through these practices of the school?

---

### Assumptions about Human Relationships

A label used by students referring to a peer as a 'teacher's pet' is most undesirable. In a staffroom, teachers may talk about an 'in-group' which influences decisions. All organizations face issues of how status and power can be distributed. In schools, the response to issues relating to power and status give rise to assumptions of how the school deals with parents, how administrators deal with teachers and also how teachers deal with their colleagues and with students. The culture of the school is built up around the human relationships within the school.

In some schools, there is a strong emphasis on status. This may be organized in a hierarchical way, or may be based on informal dimensions of the school. Status may be afforded to position (the headteacher, heads of department), to experience (seniority), to expertise (success or achievement) or to charisma. In other schools, there is little emphasis on status, and power is used in an informal and diffuse way. In general, a high emphasis on status puts an emphasis on individuals rather than on teamwork. This may result in relationships being more professional than personal, and individuals acting out of a sense of competition rather than cooperation. Some observations on teacher interaction can help illuminate assumptions about relationships. How many committees have *ex officio* officials in the school? Are people appointed to committees to represent various viewpoints, rather than in a personal capacity? How do teachers address one another at meetings — by first name, by title, or in a neutral way such as 'my colleague' — or do they avoid personal references and talk in generalities? Is special deference shown to the principal or to the chairperson at a meeting? How do teachers socialize in school — do they gather in cliques and, if so, on what basis do the cliques gather? Do teachers socialize together outside school, or is the relationship strictly within school time?

In the classroom, teachers promote a relationship between students, and also between themselves and the student. One aspect of this is the value put on homogeneity over diversity. Some teachers insist on a high level of uniformity in their classroom, trying to treat all students in the same way. Other teachers act from a high sense of the individual within the class, making allowances for individual circumstances in terms of behavioural expectations, the amount of work to be done and the amount of time given to the individual student. Some teachers develop high levels of cooperation among students, setting group projects and promoting peer coaching. Other teachers promote high levels of competition. Results of exams and tests are made public in order to keep students motivated. These teachers are working from different assumptions about the proper relationship within a classroom and communicating these assumptions to students.

Another artefact in forming relationships is the distribution of resources. In some schools, high levels of extra-curricular resources are committed to the first team, those who represent the school in the public forum. Few resources are committed to the intra-mural programme. The emphasis on performance over participation communicates a message about what is important in relationships. When applied to the academic level with streaming of classes, the allocation of different resources to the various streams can lead to different types of relationship. In one school, it was quipped that the A-stream got education, the B-stream got teaching and the C-stream got discipline! This represented a truth about the expectations teachers had for different classes, and how they reinforced these expectations through staffroom gossip.

**Reflection 1.5**

Look at some of the questions in this section about the way teachers relate to one another. Answer these questions for your school, describing the scenario as best you can. Now look over your descriptions and see what patterns emerge.

Take one of the classes you teach. How would you classify your relationship with each of the pupils in the class? What information do you have about their academic ability? What personal details do you know? How much time have you spent with them over the past month? Now, look over your list and see is there a pattern? What does this tell you about your values and assumptions?

What are the artefacts which illustrate the relationship between parents and the school? What assumptions are at work here?

### Summary

Schools differ in relation to their profiles on these five sets of assumptions: their relationship with the environment; their understanding of human activity; of truth and time; of human nature; and human relationships. Each of the sets offers a perspective on the organizational culture of the school, yet none defines it totally. The different perspectives are mutually dependent. Views on human nature impact on the way in which relationships develop. It is the interrelationship of all five sets which determines the inner world of the school. For each school, that configuration is unique. As we said about culture earlier, each school is similar to **all** other schools, to **some** other schools and to **no** other schools, all at the one time.

The distribution of culture in a school is complex. Subgroups develop which differ from the main population in their artefacts, values and assumptions. Thus, exploring organizational culture does not intend to arrive at a clear-cut description of the school. It aims at developing awareness, sensitivity and understanding of the hidden meanings and assumptions which individuals and subgroups have. The exploration does not stop with description. In describing the artefacts, values and assumptions, we are also beginning to pose questions such as whether we are happy with what we discover. We ask whether the culture we have is the most appropriate one. Sharing information about different cultures also informs us of new possibilities, new ways of looking at things. Culture is dynamic. It develops. There is a tension between being (what one is) and becoming (what one would like to be); of aspiration (what one is trying to do) and performance (what is actually happening); of goals (why things are done a particular way) and achievement (what they actually accomplish). Bridging the gap between what one is, and what one would like to be, between goals and achievements, between aspirations and performance, is the work of organization development and cultural management. However, it is not easy to change assumptions. They are deeply ingrained. In the next chapter, we will examine a model of how habits develop, with a view to finding some leverage in promoting cultural change.

## Notes

1   This chapter is heavily indebted to Schein's (1990) exposition and development of the concept of organizational culture.
2   Bower (1966) is cited frequently in organizational culture studies.
3   The concept of the reflective practitioner is well developed in Argyris and Schon (1974, 1978), Schon (1987, 1991).
4   Drexler, Sibbet and Forrester (1988) discuss models of group development through questions asked at different stages and the consequences of not answering these questions satisfactorily.
5   Wheatley (1992) examines assumptions about the nature of reality from the perspective of the new quantum science and develops implications for organizational planning. Hargreaves (1994) discusses teachers' approach to time in Chapter 5.
6   A more detailed review of assumptions about human nature as they apply to work situations can be found in Schein (1980).

## Chapter 2

# School Culture and Problem Solving

One of my favourite stories is from a class of 10-year-olds taking a course in creative writing[1]. For homework, the teacher started a story as follows:

> Once upon a time, there was a king. He had a very big kingdom, and all his subjects were very happy. The only problem was that a big dragon lived just outside the kingdom, and occasionally he came and attacked the people. This had happened a lot recently, and the people were becoming very frightened. The king sent his army to kill the dragon, but he just breathed fire on them, and killed all the soldiers.
>
> The king was very upset, and did not know what to do. He called his advisers together, and after a long discussion, he decided to offer a reward to the person who got rid of the dragon. The king would give this person everything they asked for.

The children's task was to apply for the reward and to finish the story. One little girl wrote the following account.

> I will ask the king for a blanket, two pillows, two apples, a pair of binoculars, a pair of tweezers and a matchbox. When he gives me all these things, I will use them to catch the dragon.
>
> First of all, I will set off on a picnic. When I get to the river, I will put the blanket down on the ground and put the two pillows on it. Beside one of the pillows, I will put an apple. Then, I will eat the second apple. When I am finished, I will lie down and take a nap.
>
> When the dragon comes along, the first thing he will see is an apple beside the pillow, and he will be hungry and eat that apple. When he finishes, he will be tired and sleepy, and want to have a nap as well. When he sees the pillow, he will lie down beside me and fall asleep.
>
> Of course, I will wake up first, because I went to sleep first. When I see the dragon beside me, I won't be afraid. I will take up the binoculars, and look through them the wrong way round so that the dragon seems to be very, very small. Then I will take out the tweezers, pick up the dragon and put him in the matchbox.

### Approaches to Problem Solving

In Chapter 1 we saw how organizational culture develops in response to central questions about meaning and purpose and embodies the organization's way of solving particular external challenges and internal problems. The story of the king, the dragon and the little girl illustrates how individuals and organizations face problems, and the different values and assumptions they bring to problem solving. In the story, we see different assumptions about the nature of reality (the king confronts it and tries to change it, and the little girl creatively adapts to it) and also about human activity and relationships (the king tries to dominate and kill the dragon; the little girl tries to live with him but contain him). The king and the little girl had radically different approaches to coping with external threats. The king sought to remove the threat completely, and to achieve this, he took extraordinary steps — he sent the army out. The little girl, on the other hand, sought a new way to look at the problem, to do regular things like going on a picnic but with a new perspective which would help her deal with the problem.

I have often used this story as a metaphor for the way we deal with personal problems or with organizational change. Like the king, we wait until the problem becomes a crisis before dealing with it. In previous times, the dragon's occasional raids were tolerated. They caused a crisis when they happened, but there were such long gaps between attacks that the people had time to become complacent and forget the danger. However, once the dragon attacked more frequently, the crisis had to be faced. The king decided to act and deal with the problem head on. He sent his army to attack the dragon. However, he found that the dragon was too powerful for him, and could not be removed with the resources he had on hand.

On a personal or professional level, we too put off dealing with problems until they become a major crisis. In class, teachers may put off dealing with an individual child because the problem is not very serious, and they are busy with other children whose needs seem more pressing. Unfortunately, the student continues to experience difficulties and their self-esteem becomes lower. When finally the teacher has to deal with the student, the problem is much bigger, and more difficult to solve. Sometimes, too, teachers themselves drift into ruts of teaching and thinking, without realizing that they are becoming attached to a comfortable way of teaching, rather than promoting a sense of learning among students. Once the attachment is made, it is much more difficult to change. Attacking the problem head on often brings guilt, resistance and a deepening of the crisis. In relationships with students and colleagues, the events of the past cannot be undone, yet individuals can choose to look forward rather than backward. Like in the story with the little girl, progress lies in seeking new ways to look at the problem. She used the binoculars the wrong way round. Teachers and students can also seek to put problems in a perspective that does not dominate the present in a negative way, but which gives freedom to creatively search for new solutions. Once the dragon is contained in the matchbox, it is important to resist the temptation of constantly checking the matchbox, looking inside and perhaps letting the dragon escape. The way in which problems dominate the atmosphere of the school, and the perspectives taken on them, determines to a large extent the types of solutions found and, ultimately, the configuration of the organizational culture in the school.

*Models of Problem Solving*

Facing challenges or planning for development in schools is often very reactive, and has an air of crisis management. The challenge may be external, such as changing government policies, or internal, such as new technology to be integrated into the school. The dragon is at the door before the school recognizes the problem. Then, it is faced head on, using traditional tools and concepts. The problem is seen as an undesirable effect in the school. The immediate 'cause' is identified and removed, and a new 'cause' is introduced to bring about a more desirable effect (the solution).

This model gives the impression that problem solving is a structured and linear process. Two states (present and future) are analysed as objective realities. Both the analysis of the present and the determination of the future are seen as rational processes. The problem of change is making the transition, where an individual or an organization must turn away from one state and embrace the other. The energy of change management focuses on the transition phase. Managers become concerned with the resistance that prevents people moving from the present, the sense of loss they may feel in leaving a familiar set of behaviours or attitudes behind, and their fear of the future and the unknown. Once the solution of 'killing the dragon' is proposed, it is frequently found that the army is inadequate for the task.

The linear model is not the only model of problem solving. By way of parallel, mountaineers do not always tackle an ascent by going 'straight up', but often use a longer, but gentler, system of switchbacks. So, also, in helping people and social systems to change and adapt, an indirect approach is often best. In this approach, development is seen more as a journey, rather than as an event[2]. There is no blueprint, no detailed map, although there are general directions. Along the road, decisions are taken and each of these decisions has consequences. As one problem is faced and a solution found, it gives rise to a new situation, new challenges. The commitment is to constantly seek effective patterns of response in a spirit of community and teamwork.

Journey is a powerful metaphor for the development of schools or teachers' careers. Some teachers journey into exciting new lands, with many different roads to explore, and new sights to see. The teacher discovers exciting things along the way, expanding and developing new interests and horizons. Other teachers travel along well-defined paths. They follow the guidebook, and accept the tour laid out by others. Some teachers get lost on their journey. They travel quite comfortably along the road for a while, but then they find roadworks, or even a dead end. When they decide to turn back, their momentum is such that they cannot stop, or the vehicle they are driving does not turn easily.

This image of the journey can be used to capture an individual's professional history, or indeed the past history of a school. In the journey, we can discern attitudes to problem solving — whether the teacher or school saw themselves more as nomads, travelling light in a desert of shifting sands and ever new challenges, or as settlers in an oasis within this desert, surrounded by the security of their possessions and their past history. The way individuals see themselves on a journey reveals assumptions of their relationship with the environment, their sense of purpose and reason for acting, and indeed something about relationships. Nomads and settlers tend to see the same problems in a different way and to bring different values to finding solutions. In schools, the type of journey the school imagines for itself reveals assumptions in its organizational culture.

### Problem Solving and Culture

In Chapter 1, we saw that culture can be examined on three levels — artefacts, values and assumptions. These become operative as a teacher or a school responds to inevitable challenges. In the story of the dragon, the way the citizens of the kingdom experienced life was determined by concrete realities (the dragon) and by assumptions of how to deal with these realities (do nothing, send out armies, etc.). Their lives were determined by the interaction of the actual problems and their attempts to solve them. The solutions tried were based on assumptions of how life should be, and how problems should be dealt with — tolerance, head-on confrontation, dominance, or total elimination. The little girl brought different assumptions to her problem solving. The solution she generated gave rise to a very different situation, to different perspectives on the problem and how the future might be lived.

The existence of different sets of assumptions in facing problems and planning for the future gives rise to contrasting outcomes, to different artefacts in school culture. History is an important constituent of how culture has developed. The school or a teacher may have no control over the dragons which attacked them in the past, and which might decide to attack them in the future. The dragons won't be killed or ignored. However, there are choices as to how to deal with them. A teacher can be passive or fatalistic in the face of the dragon's attacks and decide to suffer in silence. She can also seek to understand the elements and leverage points of the situation — how to set up the picnic, to entice the dragon to eat the apple, to find a pair of binoculars, a pair of tweezers and a matchbox for this particular situation.

In seeking a deeper appreciation of the organizational culture of schools and teachers, it is important to have some conceptual construct which looks at the solutions of past problems, understanding where assumptions were operative and how they influenced attitudes and behaviour. This examination helps us understand why some artefacts are so deeply ingrained in the life of the school. It can also help individuals stand back from their history and see it from a different point of view. This gives an opportunity to develop leverage points in evaluating cultural assumptions and if necessary of finding new ways to conceive of themselves and the challenges that face them. In Chapter 1 we developed our sensitivity to different levels of culture, and can identify elements which make up that culture. We now look for a deeper understanding of the artefacts, values and assumptions: why they exist, how they exert their influence. I will now present a six-fold construct for looking at various aspects of the school culture which helps us understand the way in which particular aspects of the school culture developed, and why it is as it is.

---

**Reflection 2.1**

Before we look at ways of analysing aspects of school culture, the reader will benefit by applying the approach to their own experience. One way of doing this is to take some particular aspects of their own school culture or their own career and apply the categories as they are developed. To help you choose these aspects, you might like to portray your school or career history as a timeline, indicating key events as hills and valleys in the way that the events affected morale. Figure 2.1 gives a sample timeline, where A indicates a time when a level of unhappiness crept into the school, which resulted in a crisis at B, leading to a prolonged period of low morale, which has since been solved (C). When you name some events for yourself or your school, you can apply the categories below to them.

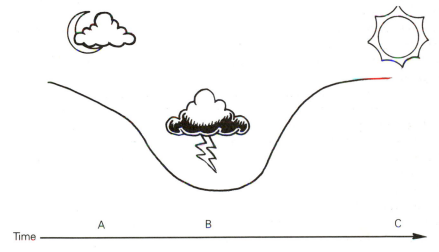

Time

A     B     C

*Figure 2.1   A sample timeline indicating three key events in a changing school morale*

---

## A Six-fold Structure of Problem Solving[3]

A basic assumption of the human sciences is that individuals and groups live according to a dynamic, an internal mind-set and external lifestyle, in which behaviour has its origin. This dynamic can be regarded as a complex matrix of six categories: context, perspective, perception, desiring, choice, and habit. In its natural setting, the matrix is like a Rubik's Cube, and the categories form the confused state of the six colours. Any analysis is akin to rearranging the sides of the cube in a uniform colour scheme, knowing that, once achieved, the cube will be returned to its natural state. These six categories form the structure of personal experience and can be applied to the structure of organizational culture, to planning for change, to understanding teacher career development, and to the analysis of issues at national, local, school, classroom, or individual level.

### Context

The country and century one lives in determine the context of space and time in which life is lived. The cultural climate of the country influences attitudes to education, prosperity, technology, travel and all aspects of life. For instance, attitudes to women and their role in the western world of the twentieth century is quite different to attitudes that existed in the eighteenth century. Similarly, the place of education in a developing country is quite different to its place in the developed world. The context therefore is the general setting of one's understanding of the world as experienced. Each person has their own context, of gender, family, rural or urban living, prosperity or poverty, good or poor health. One's personal history is the context in which one plans for the future.

Each school exists in a context. The context can be regarded as the state of the national economy, national education policy, the demands of government regulations on school governance, curriculum and assessment. A private school, well endowed with resources and tradition and serving an upper-middle-class intake gives a different context for teaching than a state school in an inner city serving students from families with high unemployment. A single gender school is a different context than a co-education school, and a homogeneous community gives rise to a different context than a multicultural one. A primary school is a different context than a post-primary senior school specializing in vocational training.

Students are affected by the context of their family, the number of children and the place of the individual among siblings; parental support levels; family resources and the level of stimulation in terms of play, friends, books, etc. For teachers, the age of students — infants, adolescents, adults — forms a context for their work and they are affected by their own age, career stage and personal circumstances such as whether they are married and have children of their own. The life context in which individuals or organizations find themselves, or which they choose for themselves, has a profound effect on their future. The context gives rise to expectations as to a possible future, and provides barriers and boosters to help create that future. The context does not predetermine outcomes, but it does have a major impact. It is important to understand the context in which a particular school culture is developing, or in which an individual is trying to live out his or her life.

### Perspective

The larger context is associated with characteristic perspectives which govern the values and judgements one makes. Victors in a war have a different perspective on history than do the vanquished, and an economist may have a different perspective on social progress to that of a social worker. Some perspectives can be pervasive, in the way that being a teacher develops perspectives on relationships with students. Other perspectives are flexible, as in the way one's perspective on music or fashion changes with age.

The context in which a school exists can give rise to perspectives on the purpose of education. In the western world, there is a history of mass education for all children up to secondary level. Governments gives substantial aid to schools to achieve this social policy, and education policy is linked to economic policy. This has implications for the balance between academic and vocational skills in the curriculum. In some schools, students are tracked into different programmes, and, in others, the school specializes in a particular type of vocational or academic programme. Some schools work from and develop a single perspective on education, while others try to cater for a plurality of perspectives.

In developing countries, there is frequently a limited tradition of mass education even at primary level. Educational provision is affected by a poor economic infrastructure and other problems related to international debt repayments. Policies other than education are higher on the national agenda. In this context education may be seen as a privilege for some, generating high levels of competition for limited places and for advancement into power positions in society. For many others in this context, education is a non-value because they are so busy with the task of short-term survival and there is no time for school.

Teachers are affected by the context of the students they teach. If the students have high ability and motivation and expect to continue study at university, this will give rise to perspectives on academic excellence, on criteria for success and standards of performance. On the other hand, teachers in a deprived urban area may take a different perspective on their social role. Many students may need help in basic literacy, which has its implications for the study of other subjects, and for the level of attainment and enrichment which can be expected. In these schools, the challenge of motivation, of classroom management and discipline requires different levels of creativity from teachers and administrators.

The context of success and failure gives rise to perspectives on school. Students who experience academic success may well be motivated to continue their education after school. They are motivated by the prospect of a future career and this perspective informs their learning, their cooperation and their attendance at school. Other students may not experience success at school. They see little connection between what they study and their likely future. For them, school is a chore. They play truant, skip homework assignments and have little interest in classroom work. A similar reflection can be made on teacher success and their perspectives on teaching as a career.

In developing countries, the numbers of girls completing education is less than the number of boys, and this is influenced by family traditions of keeping girls out of school to help with household chores, especially in the care of other children and those who are ill. Traditions of early marriage and the view that education of the boy may bring benefit to his own family whereas the education of the girl gives extra benefit to her husband's family, are perspectives influenced by national context. In developed countries, career expectations of males and females may be quite different, giving rise to different perspectives on certain subjects (contrasting patterns of uptake rates in mathematics and languages). Also, family circumstances may give rise to parental perspectives on the amount of education that is appropriate for their children before they should go to work and contribute to family finances.

Whereas context does give rise to perspective, this does not happen in a uniform or predetermined way. There are a wide variety of responses to similar contexts. Not everyone responds to reaching 50 in the same way! Not every bright student is highly motivated to use their intelligence, and many students who are academically less gifted are highly motivated and appreciative of school. Some people are overwhelmed by the context of their lives and accept it fatalistically. Others rebel against their own context and seek to escape from it, whereas another group brings a level of creativity to their context, transforming it for their own advantage and that of others around them.

The perspectives that individuals and groups develop are a unique response to their circumstances. They reflect the assumptions that have been brought to solving the problems posed by their context in time and space. These assumptions define their relationship with the environment and have helped establish their identity and unique organizational culture. A frequent requirement for growth and development is a reinterpretation of one's context and the development of new perspectives. As in the story of the dragon, the key to development and progress may not be changing the context so that one can see something different, but rather to change one's seeing, so that the problem takes on a new appearance.

---

**Reflection 2.2**

Look back on the key events you have chosen in the timeline in Reflection 2.1. Outline the general context at the time — what was happening internationally, nationally and locally? What were the educational policies at the time, and how might the understanding of these have affected the way in which the events of that time unfolded? Examine them from different perspectives — conservative, liberal, religious, cultural, economic. What were the dominant perspectives that operated in the solution of past events? What elements of the context supported this perspective?

How does this context differ from the context which exists currently? Does this reflection on the general context help you understand past events in a richer way? What perspectives are operative at present? What artefacts represent the different perspectives?

If you try to plan for the future, can you imagine the context which will exist in 5, 10, 20 years' time? What type of impact will this have on schools, teachers and students? What are the implications of this changing context?

*Perception*

Context and perspective determine what one perceives. Beauty is not the only thing in the eye of the beholder. Every value resides there in some measure. It is not that one sees what one wants to see, in a merely wilful way; rather the eye embodies the history, the context and the perspective into which one has grown. Art regularly tricks the eye in matters of shape and size by changing the background context of an object. The context in which we view things and our own sense of perspective sometimes fool us about what we really see. If this is true with the physical environment, then it is much more likely to be true in the area of feelings and personal judgements. To an extent, familiarity breeds myopia, and our perspectives on life can be self-fulfilling.

Perceptions are influenced by perspectives. Take for instance a homework assignment which has been awarded a mark of 95 per cent. One student sees the mark and immediately celebrates success. For another, however, what stands out is the red mark around the mistake. This student focuses on the missing 5 per cent rather than the near perfect achievement. The different perspectives and expectations of these two students actually conditions what they see. The perfectionist perspective of one of them actually prevents them noticing the high degree of success achieved. In extreme cases, this perspective can be pathological. Sometimes schools unintentionally promote an academic self-image among students by the way students are organized into different streams or tracks. For some students, the image promoted is quite positive, but others unfortunately develop negative self-perceptions.

One way in which teachers are socialized to the values and artefacts of school culture is through staffroom gossip. When teachers are assigned to classes at the beginning of the year, colleagues fill them in on positive or negative stories about the class. During the school year, teachers talk about their experiences and add to the common stories. Individual students or a whole class may be stereotyped as troublesome or cooperative. The perceptions shared in this way form a perspective on such students and classes. Teachers come to expect 'typical' responses and behaviours from certain students or classes. In a way, the previous perceptions form a perspective which conditions future perceptions.

The same process operates for students — they also see teachers in a particular way. Students talk about teachers to one another and at home. Stories of teacher eccentricities are recounted at length and become legend, and reputations are passed on from one generation to another. These are often embodied in nicknames. They condition expectations of that teacher in terms of classroom discipline, intensity of learning as well as standards of homework and examination performance. The perspectives students have determine what they actually see and pay attention to in the classroom. Some teachers struggle with a reputation built on 'battles' in their early career, whereas others rest on the laurels of early successes.

At a school level, tradition and prestige form a context and perspective which influence perceptions of what the school is offering. The perspective validates some practices and allows them to be seen in a particular way. The film, *Dead Poet's Society* illustrated the tension that can exist between different perspectives on education. Two teachers, with very different perspectives on teaching poetry, used the textbook in different ways. One saw it as central to teaching and followed it slavishly. The other saw it as a hindrance to true appreciation of the subject, and ripped it up. In the same film, different assumptions about personal development and growth led to a clash of perceptions between parent, student and teacher on acting as a career. The consequence of these different perceptions eventually led to the student's suicide.

Perspectives can also give rise to problems related to the parity of esteem between subjects in the curriculum. In some schools, the sciences and mathematics are held in high regard, whereas subjects such as music and art are seen as optional extras. At another level, physics, woodwork and engineering may be seen as 'male' subjects, where home economics and the language arts are often seen as 'female' subjects. These perceptions are often deeply embedded not only in the school, but also in the assumptions and values of society itself.

In moving from perspective to perception, two problems emerge. The first of these relates to the complexity of the relationship. The perspectives people bring to a particular artefact can be contradictory, and give rise to very different views. One school I worked with focused on their discipline sanctions. They had developed procedures of excluding or suspending students who had been truant. There was a system of detention which involved extra written work for students who failed to produce homework on time. At one level, there was the conflicting perception of school or homework among the students and the teachers. The former did not value it and failed to attend or produce. The latter thought that these artefacts (attendance and homework) were important and sought to convey this to the students. The teachers regarded the sanctions as very serious, and this reflected their perspective and value system. However, the suspended truants saw their now 'legitimate' absence as a reinforcement of their own perspective, and the non-producing student in detention now viewed homework with even more distaste.

The second problem is that not all aspects of our context impinge on consciousness. In one sense, it is easy to examine those things we are aware of and which we perceive as real artefacts. However, equally important are the things we miss, the artefacts and opportunities which we do not refer to, which pass us by. In many ways, these subliminal perceptions create the most powerful influences on the behaviour of the individual and the organization. For instance, the way in which two people, one with a trained and the other with an untrained ear, listen to a piece of music is quite different. The notes played are the same for both, but one listener attends to patterns and nuances which the other person misses. In effect, they hear two different pieces. One of the most affirming experiences of teaching is when students learn to deal with material and see patterns they could not see before. At the beginning, they are blinkered by their past experiences. As the process of learning develops, wider perspectives on the subject allow them to see clues that they missed before. They now see different things, and their perception of the material as a whole is different.

The pattern of perceptions — what is seen and what is missed, what is attended to and what is ignored — makes up the world view of individuals and determines the most powerful aspects of organizational culture in groups. It follows, therefore, that helping people acknowledge what they see, and then to look more closely to see what they have missed, and then perhaps to see some of these things differently, is a key function in the management of culture.

## *Desiring*

The human person is not a passive observer of the universe, but is attracted or repulsed by what is experienced. The characteristic shape of one's desires arises from the context, perspective and perception which has been inherited or adopted. For instance, the perception of certain foods as good and others as inedible shapes the desire to eat them. A plate of 'escargot' gives rise to different feelings in someone who likes gourmet food and the person who has always thought of snails as garden pests. Similarly, the problem-solving perspective of technological culture, in which every difficulty is seen as a problem waiting for a logical solution, can lead to considering all human affairs from a similar perspective. This may evoke a desire to end human ambiguity by addressing entangled human relationships in much the same way as one solves problems in technology. One is drawn into a mode of action in which people may be thought of as numbers or issues.

In general, we do not follow the precept, 'Don't judge a book by its cover'. How we see other people to a large sense determines our willingness to approach them. This sets the type of relationship we seek with them and the level of cooperation extended. In school, the perception of others as friendly and accepting sets up conditions of trust and willingness to communicate, which are so necessary to establish the relationships which lead to good teaching and learning. These conditions are also essential for the growth of a good staff development programme and for healthy cooperation and communication between parents and teachers.

Desire is the basis of motivation. The traditional approach to motivation tells us that people will expend energy if they see that the effort produces an effect. And they will continue expending that effort, and trying to bring about an effect, if they believe that the reward is linked to the effect. For instance, a teacher will prepare classes (*effort*) in order to teach well and help students learn (*outcome*), and will continue this pattern of preparation and work as they see it leading to promotion and career advancement (*reward*). There is a perceived connection between the effort, the outcome and the reward. However, if the teacher sees no connection between lesson preparation and what happens in class, or between good teaching and promotion, then there is a break in the link, and the pattern of motivation breaks down. The valence model adds an extra dimension to the traditional model (see Figure 2.2). The effort spent in acquiring rewards is also influenced by the value put on the reward on offer. Frequently, external rewards are not of great interest to teachers. Of much more importance to them are internal rewards such as status and a sense of achievement. For instance, the teacher may not be interested in a promotion which moves them out of the classroom, or to another school. They see the link between effort, effect and reward, but are not motivated by the prospect of

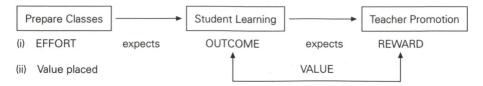

Figure 2.2 *A Contingency Model of Motivation: (i) motivation is based on the expectation that effort will produce a particular outcome, which in turn will bring a reward; (ii) recognizes that the promise of a reward only motivates effort if the reward itself is something that is valued*

this promotion. This particular reward then fails to motivate them. It is the way the reward is perceived which gives rise to the desire to obtain that reward, and which fuels motivation (Vroom, 1964).

A student who has decided on a career in medicine will experience a different intensity of desire for study and academic success than a student who has no clear direction. Similarly, a student who experiences success at one subject, say history, or who becomes fascinated by some historical figure, may find the desire to read more about a particular period. Their interest fuels the desire for more. When students do not see the possibility of success, then motivation can be difficult. For instance, students may be reluctant to make suggestions for a solution to a mathematics problem. They see themselves as weak at mathematics, and won't take the risk of giving a wrong answer. The fear of failure outweighs the possibility of success. In the same way, students who are good at sports or athletics do not forget to bring equipment for gym class, whereas students who feel themselves as awkward often seek excuses of forgotten gear or some minor ailment — anything to avoid participating.

A prerequisite for problem solving is the desire to solve the problem. When this desire is harnessed and alternative scenarios developed, individuals or groups must then want one of the new scenarios badly enough to implement it. This focus on perception and desire, helping people see things in a way that brings about a response, can be applied to many aspects of school life — to organizational change in school structures, to curriculum change, to the strategies of teachers in the classroom and to students developing good study practices. Perhaps the single most important factor in development is the desire for growth. Without this desire, the inertia can be too powerful, and new directions are not taken.

## Choice

Desires focus intention, enabling decision or choice. One can be faced with a myriad of desires, in the way shelves of a supermarket present many different products and brands. We cannot respond to all our desires. Some are mutually exclusive — we cannot choose to diet and eat ice-cream at the same time. We either decide to diet and forgo the ice-cream, or we take the ice-cream and postpone the diet. At other times we are faced with direct choices: to be nice to someone or

---

**Reflection 2.3**

Return again to the timeline for your own career or for school events. Apply the categories of perception and desire to these events. Is there any evidence that people saw the same thing in a different way? What did they want out of the situation? What motivated them? How is this linked to the context and perspectives outlined earlier? In coming to a resolution of the different events, did perceptions or desires change? What brought this about?

How does this model apply in the classroom? How do students view the school, or the subject you teach them? What strategies do you use to help them see their work in a positive light? How do you motivate students to work? What makes for a successful strategy? What does this tell you about the value system — the perceptions and desires — of the students?

---

to ignore them; to cook a meal or to eat out; to live in one area of town or to move to another; to change jobs or stay where one is; to look for promotion and different responsibilities, or to develop the responsibilities one has.

Choices can involve major directions in our lives, or they can reflect relatively trivial decisions of what to eat or wear. Some choices force us to embrace the context of our lives more fully and deeply. For instance, the decision to marry and have children brings with it obligations of home and finance which impact on other decisions. Similarly, when an organization invests heavily in new equipment, hires new personnel, or enters into contracts, these choices make commitments to the future context and perspectives of the organization. Other choices are characteristic of a certain perspective. A decision to volunteer one's time working in a soup kitchen reflects a commitment to share some of one's wealth, and to be concerned for others. An organization's decision to lay off workers may reflect its profit-making and 'bottom-line' perspective.

Schools make choices all the time. Teachers are hired and assigned to teach particular subjects at particular levels. Students are allocated to classes according to some principle — on merit ratings or a random basis, on the basis of past performance or because they want to take the class. Budget allocations are made to particular projects, to maintaining the cleanliness and state of repair of classrooms and corridors, to buying equipment and resource material for teachers, to acquiring resources for the school library and for particular subject areas. Choices are also made on priorities within the life of the school. Some activities have a high visibility in celebrations, such as the extra-curricular sports programme or the school drama. Prizes may be given for achievement in music or art, languages or science but not in areas such as effort, punctuality, helpfulness, etc. Schools choose to have students wear uniforms or to dress according to individual fashion. Choices also determine the style of discipline. The discipline code may consist of a detailed list of rules and regulations, or else of general guidelines. The code may be interpreted strictly and in a literal way, with everyone treated the same way, or the interpretation can be liberal and infractions are dealt with on an individual basis.

Schools allow different levels of choice to students in the subjects they take and in the teachers they have. Some schools place a strong emphasis on parental contacts, and parents are free to come and visit at any time, and in some cases even help out in the school. In other schools, parents are not encouraged to visit except at times specified by the school. The principal chooses a style of management — to consult with students, teachers, parents and other stakeholders about the running of the school. Teachers choose a style of classroom management which reflect their beliefs about learning and the nature of knowledge, about themselves and their students, and how that relationship should develop. Students choose levels of participation in school — to work hard in class, to volunteer answers, to initiate questions, to become involved in extra-curricular activities after school. Choices pervade all levels of the life of the school. They give rise to the artefacts of school culture, and reveal the underlying values and assumptions on which that culture is based.

Choices also have qualitative aspects. To choose from a number of clear alternatives after much thought and deliberation means something different than when the choice is coerced, or made from limited possibilities. For instance, a student who takes physics as an option from among a number of subjects because she likes science and is thinking of becoming an engineer, is likely to have a different experience of the class than the student who takes physics as 'the best of a bad lot' on offer in that slot of the schedule. A teacher who chooses a particular approach to teaching a topic from a number of possible approaches, is likely to be more flexible in the actual classroom situation and to the difficulties of students than a teacher who knows only one way of teaching for all topics. Central to choosing is the decision-making process in the school. Frequently, people in organizations are alienated, not because they disagree with the content of decisions made by management, but because they feel they have no influence over the decision, no power to determine their own future. Another aspect of choice in the school is the degree of participation of teachers, parents and students in the deliberations. Decisions consciously and deliberately taken from among alternative give a sense of ownership, direction and empowerment.


*Habit*


The five aspects outlined above give rise to habitual ways of thinking and acting. Both individuals and groups grow accustomed to how things are, to particular attitudes and values, to wanting and doing things in a particular way. At an extreme, this becomes a compulsion or obsession. Our need for some particular object, or some particular ritual becomes all encompassing, and we would go to any lengths to ensure it. At another extreme, one finds oneself in a behavioural rut, doing things in a mechanical and mindless way. We drift into decisions without thinking, because this is the way things were always done. We never stop to examine a changing context, or to ask if maybe there is a better way.

Schools develop habitual ways of dealing with teachers, students and with parents. This can be seen in the structure of the school year, the rhythm of the daily schedule with regard to classwork, homework and examinations. It can also be observed in the emphasis and energy that are put into seasonal sports, school drama productions, tours and visits to places of historical or scientific interest. Habit is also built into relationships. As students get to know teachers, they expect them to manage their classes in a particular way. They come to sense the mood of the teacher, to know whether the discipline in the class is strict or relaxed, whether the demands of study are externally enforced or whether they must take the initiative themselves. A teacher sets a pattern of asking a lot of questions in class, or encouraging students' questions. Some teachers work at a fast pace within the class, and most of the work is covered there, and others require a lot of written homework and home study. Students also pick up cues as to the nature of examinations, and how to study for them. They quickly learn their own place in the ranking system of the class, and this often sets their expectations of regular grades and marks. The routine and ritual of school life give a sense of security to most students — they know what to expect and they do not feel threatened by the possibility of new demands every class. Some students flourish in such an atmosphere. They form habits of work, and develop at a regular and even pace. However, others form habits of passivity and compliance in which they avoid challenge and do not reach the fullness of their potential.

Teachers also have habits. In their teaching, they try out various strategies, and if these work they are used again and again. Once teachers observe a pattern of success with a strategy, they expect the same success each time the strategy is used. They may begin to think that this is the only way to teach a particular unit, and are reluctant to use new strategies that have not been proven in practice. Relationships with colleagues can also be ritualistic. Staff meetings take on a familiar structure, with certain teachers making predictable contributions. Even the arrangement of the staff common room takes on a predictable shape: during the school day, teachers who are free at the same time talk together, and during a mid-morning or lunch break, the same group of teachers tend to congregate together and talk about similar interests. Teachers also develop roles within the school over and above their classroom teaching duties. They take on voluntary responsibilities for running the school or for extra-curricular activities. Sometimes these roles and activities become valued status symbols for individuals.

These habits are the ingredients of the school's organizational culture, but frequently the importance and impact of the habits are not immediately available to the members of the school. We only become aware of habits in comparison or contrast with other schools or individuals. Frequently an individual is unaware of the impact of their own generosity or character, because they see nothing unusual in it. For them it is a normal way of behaving, the natural thing to do. It is only when others observe it that it stands out from the general mass of behaviour. School patterns are similar. Those in the organization become used to the behaviour and accept it as the way to do things. It takes time to help schools appreciate the nature of these habits, and the possible contribution the habit may be making to the organizational culture.

**Reflection 2.4**

Return again to the timeline you developed in Reflection 2.1 (p. 29). Examine some of the decisions that were taken at key events, and how the consequences of these decisions became evident subsequently. How deliberate were the choices made, and how much did the context or perspective affect the way alternatives were seen in the decision-making process? How effective were the decisions in building up habits which supported the decisions?

Apply this model to the classroom. What choices and habits are evident in the way you teach? In the way that students approach work in class, or homework? How deliberate are these choices and how influenced are they by context? How easy is it for a teacher or a student to make a new choice and develop a new way of working?

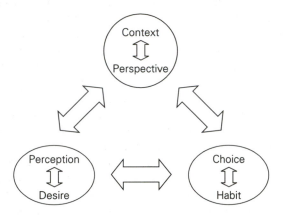

*Figure 2.3   The interdependence of the six dimensions of Tetlow's model adapted for problem solving*

## Using the Structure to Solve Problems

The six-fold structure of context, perspective, perception, desire, choice and habit might appear as a linear progression. However, there are many feedback loops within the system and deciphering the influences requires a systems approach, where the six factors are seen in an interrelated and interdependent way. The approach seeks to understand the relationship between the chicken and the egg, rather than trying to solve the riddle of which came first. The six components are seen as both cause and effect of one another. Just as choices lead to habits, so also habits give rise to choices. Over the years you develop the habit of sitting down with a book or listening to music in order to relax. If for some reason you don't get time to do this, then you begin to miss it, and the desire for time alone comes back intensely. If you are someone who likes to walk for exercise, and the weather prevents you going out, then you feel something missing from life. We return to our favourite restaurant, we meet with the same friends, we persist with the same hobbies and ways of doing things because we can anticipate with confidence the choices we will have to make.

Some habits are learnt through imitation, as children learn to do many things. Parents try to inculcate good habits in their children. A well-developed habit pre-disposes the person to making particular choices and behaviours. When faced with choices, our habits make it more likely that we will choose in a particular way. In fact, the familiarity of habit creates a comfort zone which drives us to seek situations where a particular choice is available to us. Thus the development of a habit also acts to reinforce perceptions and perspectives. Our habits create a context in which our actions and attitudes are validated, in which our choices are seen as the only valid options, and in which other options fade into the background and are not even considered.

Different aspects of our world view can also exist in an uneasy incongruent symbiosis. For instance, many of our desires are experienced at a subconscious level. I may proclaim a perspective on teaching which seeks to do something for students, to help them develop their talents and to succeed in life. I refer to these desires and assume that these drive my behaviour and approaches to teaching. However, I also have need of acceptance and control which I do not experience on an explicit, conscious level. In practice, I organize my classroom in a particular way to do what I think is important for the students. The perspective I use is my own philosophy of education, and this governs my perceptions of what is happen-ing in the classroom. I do not check anything out from the perspective of the students or their parents. If there is a mismatch between my expectations and their response, I put it down to a lack of maturity, a lack of appreciation on their part. I congratulate myself on my ambition for them, and choose to suffer as a martyr in their cause. I do not see a contradiction in my espoused desire to help students, and the desires which actually control behaviour and make me a (benign!) dictator.

Incongruities also exist in how schools are run. What the school aspires to and values is not always the same as it achieves and this sometimes goes unnoticed because of habits of mind which distort perception. For instance, a school may insist that students wear a uniform to help develop a sense of identity with the school. However, the way the dress code is implemented is more consistent with developing conformity and denying individuality in students, and they come to resent wearing it. For them, it is a symbol of oppression and alienation. Schools also profess the development of personal and cooperative values, but they exist in an environment where the primary focus is on students' achievement in examina-tions, and the school unwittingly adopts structures, motivational strategies and reward systems which promote high levels of competition between students. The espoused values of cooperation and sense of community have second place.

Understanding the inner world of the school means understanding the world view of the school. It means understanding at a deeper level the assumptions which operate in the context, perspectives, perceptions, desires, choices and habits which make up that world view. The interaction of the six levels poses a dilemma for the organizational leader or consultant who wants to help a school develop its culture. Where does one begin with change? Does one start with understanding context and developing new perspectives and perceptions as in psychoanalysis, hoping that it trickles down to new behaviours? Or does one try to build new habits through behaviour modification and hope that this leads to changed perspectives and a more meaningful context. There is a great danger in being too linear in one's thinking, moving from context to habit, or habit to context. The interactions and high levels of interdependence of one factor on another suggest that no single focus is enough. To change and maintain new habits will require the support of a new way of looking at things, and possibly a new context for the behaviour. Alternatively, to develop a new context, one also needs to take different decisions and develop new habits, or else one is condemned to reproducing the old context in a new situation.

The key to understanding and developing culture is to work on all six aspects of its structure together, incorporating an awareness and appreciation of context and perspectives when individuals are sharing their perceptions, as well as when they review their own habits and choices in the organization. In proposing changes of behaviour, the school must also give time to the transition of perspectives and perceptions which will be necessary in reinforcing the change. As in the creative writing exercise quoted at the beginning of the chapter, teachers inherit stories in their schools. Like the king in the story, they have a context set for them, with its own dragons, its history of ignoring them or sending out the army, and the legends of victories and defeats. Principals, as the architects and managers of school culture, must learn to read the story, to assess the resources available to them and to creatively propose new perspectives and perceptions which cage the dragon and empower the school to develop a fuller life for itself. The process of empowerment is built on being attentive to all aspects of the story and being realistic in how much of the problem can be 'solved', and how much of it can simply be 'contained' to allow for a more wholesome development.

### Notes

1   I first heard a version of this story from Don Clifton at a training course with Selection Research Inc. at Lincoln, Nebraska in 1982. It has been adapted in the telling and application over the years. Clifton's approach to story telling, and getting people to tell their own stories, had been a major influence on my own approach to working with teachers.
2   Fullan (1993) uses this image as one of his lessons of change. The image of journey allows for non-linear elements to be dealt with in working out the solution to problems.
3   This structure is based on the work of Joseph Tetlow, with whom I studied in Texas in 1990. He based his approach on the process philosophy of Whitehead, although the application here is not from a theoretical perspective. Tetlow's main focus is on individual spiritual development.

## Chapter 3

# Participation and Culture

In the previous two chapters, I have outlined three components of culture — arte-facts, values and assumptions. We saw how these components become powerfully embedded in a culture through the process of problem solving. The focus has been on the way individuals act. They respond within a particular context, and develop perspectives and perceptions which give rise to desires and values. They make decisions and form habits around assumptions which reflect their experience of how schools work. As well as this individual dimension, there is also a relationship which exists between individuals and an organization's culture.

Participation in culture is not uniform. Subcultures nuance what is meant by a common culture. In schools, the quality of the relationship between the individual and the school is very important. The meaning and value individuals place on structures and procedures — the artefacts of culture — give a qualitative dimension to their participation in the school. Meaning and value are given by individuals: artefacts are 'allowed' to affect the life of the school by the response and valuation processes of individuals. Certainly, artefacts are important ingredients in culture. Equally important is the process by which value is attributed by individuals and groups to these artefacts. In particular, the openness and ability of teachers, parents and students to change and integrate new values is an essential part of a living school culture. In this chapter, the focus is on the ways individuals participate in school culture. Reflection on the dynamics and structure of participation gives a deeper understanding of organizational culture, and gives insights into possible interventions which improve the quality of individual participation, and thus pro-motes the development of the inner world of the school.

## The Concerns of Participation

The success of any organization in achieving its goals depends on acquiring a language, a common body of terms and meanings so that members can commun-icate with one another efficiently. Commentators on group dynamics outline two main concerns of membership: the orientation to authority (power and the leader); and an orientation to intimacy (commitment and other group members)[1]. As indi-viduals come to a school, they bring with them a personal perspective on life and, in particular, on the school itself. Their first concerns are to define a suitable role for themselves in the school — one that conforms to their own expectations and that of management. As the participation develops, a psychological contract is formed and concerns of the individual turn to the development of identity and influence within the school. The growth of this sense of identity with one's role in the group is a form of personal intimacy, as the role determines a level of relationship with the other members of the group or the organization.

When students join a new school, their first concerns are with rules and regulations — what do they have to do, where do they have to be. Once the students have mastered the basics of transition into the school, and can find their classroom and understand their timetable, they look for friends and a group to identify with. They seek a sense of belonging among their peers, in their classroom, in their year and in the school. Among their peers, individuals makes friends with the person they sit beside, with others around them, perhaps with other students from their previous school. They decide to make new friends and develop new interests by joining clubs or sports teams. They learn how to relate to the expectations of teachers and quickly come to appreciate their status in the social system of the classroom. In much the same way, new teachers also get to know their own timetable, and the curriculum to be taught. They then get to know other teachers, those in the same department or those teaching the same students they teach. They also learn the social system of the staffroom and begin to identify with certain groups or cliques: the group which talks politics, the other which discusses sports and the third which swaps gossip and scandal.

The initial basis for joining a group is some degree of similarity or a way to complement one's own talents. Individuals look for friends or patrons, people who will help them belong to the organization. A sense of belonging to a small reference group gives confidence to test influence in the larger environment. At this stage, individuals seek to establish their identity by influencing those who were initially classified as dissimilar. They begin to take responsibility for the ideas and norms they have discovered in the small group and to promote these ideas with others, thus influencing other individuals and groups. However, identification with a small group sometimes brings with it a fear of being regarded as a peripheral clique with consequent isolation from meaningful experience in the school. Small mutual support groups experience a need to be involved and cooperate with other groups. This stage represents a transition from a need for influence to a need for intimacy. As groups experience this sense of belonging in a school, they may also feel a need for the integration of all the different roles within the school, to find some underlying unity and to make the most of everyone's capacities. Individuals idealistically see themselves and others in a state of interdependence.

The task and the social system of the school evolve through a complex set of relationships in which meaning is given to artefacts in the school, is shared with small groups of similar minded people and later negotiated with other groups of differing and contrasting views. As participation in the life of the school deepens, the reality of the shared meanings becomes the accepted norm of being, feeling, thinking and doing. The assumptions behind the activity and the relationships are taken for granted. They exert their influence in imperceptible but powerful ways, and are pervasive in the life of the individual and the school.

## Rashford and Coghlan's Four Levels[2]

The process of socialization deals with the development of the psychological contract in the individual. However, the participation of the individual in the organization is a complex matter, involving both personal factors and different degrees of interaction and cooperation with others. Therefore, it is important to have a framework in which to understand this participation, and also to have means of planning interventions which help develop the culture of the school. Rashford and Coghlan (1994) developed such a framework, describing four levels of participation which affect organizational culture: individual, team, group and organization. These levels can be applied to schools, particularly to the work of teachers who are the most stable population within the school. The pattern of participation also helps one reflect on the basic assumptions which individuals and schools have about the distribution of power and decision making within the school.

Level I, *the individual level*, describes the relationship which exists between the individual teacher and the school in which he or she works. For the individual teacher, this relationship involves a participation in the life and work of the school as part of a wider framework of personal life and career goals. The outcome of this relationship between teacher and school is an appropriate *bonding* relationship. A more complex approach to participation exists in establishing *effective working relationships in a face-to-face team* (Level II). An even more complex involvement exists in terms of the interdepartmental group where the work of multiple teams and groups must be *coordinated* in order to achieve interdisciplinary and interdepartmental tasks and maintain a balance of power among competing interest groups (Level III). Finally, the most complex, from the point of view of the individual, is the relationship of the school to a changing external environment. The key task for any organization is its ability to *adapt* to environmental forces which drive change (Level IV).

### *Level I — Individual*

The analysis of individual participation focuses on the way in which the school is integrated into the wider framework of personal life and career goals. From a school perspective, this involves having the individual committed to the goals, values and culture of the school. This refers to both students and teachers and can be extended to parents and other groups.

Students participate in the school against a general background of family support and values, developing personal identity and peer affiliations, and later focusing on future career aspirations. A major concern of schools is to develop structures which help individual students to integrate these areas of development with the values and culture which the school promotes. This is done through induction programmes at major transition points and a pastoral care system which is geared to the individual student to ensure that any difficulties in adapting to school can be dealt with quickly.

Promoting a sense of teacher bonding with the school involves understanding the psychological contract and career motivation of the individual teacher and how this is integrated with family interests and external attractions. Teachers respond to different forces in developing their careers. These can be broadly classified in three groups[3]:

(i)   *extrinsic* — the societal factors such as pay levels of teachers, opportunities for other employment, the status of teaching as a profession;

(ii)  *personal* — getting married, having children, personal ageing, illness, winning the lottery;

(iii) *intrinsic* — changing views of teaching, satisfaction from the experience of school, opportunities for professional development.

In forming a career bond with a school, individual teachers seek their own unique and personal satisfaction in the world of school work and relationships. When bonding is successful, there is a match between individual and school goals. Individuals can allow the school to become a source for their own personal goals, and the school accommodates individuals so that they retain their own individuality while 'belonging' to the school. For individuals embracing a career in education, this bonding has both a personal and a professional dimension.

An important issue in understanding career is the image people have of their careers. For some, the career is often seen as having a particular goal, a destination. Progress on the career journey is charted, and success is defined in terms of key events: — first job, a car, a particular salary level, marriage, a house. These are seen as intermediate destinations towards the final one. Yet, frequently, in middle age, a pinnacle is reached only to find there is no 'there', only further journeys, this time with more side roads, and almost inevitably delays and road-works with which to cope. The realization of mortality reveals that there are some 'nevers' in life — things that will now never be done or achieved. Success is now measured in terms of process rather than outcomes. For instance, the decision to marry and raise a family gives rise to a developing set of personal concerns. The first half of adult life is taken up with raising the family, and is interspersed with key events related to family life as children grow and develop, become enmeshed in the educational process themselves and finally in the search for employment, career and family of their own. In the latter half of adult life, the focus of relationships with children and grandchildren is more on process and quality rather than having active responsibility for making things happen. This personal process has implications for career development.

As they move through these personal life stages and the age gap between them and the students widens, the teacher's perspective on the teaching career alters. The young single teacher in the early stages of the teaching career may devote a great deal of physical energy to coaching sports, to field trips and to other extra-curricular activities. Later in life, when that teacher has his or her own family concerns and the energy and inclination for that earlier form of involvement no longer exists, there needs to be new ways of developing participation which is appropriate to age and experience. In the same vein, when a teacher has been in the same school for many years and when opportunities for development have not been provided or availed of, bonding may take a negative turn and give rise to alienation and disengagement.

Commentators on the world of work indicate changing attitudes to employment, where there is an increasing sense of commitment to a 'professional ideal' rather than a loyalty to a particular school, institution or organization (Handy, 1994). When teachers come to a school, their loyalties to the school are very varied. For some there is a willingness and openness to develop a strong bond with the particular school whereas others are focused on using their present position as a stepping stone to some further advancement in their own careers[4]. The focus of individual teachers in their own professional development, and their use of external or internal reference groups, dictates a quality of bonding with their individual schools.

For some, the progress through the personal life and career stages is quite calm, but not for all. Personal life histories may (but equally may not) have significant impact on the individual's bonding to the school. However, an understanding of the changing personal perspectives and energy of the individual teacher is a key to understanding the psychological contract made with the school, and the centrality of meaning that arises from participation in the school culture.

*Level II — Face-to-face Team*

From the individual's perspective, entry into the school means meeting with other people and working with them. This happens in teams. Teams are typically formal groups and defined in terms of: face-to-face interaction; common objectives; psychological awareness of other members; and self-definition as a team with boundaries between members and non-members clearly defined. The team level is a more complex level than the individual because of the increased number of participants and interactions. Teams are parts of a wider system in organizations and some of the dysfunctional issues that arise within the team may originate beyond the team in its technological and political interface with other teams. Problems which arise between teams are considered at Level III.

Teams give an increased sense of community and shared ownership with the task of the school. Ensuring that students are offered opportunities to learn through cooperative projects within the curriculum, through community service projects involving people less fortunate than themselves, and that they begin to understand the use of power and process by running student societies and committees, are all aspects of school life which involve students in teamwork.

Typically teaching has been classified as an individual, private activity. Teachers have been masters in their own classroom, and there has been no reason or need to engage in meaningful teamwork with other teachers. Any participation at this level occurred on a purely voluntary basis. However, modern schools show a growing need for teamwork among teachers. Teachers may be involved in teams relating to a particular subject department, curriculum development or team-teaching project, or they may be involved in a devolved management team. To move beyond the stage of being a collectivity — individuals who come together — to that of a team, strategies need to be developed in terms of (a) setting goals and priorities (b) allocating work (c) evaluating processes within the group and (d) evaluating the relationships among group members. Interpersonal problems between team members can result from a lack of clarity about team goals, procedures, responsibilities or roles. Similarly, procedural problems can result from a vagueness about responsibilities, roles and goals. Alternatively, problems about roles and responsibilities can arise because of a lack of clarity about team goals and priorities. Thus, team development focuses on the clarification of the content and process of task accomplishment and the maintenance of working relationships.

Process refers to how a team works to achieve its goals. In some schools, the procedure for meetings may be very traditional and well established. (The principal chairs the meeting and the junior member of staff takes the minutes!) Sometimes, such procedures may be unsuitable for the particular task. For instance, a meeting which proceeds in terms of motions proposed, seconded and voted on, would seem to be counterproductive to a discussion on pastoral needs. More important, however, are the informal procedures which give high or low status to some individuals, which attach blame to some individuals and regulate how minorities (students!) are treated — even in their representation on such committees.

Requirements for teamwork in schools typically arise from: (1) devolved management structures; (2) educational planning groups; and (3) pedagogy. These afford teachers an opportunity to develop essential team skills.

## Management structures

Increasingly, teachers are involved in management teams in schools. The development of middle-management structures requires team skills which focus on agenda setting, chairing meetings and motivating others. This level requires members to think beyond their own personal needs in terms of team needs. Typical teams at this level are Boards of Governors, year heads, pastoral care personnel, subject departments, subcommittees dealing with issues such as discipline, staff development, finance and fundraising. Team skills can also be applied to teacher union meetings and student council moderation. Some of these teams have very clearly defined functions. Others run into difficulties because of different expectations of roles — whether the primary function of the team is support for individual members or involved in policy development (e.g. a pastoral care team in a school). Another source of confusion with some committees is whether their role is advisory, or whether it is a decision-making group (e.g. in the case of year heads discussing issues, and the subsequent role of the principal or vice-principal with regard to the decision).

## Educational planning

A second form of involvement of teachers in teams is in educational planning. For instance, subcommittees set up to examine issues of new programme development,

the introduction of new curricula, or the educational impact of organizational structures such as streaming, focus on an area of professional expertise and competence
for teachers which differs from the management concerns outlined above. Team
skills here focus on listening, evaluating data and developing consensus. Some of
the same issues arise for process as in management teams. Is the team advisory or
decision making? Does the team make recommendations only or is it responsible
for implementation as well? Lack of clarity on the fundamental purpose of the team
gives rise to frustrations both within the team, and with the team. Developing clarity
on these issues allows members to plan their participation and focus their energy on
the task at hand.

## Pedagogy

Level II issues of teamwork also apply to the area of curriculum delivery. There has
been a growing awareness of the discontinuity of approaches between primary and
post-primary schools. In secondary schools, which have traditionally been more
subject oriented in the approach to teaching, this has posed a challenge to focus on
a variety of learning processes in students, and for teachers to adopt their strategies
to these different learning styles. Projects, discovery learning, group work, peer
learning and portfolio assessment are words which have found their way into current pedagogical philosophy. These approaches have implications for the type of
relationship that exists between teacher and learners and require the development
of team skills. As well as the demand for a changed pedagogy, with the emphasis
on the teacher as a facilitator of learning, there has also been a development of
curricula which promote an interdisciplinary approach to teaching, and see a role
in team teaching. This proposed change in 'peer relationships' between teachers in
their professional work is a radical shift in thinking, and demands skills of cooperative
teamwork, in planning and delivery.

### Level III — Inter-departmental Group

In its essence, Level III comprises any number of face-to-face working teams
which must function together to accomplish school goals. This inter-departmental
group level needs to have critical information which passes beyond the boundaries
of particular teams in order to implement programmes and projects at a range
beyond their direct contact. In large organizations, where size and distance dissolve
immediate personal relationships, it is imperative that this third level functions
well. From management's standpoint, each team's tasks within the overall group is
to perform effectively in its own right, while at the same time having a clearly defined commitment to the whole school. When this third level is working effectively,
people in the middle-management group are capable of obtaining information and
converting it into decision processes, enabling the implementation of complex programmes or operations. The task at this level is to map the flow of information and
partially completed work from one team to another. Management needs are that
these teams form an integrated whole.

The identification of the need for integration of teams within the school is a response to the identification of legitimate stakeholders within the school. Teams formed for specific functions within the school obviously have to be coordinated, but so also do less formal teams, such as parents and non-teaching staff. The development of ownership of the educational goals of the school is determined in large part by building a climate of trust, cooperation and commitment to participative responsibility on the part of the different teams and commitment to listening and responsiveness on the part of management.

There are many obstacles to cooperation at this level. In Western society, the role of education has become a critical element in selection for employment. Second-level education is no longer a terminal stage for many students. They aspire to places in third-level institutions with a view to better qualifications and entrance into highly paid work. Competition for such places is often very keen and schools are no longer regarded as 'finishing academies'. In their new role as 'means to ends', they are strongly influenced by the need to produce good results and place their students. For students for whom second-level education is terminal, chances of employment are largely determined by performance on school tests. This has further increased the 'sorting and labelling' function of second-level schools, and created a high level of competition among students for the necessary credentials. This competition has been extended to inter-school rivalry, with the development of league tables based on academic results.

As well as this academic concentration, the increased participation rates in education have shown up needs for non-academic programmes more responsive to student and community needs. This requires new resources, especially personnel, for such functions as home–school liaison, remedial work, guidance and counselling. It seems that an inevitable consequence of these developments is an increased tension within schools as they seek to provide the resources to respond to the specific needs and demands of students and parents. This can give way to rivalry between subjects — science and language, practical subjects (woodwork, computer studies), cultural subjects (art, music), as they seek quality time on the schedule, as well as teaching resources and equipment. In some cases, the resourcing of some subjects is the cause of acute envy and dissatisfaction within the teaching staff.

As well as the status of individual subjects within the curriculum, there is also competition for status between curricular and co-curricular activities. Participation in activities such as games, school drama and field trips can impinge on the academic programme of the school, and the demands of both areas need to be coordinated. In other schools one sees a tension between pastoral care and academic programmes, or between religious goals of community and secular goals of individualism. One gives rise to cooperation and the other to competition.

Level III can be a highly political situation in which the in-built structural conflicts of multiple-interest parties need to be resolved. As an inter-departmental group, this diversified mass of differing functions and interests must negotiate an outcome that adequately reflects the balance of power and a distribution of resources among competing coalitions. Essential elements in Level III dynamics centre on issues of power and on how power is exercised in the allocation of resources and the accessibility of information.

### Level IV — Organizational

The fourth level relates to the organizational goals, policy and strategy level, which constitutes the fusion of all three levels together to form a working, cohesive organization. A school promotes itself as having a clear purpose and identity in a highly competitive environment. Consequently, a school needs to be capable of reflecting on its own strengths and weaknesses, as well as engaging in proactive relationships to determine and deal with the opportunities and threats from the external environment. The assessment of strengths, weaknesses, opportunities and threats results in a selection process which establishes programmes and services. These procedures aim at accomplishing the goals of the school and adapting to external environmental demands. An awareness of the cultural assumptions which underlie any school's policies, strategies, structures and behaviours contributes to the successful completion of the tasks at this level.

At this level, education policy is seen as part of a broader social policy, and the provision of educational services is examined in the light of other social demands. Social policy is affected by demographic issues such as birth rates, the proportion of younger and older people in a population and levels of unemployment among the workforce. These factors place demands on government for the provision of health services, pensions and social welfare. This gives rise to competition between educational needs and these other social needs in the national budget. In seeking to provide these services, governments are faced with options of borrowing, increased taxation or cut-backs in public expenditure. The net result of this dilemma is a lack of what might be termed 'discretionary funds' — funds earmarked for non-essential desirable and/or experimental programmes.

In such an environment, the development of a mission statement gives direction to school policy and decision making. A mission statement states a school's unique 'reason to be'. It says what the school does and what it promises. The mission statement therefore gives direction and sets expectations for people inside and outside the organization. It gives a description of the preferred future of the organization and becomes a foundation and energy source for all the organization's stakeholders — those who have a clear interest in the school's future. It serves as the basis for every important decision, and shapes the day-to-day activities (and thus the future) of the school. The development of a mission statement is therefore part of a strategic planning process, involving external and internal stakeholders, which aims at clarifying the aims of the school and how the school's value system underpins these aims, understanding the many forces which promote and hinder its goals, assessing the strengths and weaknesses of the school, deciding on policy priorities and on practical steps to implement that policy.

The educational system has already responded to some of the environmental changes. There is a growing awareness of the link between education and employment and there has been a growth in investment in new vocational courses, and in particular in training students in new technologies. The European Union had made substantial investment in such training programmes in its own jurisdiction, giving rise to a 'training versus education' debate which helps clarify the core mission of a school, and expose the underlying assumptions and values of the stakeholders in education.

New forms of governance in education, with increased parental participation in management structures and with advisory functions to curriculum planning are the result of a new sense of democracy in public education, especially in Europe. The ideal of this increased participation is to provide leadership and vision for the school, to ensure that it becomes a reflective organization, involved in not only 'doing the thing right' in being an effective and efficient implementor of policy, but also an organization which 'does the right thing' (Bennis and Nanus, 1985). This latter leadership role embraces the moral dimension of education and reflects not only on effective and efficient, but also on appropriate, policy.

### Inter-level Dynamics

The framework of the organizational levels does not confine itself to a description of what takes place on each of the four levels. A significant element of the framework is how the four levels are integrally linked and interdependent.

In viewing the interrelationship and interdependence of the individual level with each of the other three, it is clear that an individual's attitudes and behaviour can affect the working of the team, the coordination of the inter-departmental group and the effectiveness of the school. If a principal or vice-principal is having personal problems or is alienated and demotivated (Level I), this will affect the formulation and implementation of policy (Level IV), and the coordination of the multiple activities in the school (Level III). The whole school may be afflicted with a malaise. Similarly, a change in school policy may affect how an individual feels about being in the school, either positively or negatively. For instance, the introduction of co-education or an amalgamation with another school (Level IV) may give a new sense of direction to some teachers (Level I), and facilitate their commitment to participation in teamwork and management structures (Levels II and III).

The development of a mission statement is typically a Level IV activity. A mission statement which has clear values becomes a standard against which future developments and proposals can be discussed. This focus has the potential of raising the quality of debate on educational issues, of giving clear direction to teams working in the school, and their coordination (Levels I, II and III). The effective working of teams and committees may provide added motivation and help develop individual skills and contribute to the overall quality of the school (Levels I and IV). Mission statements are also an important part of the induction process of new teachers, and provide direction for personal in-career development decisions (Level I). There is always a danger that a badly developed mission statement will be seen as a blueprint for the future, developed externally to be imposed on other levels.

It may very well come to haunt administrators and staff alike. It becomes a tool in bargaining, subject to minimalist interpretations on the one hand, leading to destructive inter-team relations or excessive competition affecting morale and the school's performance (Level III). On the other hand, the mission statement may be used as a means of coercion, thus alienating teachers who do not 'own' the mission (Level I).

Another Level IV activity is the analysis of the changing environment of the school. The changing social situation of students — family structures, attachments and values, participation of students in part-time work to supplement family income and personal lifestyle — has major implications for school discipline and attendance. These changes often present problems at the classroom level for the individual teacher, who has to develop new skills to cope with new situations (Level I). Failure to cope with such changes can lead to stress and burn-out. At school level, there is a continuing need to co-ordinate approaches to discipline and pastoral care, which involves teachers in teamwork to ensure a just response to all situations (Levels II and III).

The four levels are integrally interrelated and interdependent. The implication for the management and leadership of schools is that not only must the issues at each level be consciously managed but also, the effects of one level on the others need to be afforded equal attention.

The four organizational levels are a framework for integrating policy formulation and development (Level IV), resource allocation and inter-departmental coordination (Level III), teamwork (Level II) and teacher development (Level I). The framework can also be applied to more complex systems than the individual school. Clearly, the four levels can be applied equally to the education system, where the development of national policy constitutes Level IV, the coordination across the schools in the system Level III, how individual schools work to meet the policy requirement Level II and how individual teachers bond to their work Level I. The framework also applies to students in school — how individual students bond with the school (Level 1), how they co-operate in the classroom with a teacher and other students (Level II), how they coordinate and manage the demands of different classes and choose elective subjects (Level III) and the relevance of the curriculum offered by the school to meet personal and vocational needs, and their involvement in decision-making processes within the school (Level IV). Parental involvement in schools can also be viewed from the perspective of the four levels. Parents may be consulted individually with regard to their child's needs or progress (Level I). They may sometimes work together for some project — fundraising, open days, sports day (Level II). These efforts may be co-ordinated through some kind of Parents Association (Level III). Parents may also be involved as a recognized stakeholder on Boards of Management, or may be consulted with regard to the development of school policy (Level IV).

Viewing schools as social systems in which there is a integral link between how policy is formulated and implemented, how the work of the school is managed and coordinated, how people work together and finally how the individual teachers, students and parents find satisfaction and contribute actively to the work of the school is essential for coordinated renewal. The construct of organizational levels is a useful tool in understanding the nature of individual developmental needs, focusing on team function and coordination within the school, and the development of policy and vision which both inspires and sustains development at an individual and a team level. Each of the levels makes an important contribution to the organizational culture of the school and can help develop guidelines for interventions which develop that culture. The levels are also integrally linked, and each individual level affects and is affected by the other three levels. The development of one level gives rise to a changed context and perspectives at other levels, and these changes give rise to new choices and habits, affecting organizational culture. Consequently, effective school development involves not only the development *of* each level, but development *between* each level. In Parts Two and Three we look more specifically at interventions at each of these levels.

---

**Reflection 3.1**

Apply Figure 3.1 to your own school. Typically, you will need one sheet of paper for each of the squares.

| | Level I<br>Individual | Level II<br>Team | Level III<br>Internal | Level IV<br>Organization |
|---|---|---|---|---|
| Individual | | | | |
| Team | | | | |
| Internal Group | | | | |
| Organization | | | | |

*Figure 3.1   Grid to develop the inter-level effects of Rashford and Coghlan's four levels in a school setting*

- Draw up your own description of health and good development at each of the four levels — individual, team, group and organization. Place these in the shaded areas of Figure 3.1. Now, work along the lines. How does the climate of the shaded square impact on other squares on the same line? Write a description of the effects for each box along the line.

- Repeat the exercise using negative developments and dysfunction in the four levels. These are placed in the shaded square, and again you work your way along each line, filling in the effects of negative development on each of the other levels.
- Now compare the two sets of data. Which areas are most relevant to your school? Does this give cause for celebration, or for reorganisation? What stands out as priority?

Take a proposal for restructuring or intervention. Outline the possible effects on each of the four levels, positive and negative. What are the areas that are most likely to hinder the success of the project? What areas are likely to promote the project?

## Notes

1 These concepts are dealt with in most books on group dynamics. A summary can be found in Schein (1980).
2 Rashford and Coghlan (1994) have developed their scheme in the world of business. Applications of this scheme have been used for schools and for teachers by Tuohy and Coghlan (1994, 1997).
3 This conceptualization is a development of Herzberg's hygiene and motivating factors and Alderfer's categories of existence, relatedness and growth needs.
4 An application of this sense of belonging is discussed in Chapter 8 using the categories devised by Gouldner (1957).

*Part Two*

*Exploring Assumptions*

## Chapter 4

# Personal Metaphors of School

In Shakespeare's *As You Like It*, Jacques reflects on the wide and universal theatre of life and claims:

> All the world's a stage, and all the men and women merely players. They have their exits and their entrances, and one man in his time plays many parts, his acts being seven ages. (Act II, scene 7)

He goes on to describe the unfolding drama of human existence in the different stages of the lifecycle — from the baby 'mewling and puking in the nurse's arms' to the last scene 'which ends this strange eventful history, in second childishness, sans teeth, sans eyes, sans taste, sans everything'. In *Hamlet, Prince of Denmark*, the power of drama is used to reveal the dark inner secrets of the regent king and his consort. Hamlet suspects his uncle of murdering his father and usurping his position as king. Unable to find proof, he persuades a band of travelling players to put on a play which re-enacts the way his father has been killed. He plans to confirm his suspicions by watching his uncle during the play:

> I'll observe his looks: I'll tent him to the quick: if he but blench, I know my course. . . . The play's the thing wherein I'll catch the conscience of the king. (Act II, Scene 2)

Since earliest times, people have enacted the drama of their existence in art and story-telling. Stories expressing the common truths, beliefs and hopes of life are universal. The oral tradition of primitive tribes was a means of preserving and transmitting images and meanings. Key events in their history were recorded and heroes and heroines honoured. Children were taught the distinction between good and evil and were inducted into the tradition of the community or tribe through stories. Although the modern world has a much greater reliance on the written word, children still love stories at bedtime, and their stories are often designed to give a sense of confidence that the world is good and that 'all live happily ever after'. Adults, too, love stories and these are often repeated at family gatherings, meetings of friends and school reunions. The phrase 'Do you remember the time . . .' is the occasion to introduce the well-rehearsed story of the fish that got away; Grandpa's reminiscences of the good old days and family memories of the eccentricities of Aunt Jemima — the stories which make up a personal and a family tradition. The story implies a relationship between the story-teller and the audience, as well as between the audience and the story itself. The telling of the story unites the audience. Everyone enters into the same story, visualizes the same thing and focuses on the same emotions. Images and meanings are shared together and the audience is caught up in the flow of the story.

Story-telling depends on images and metaphors. Characteristics are attributed to an object which are not strictly true, yet the analogy conjures up a creative relationship and meaning. Metaphors do not record already existing similarities in objects or situations. Rather, they are artefacts of language which bring diverse and dissimilar thoughts together and reframe our perceptions of the world. The metaphors we construct of our world are also powerful determinants of future experiences. In some cases, our metaphors create reality. They influence our perceptions and guide our actions. In a sense, the metaphor becomes a self-fulfilling prophecy of life[1].

The relationship between perception and action, however, is complex. Argyris and Schon (1978) claim that all deliberate human action has a cognitive basis and reflects 'espoused theories' and 'theories in action'. These theories are built from norms, strategies and assumptions or models of the world. 'Theory in action' is reflected in personally constructed representations or images which often exist at an unconscious level. 'Espoused theory', on the other hand, represents the inherited wisdom and image which can be referred to at will. Grady (1993) used a powerful example. No educator seriously espouses the metaphor of a school as a prison. Yet some people remember their schooldays as if they were in a prison, and the teachers worked in custodial roles. The inmates (students) were physically abusive to one another, and they and visitors (parents) had no rights while the officers (teachers) and warden (principal) had all the rights. Teachers who act in such a manner are said to have school as prison as a 'theory in action'. The effect of this subconscious mental model is that any discussion on school improvement with these teachers would, at best, centre on making the prison a better prison, with improved security and better control, without ever questioning whether this was an appropriate image for a school or not. To change the metaphor then is to change the theory for this individual[2].

Organizations are complex, ambiguous and paradoxical in nature, and they can be many things simultaneously. The individual may move between many images of the school, oblivious to the controlling metaphors, and referring only to a single espoused theory. The process of exploring metaphors is similar to the Freudian technique of eliciting responses to images, entering into them and exploring their influences on attitudes and behaviours.

In assessing an exercise on metaphor development, success does not depend so much on the actual metaphors developed, but on the quality of interaction between group members as they share insights and images with one another. This quality can be determined by the elaboration of aspects of the initial metaphor proposed to the group and how they apply it to schooling. A facilitator can help this by encouragement and reinforcing feedback, and occasionally by probing questions and challenges about areas not addressed. In applying the metaphors to schooling, the

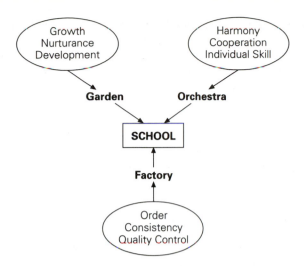

*Figure 4.1   The structure of Chapter 4: Areas of underlying assumptions about school revealed through metaphor*

individual or the group might explore what the metaphor reveals about assumptions such as those outlined in Chapter 1 on the relationship of the school to the environment, the nature of human activity, truth, reality and time, human nature and human relationships. Alternatively, the group might reflect on the context–perspective–perception–desire–decision–habit complex which the application of the metaphor reveals. With this in mind, the rest of this chapter develops three metaphors which have proved very successful in my own work with teachers (see Figure 4.1). The three metaphors of school as garden, orchestra and factory each stand for a particular aspect of schooling, but there are areas of overlap common to all. The metaphor of the garden is broken down and explored in some detail to illustrate levels of the creativity which groups have brought to this exercise. The metaphors of orchestra and factory are slightly more compact, and illustrate different ways in which metaphor can be explored, depending on the time available. The treatment of the images here is not exhaustive, and the reader's own experience can add to the richness of both the image and its interpretation.

### The Garden Metaphor

The metaphor of the school as a garden is not exactly original. It goes back at least to the days of Pestalozzi, and is the basis for the term Kindergarten (garden of children). However, the metaphor still appeals to teachers and parents because it is associated with growth, nurturing and development. Depending on the type of assumptions you wish to explore, you may focus the exercise on particular aspects of the garden. Figure 4.2 illustrates some of these aspects.

*Figure 4.2   Aspects of the garden metaphor and the focus of application to schools*

---

**Exercise 4.1**

Before going any further, you might like to anticipate the exercise for yourself. There are two parts to the exercise. First, describe the garden, and then apply it to the school. Do not mix the two parts by jumping into the application too soon.

Focus on your own image of a garden. Describe your favourite garden, or an ideal garden. Note its salient features — its size, its design, its location, the types of plants there, the people who come to the garden and the use they make of it. What is the purpose of the garden?

The second part of the exercise asks you to reflect on the question 'How is a school like a garden?' Take some of the images you have described in the first part of this garden exercise, and ask yourself what these stand for in a school. What do the different types of gardens represent in education, or in an individual school? What do the different layouts of gardens represent?

---

### The Garden

If you have completed Exercise 4.1, either by yourself or with a group of colleagues, you will have anticipated much of what I will share with you here — images of gardens and their application to education that arose in my own work. You will be interested to see the common ground your own thinking has — and where it diverges. You may find yourself affirmed or challenged in your thinking about schools. The reflection on the type of garden you cultivate reveals the context you have for the school. The type of garden you imagine says something about your concept of growth and development, your preference for how things should be arranged and ordered, and the type of work which has to be done to make that garden a reality. As such, exploring the metaphor and applying it to education can reveal assumptions about teaching and learning, about the organization of the school and the role it plays in society.

### Developing the image

Gardens have sacred associations. Paradise is depicted as the Garden of Eden, a place of tranquillity, harmony and peace. In it humankind was at one with God and at peace with itself. The Garden also contained the tree of knowledge and wisdom, and hidden there was temptation and the danger of self-destruction. In Christian spirituality, the garden has been one of the central images. Spiritual development has been variously compared to the growth of the seed, a battle with weeds and producing a hundred-fold harvest.

One of the fascinations of the great houses of Europe was the development of formal gardens. Botanical and horticultural societies as well as wealthy families went to great lengths to design gardens of distinction, importing trees and plants from different climates to bring colour and enhancement to an indigenous land-scape. These gardens, once designed as part of the private wealth of individuals, are now more in the public domain, although the public may well be charged to enter and look back on past glories.

Some gardens are designed for play. The serious play of adults is simulated in the philosophical symbolism of life found in the design of Japanese gardens, which use the arrangement of water, wells, bridges, altitude, stones and ornaments among delicate plants and special bonsai miniatures to create a reflective theme on the human journey through life, and beyond. The development of hedged mazes such as that at Hampton Court reveal a fascination with mathematical playthings. Other gardens are designed for recreational play, with a tree-house or children's swings hanging from sturdy branches, croquet or bowling lawns, large spaces to run on, even to transform in the imagination into the great stadia of the world where children (and sometimes their parents!) perform spectacular athletic feats. There may be bushes to hide in, where they become artefacts in games of great mystery, adventure and intrigue.

Fruit and vegetable gardens are also popular, where the emphasis is more on utility. In some estate gardens, the vegetable garden was a large area specially set aside and cultivated to provide fresh vegetables for the household all year round. In Africa, vegetables dominate the garden, with little space (or precious water) alloc-ated to flowers. Sometimes the growing of such plants, especially fruit, demands security and protection, with houses guarding their apple trees against the orchard raids of the neighbours' children. In the concrete jungles of urban areas, where houses are built without gardens, people buy or rent allotments in order to have their own 'patch'. If people cannot manage their own garden or allotment, they develop windowboxes and hanging baskets, creating miniature gardens of their own.

A commercial focus can be found in garden centres. Seedlings, shrubs and bushes are grown in sheltered or protected areas and sold to the public for trans-planting in their own homes. They are sold in a reasonably well-developed state, where they have a better chance of survival and require less care than raising them from seed. When one enters the Garden Centre, the plants are carefully sorted to facilitate selection — indoor plants, others for outdoor bedding, plants for ground cover, for climbing. They are marked and priced.

Not everyone treats a garden in the same way. As one walks through a suburban area, gardens may be open to view, or may be well hedged, to emphasize privacy. Some gardens are not well cared for. The family (or worse, the neighbour's) dog or cat may like to come in and root in a newly planted flower bed. Sometimes, pests such as slugs, greenfly and different fungi attack the plants. Weeds are a constant hazard, and some are quite persistent, quickly taking hold to spread throughout the lawn or the flowerbed. If lawns are not cut, they develop weeds and look unsightly. If neglected, gardens become overgrown and return to a wild state. In some places, people lose interest in or do not value the idea of a garden, and they put tarmac over the area, using it to park their cars.

## Application to education

Like gardens, there are different images of schools. They too have sacred associations. The history of education shows that early attempts at formal education were often centred around a religious settlement where the druids or the temple priests were inducted into the history and the sacred practices of their culture and religion. In western history, formal education consisted mainly of reading the Bible and the study of philosophy and theology. It was conducted in the great monasteries of Europe, and when lay people were included, it was to share that same education, to learn to read the scriptures and the theo-centric interpretation of world history. The philosophy of education which focuses on the development of holistic human development — physical, emotional, social and spiritual — echoes the images of religious growth and development.

Like the stately gardens, the historical content of education was largely formal, concerned with the beauty and the symmetry of creation. It concentrated on the classical texts, seeking to enhance the lives of individuals by reference to the lives and philosophy of the great civilizations of Greece and Rome. The study of these texts aimed at enlightening people as to the good life and inspiring them to embrace it. In many ways, education aims to form new landscapes of thought patterns.

The twentieth century has seen the development of mass education, the purpose of which is influenced by industrial needs and developments. Just as the stately homes no longer dominate the countryside but have become part of a public domain, education is no longer the exclusive domain of the rich and better-off classes. The classical approach no longer suits the new clientele, and so new curricula have been developed. Although students are occasionally taken to visit the historic landscapes, schools organize themselves to promote different types of plants and to show them off to the best advantage.

Different types of schools reflect different concerns and goals. The pre-school atmosphere which encourages development through play reflects the family or leisure garden. The formal school of primary and secondary levels reflects various concerns of order, exploration, productivity, appreciation of beauty and other cultures, creativity and understanding the meaning of life. These too have their parallels in garden designs. Just as vegetable and market gardens became popular, so also in education there was a greater demand for relevance, for an education suited to local needs and environment, rather than a reliance on 'imported' ideas and concepts. Some schools have responded by specializing in a particular type of curriculum (e.g. vocational education, sixth-form education) whereas others have remained comprehensive and general. In Africa, for instance, the focus on vegetables in the garden is reflected in the allocation of education resources to developing practical and useful skills which focus on employment and economic development. The curriculum is very focused on the pragmatic, with little place given to history, music and art. It is assumed that such values are transmitted in the local community and school has a different focus.

Productivity and the ability to sort students into vocational skill categories tend to dominate the development of some schools. As with the arrangement of plants in a market garden, the arrangement of schooling and of assessment procedures helps employers to find different types of students and to identify their skill level. Just as gardens can be compared on the level of complexity of plants grown, the care taken of them and the way they are displayed, so also schools can be compared on the basis of the curriculum and the attention given to students. Some schools are very open to public view, others are quite private. Some schools unfortunately resemble neglected gardens, and other schools are quite barren, resembling tarmac spaces requiring low maintenance and low interest.

The point of this exercise is that images of growth and development in the garden can be transferred to the school context. The application of the metaphor reveals hidden assumptions about schooling and the importance of some practices to the 'espoused theory'. It helps us understand the type of garden we want to grow ourselves, and to understand the gardens that colleagues may be cultivating. A source of tension in schools is that teachers may be developing different types of 'gardens'. Schools may need to decide to work on one type of garden, or to allow different teachers to develop their own garden within a single estate. By sharing images of gardens, teachers come to appreciate new possibilities for their own gardens. They develop plans to incorporate new elements into their design. They also come to see other gardens in a new light.

---

**Reflection 4.1**

You might like to go back now to your own image of the garden. You may see possibilities for a new design in your 'school/garden' — a new flowerbed, or a new arrangement of plants, or perhaps even a new section in the garden.

Compare your own imagery and that raised in the text. What is the common ground? What is different? What did you include? What did you omit? Does this point to assumptions about human nature, human activity, relationships, the environment, etc. such as those raised in Chapter 1. What does it say about the different context, perspective, perceptions, desires, decisions and habits of thinking you and I might have?

---

*The Plants*

We now expand the metaphor of the garden, with a slightly different focus. This time we focus specifically on the plants in the garden. Again, the reader might like to do the exercise before reading any further.

---

**Exercise 4.2**

As before, we start with a description of the different types of plants. Make a list of different types of plants and their characteristics.

Now apply the metaphor to schools. We ask ourselves what do the plants stand for. How is a student like a plant? How is a teacher like a plant? How is knowledge like a plant?

Complete this exercise by yourself before you read any further, where you can read how other teachers have used the imagery of plants in a similar exercise.

---

Plants exist in a bewildering variety of shapes and sizes. There are large trees, which survive for hundreds of years, giving shade and shelter. Some are evergreen, and change very little during the year. Others are deciduous, changing with the seasons, giving delicate green colours in spring, a solid green through the summer, delicate shades of yellow and brown in the autumn, and a skeletal outline in the winter. Trees tend to dominate a landscape, towering over other plants and controlling the amount of light available. In some landscapes, a lone tree stands out. Other varieties grow in little plantations or great forests. These may be made up of the same variety, or may be mixed with other species. Some trees are commercially valuable, whereas others are more decorative and interest in them is more specialized.

Shrubs and bushes also give shade or ground cover. Like trees, they come in different shapes and sizes. Some produce brilliant flowers and great displays which last for a long season. The flowers of other shrubs are more ephemeral, lasting only a short time. Some of these shrubs are also evergreen, and can be cut to form exotic shapes and images. Some protect themselves from damage through defence mechanisms, by developing thorns, stinging capacity, odour or simply entwining themselves around other plants.

Some plants are cultivated for their colourful flowers and foliage, others for their nutrient value. Some of these plants have been cultivated from a wild form, through years of experimental cross-pollination or grafting. Some plants are hardy and survive in most environments whereas others are delicate and choosy, requiring a very precise habitat. Delicate orchids for example are raised in glasshouses, with carefully regulated heat requirements. Some plants start off in glasshouses during a period of cold or frost, and later are placed in the open, to survive the buffeting of the elements. For many plants, a typical garden is not their natural habitat, but something artificial. Being cultivated changes the pattern of competition for light and nutrients and allows the plant to flourish in a way not possible in the wild. Some plants require regular feeding, whereas others die if they are given too many nutrients. Some plants grow quickly and spread rapidly, climbing over walls or trellises, whereas other plants take years to develop, growing very slowly. Perennials flower regularly from year to year, whereas other plants have a short lifespan, flowering once and are not seen again.

Plants also reproduce in different ways. Some are wind pollinated and must depend on what it blows in their direction. Others depend on insects, often in a very specialized way, to carry the pollen to a receptive plant. When pollinated, some plants produce thousands of seeds, and spread them to the air in the hope of finding a place to rest, whereas other plants produce very few seeds, reasonably confident that they can find a place to grow and develop. Indeed, some plants do not produce seeds at all, but depend on vegetative growth, or grafting, to establish a new colony.

In cultivated gardens, plants are often protected from competition from other plants — weeds. Weeds are not wanted in a garden. Although there is plenty of room for them, they never get established before being forcibly removed. In the wild, these same 'weeds' might be admired for their survival capacity. There they struggle for survival, finding a precarious niche among the other plants.

There are many ways in which the metaphor can be developed. The plants may be thought of as students, as teachers and as knowledge itself. Just as there are many different types of plants, so also there are different types of students and different learning styles. A tree may represent the student who sets down deep academic roots and stands out for their brilliance in a class. Bright students such as this are sometimes organized into their own class — a plantation or forest. Some students seem to be delicate, and need a lot of attention. They are sensitive to changes in classroom climate and in work methods, and are easily put off. Like a plant which starts off in the greenhouse before planting out, special care must be taken of these students if they are to function properly in school. Others are more sturdy, and seem to take everything in their stride. They are unaffected by changing grades, by different teacher styles, by praise or by criticism. They present a hard exterior which is unaffected by the environment. They develop defence mechanisms of aggression and cynicism (stings and thorns) which make them difficult to appreciate and teach. Some students flower early and keep flowering right through their time in school. Others take a long time to flower, to find the right subject or niche. Some students go virtually unnoticed during their time in school, fading into the background and becoming part of the ground cover. Some students work best by themselves, whereas others are better in groups where they can exhibit leadership or support for other students. Some students have very cooperative learning styles and enjoy sharing their knowledge with others. They enjoy being with other students and sharing both the product and the process of learning. Others are competitive and seek to establish themselves against others. They seek the best of resources and the best of attention, at the same time depriving others of these resources.

In the classroom some students are colourful and showy. They are readily noticed and attract attention. Sometimes the attention is well deserved, and at other times it is very ephemeral. They work in spurts, and have moments of brightness, but they do not sustain it. Some students can be considered as vegetables — they are steady workers who produce the nutrients of education — solid performance without much show. They are the staple diet of teachers, and indeed also of the economy when they graduate. Other students might be considered as weeds in a classroom. Their persistent lack of discipline or disruption of work absorbs time and resources which might be used by the other students. Unless controlled, the lack of discipline can be contagious and spread rapidly, giving a malaise to the work of the classroom.

After school, students may choose to continue their educational development. Some travel abroad and influence many people. They migrate to other towns and cities to find work, to establish families of their own and make new friends. Others remain in their local area, take up steady employment and live steady if unspectacular lives. Some people thrive on being transplanted out of school, whereas others seem to lose their way and cannot survive outside the protected greenhouse environment of school.

A similar application of the metaphor might be made with the focus on teacher talent — the ability of the teacher to provide sustenance and shade, to attract students, to spread the seeds of knowledge, are easy aspects of the metaphor to develop. It can also be applied to some subjects; for instance, religious studies, or English literature might be considered as a tree, setting down deep roots which correspond to values which are meant to survive over time. Mathematics and science might be considered as vegetables, and subjects like music and history as flowers and shrubs which decorate the environment. As teachers apply the notion of plants in a garden to the process of schooling, they reveal something of their own concerns. What they find attractive in plants may have parallels in what they like about students or their own subject. As they reflect on their imagery and the meaning they give it, questions can be asked about the variety of plants they see in the garden, whether their gardens cater for many different types of plants, or for a very narrow range. Perhaps they specialize in rare orchids, or perhaps they have become vegetable gardeners, determined to turn every plant into a prize vegetable. Reflection may affirm the teacher in his or her appreciation of different talents in the classroom, or among other teachers on the staff. It may give an appreciation of the role of different subjects in the curriculum. Teachers also come to realize that they may have missed some plants in their own garden, and failed to develop them. They reinterpret their 'weeds' as 'wild flowers' and help them find a niche in the habitat of the school.

For some teachers, this application of plants to students is difficult. What a seedling becomes is predetermined by the genetics of the plant. All you can do is to ensure that it grows up strong and healthy. They believe that this is an inappropriate image for the student who is searching for their identity and choosing their own direction. It is frequently pointed out that stereotyping students as particular types of plants is false. It is more productive to see the plants as individual talents, and each student as a garden, with a unique combination of trees, shrubs, flowers, vegetables and weeds. The skill of teaching then becomes one of helping the student become a gardener of their own talents, rather than the teacher cultivating a particular type of plant. This image would give rise to a different type of teacher, and a different mindset in developing relationships between the student and the teacher. However one develops the image, it is a powerful stimulus for reflection, and sets the agenda for understanding the different types of plants in the school garden, and how they may be cultivated.

**Reflection 4.2**

We now have an enriched view of the nature and variety of garden plants. We can assess the importance of this image by asking questions such as: what was our spontaneous identification of plants and what implications might a shift of emphasis have for classroom management or relationships within the school? Other suggestions for application may arise from your reading of Part One. When you finish reading the section, you might again reflect on what was common and what was new to you, with a view to discovering your own 'theories in action' as opposed to 'espoused theories'.

*The Gardener*

At the end of the last section, we saw how one's perspective on the plants in the garden affects the image of what it is like to work in the garden. In this section, we expand the metaphor even more by examining the work of the gardener.

**Exercise 4.3**

You may continue to reflect on the metaphor of schooling by describing the work of the gardener. Describe the work either in terms of its content, the disposition of the gardener or the relationship of the gardener with the plants.

Gardens need regular care and attention. People respond in different ways to their responsibility. For some, working in the garden is a chore to be endured at the weekend, cutting and edging lawns, trimming hedges, weeding flower beds and occasionally watering plants and pruning roses. If possible, they will pay their children, or the Boy Scouts or some enterprising neighbour, to do the work. For them, gardens are places to be in, or to look at. They expect them to be there, and to be 'right', but they don't like to have to make it so. At the other end of the spectrum are those people who love working in the garden, for whom it is an experience of being at one with nature, at once refreshing and calming. They enjoy the changing texture of the plants with the seasons, and look forward to the creation of new landscapes, however small, as they move plants from one bed to the next, set out new plants in season, carefully weed and water, and prepare for the following season.

Some gardeners have 'green fingers'. Give them any plant, and it flourishes. They seem to know what it needs: the right amount of water, the correct balance of sunlight and shade. These gardeners instinctively choose the right place to put a plant. They know what type of soil is needed to help it thrive. On the other hand, give some people even the hardiest of plants, and somehow it shrivels up. They overwater, or forget to water. They put plants that need shade in direct sunlight, and leave those that need sun in shaded areas. They forget to check the plant for disease, for greenfly, or any other symptoms which might indicate ill health. With them, the plant is meant to survive on a haphazard and random level of attention.

One type of gardener goes to the shops and buys a packet of seeds. These are sown together in large trays. Once germinated, they are regularly thinned out, and only the best survive. They are all treated the same way — they are watered together, often with a sprinkler, each getting the same amount of water, the same fertilizer. This gardener judges success by the end product, by the number of blooms, the array of colour, the size of the fruit. If one plant does not do as well as another, it is taken as the luck of the draw, something that was wrong with the seed. Perhaps the gardener will have better luck the next time, and maybe will take more care in selecting the seedlings. The opposite type of gardener is the one who tries to make every plant grow. She wants each seedling to develop. Plants are treated individually. The hardy ones are left by themselves, others are planted in pairs, or in larger clumps. Some are brought to the front of the bed, others are left further back in the shade. When it comes to watering, the gardener does it individually with a watering can, so that she can vary the amount of water given to each plant, adjusting the amount to the needs of the plant. This gardener is at one with her plants, and enjoys the survival of the weaker plants as much as the full blossoms of the healthy ones.

The teacher might be considered as the gardener in this metaphor. Students intuitively recognize a good teacher, someone who knows what they need and can respond to these needs. They know when a teacher gives attention to detail, or is careless in the preparation of classes, the explanation of concepts and the correction of homework and examinations. Teachers bring different levels of interest and energy to the work of teaching, and this can be compared to the interest a gardener takes in the development and care of the garden. Some teachers are gifted with a sense of the individual student in the classroom, whereas others are more taken with their subject, and are prepared to 'thin out' students who do not develop as they should. Some teachers have a wide range of options which they use to develop their students, whereas others are limited in their approaches and in their knowledge of what might work. They understand students' need of attention, information, discipline, encouragement and guidance in much the same way as the gardener appreciates the need for shade and sun, for water and nutrients, for pruning and weeding.

However, choosing the teacher as the gardener is itself an assumption. One might just as easily choose the student as the gardener, where the student takes responsibility for the development of the garden of knowledge. In this case, the teacher becomes a resource — a garden centre — for the student. The point of the exercise is that if you went to visit classrooms which worked from these different images, you could reasonably expect to find different contexts, different perceptions of the learning–teaching situation, different choices of strategies and behaviours. It is not that one is necessarily better than the other. However, the exploration of the metaphor, and its application to education and schooling, can reveal basic assumptions and help us to examine them. At times, the examination will be self-affirming and give rightful cause for celebration. At other times, it will give cause for further reflection, judgement and perhaps a new decision.

---

**Reflection 4.3**

The three different aspects of the garden metaphor reveal rich details of assumptions about schools and relationships within schools. If you have worked on the three different aspects, you should now look at them together, and evaluate some of the discoveries you have made.

What aspects of the metaphor are most appropriate to education?

What new things have been revealed to you that you would like to integrate into your working image of schools and schooling? How might you set about integrating this in practice?

What have you rediscovered about schools through the use of this metaphor — things that you knew once but had faded from consciousness?

What aspects of the garden are inappropriate to schooling? How can you deal with these aspects in practice?

---

## The School as an Orchestra

School as orchestra is another metaphor which can be used to explore the context and perspectives which guide choices and behaviour in schools. The metaphor of orchestra evokes images of community and cooperation, of mood and harmonized melody, of individual technical skill and collective interpretation. In an orchestra, many people work together, each with their own individual role, to produce a harmonized output. As such, the metaphor of the school as an orchestra appeals to those who see school as a preparation for living in community. It helps students understand and appreciate their common humanity and the need to work together in peace and harmony. Also, students are helped to develop a high proficiency with their own individual talent while at the same time, they see that talent in the context of the total community. The implications of an orchestra having to play to a prescribed score finds parallels with the way schools are run, and can be explored as a metaphor for their response to external forces, particularly government policy in education. As in the metaphor of the garden, different aspects of the orchestra can be examined: the orchestra itself, the players and their instruments, and the score they play (see Figure 4.3).

| Orchestra | Players | Score |
|---|---|---|
| Specialized types of music<br>Spirit of cooperation<br>Harmony | Variety of sounds<br>Individual skills<br>Individual and group | Set curriculum<br>Specialized language<br>Composer and conductor |

*Figure 4.3   Aspects of the orchestra metaphor and the focus of application to schools*

## The Orchestra

---

**Exercise 4.4**

The reader might like to try this exercise for themselves before reading on. Just as with the garden metaphor, the first stage is to list different characteristics of the orchestra, or different kinds of music. A second phase of the exercise might look at the different instruments of the orchestra, and then move on to consider the score the orchestra plays.

Take three sheets of paper, one for the orchestra, one for the instruments and the third for the score. Write what comes to mind about each of these aspects of the orchestra. When this descriptive exploration of the metaphor has been completed, then ask yourself 'How is a school like an orchestra?' and identify each of the different elements on your list with some aspect of school life.

This section of the chapter reflects on different images and applications which have been used in the course of my own work. You may find that sharing with others on the way they see the school enriches your own appreciation of the school. It may also challenge the way you think about your work by revealing patterns of assumptions which you bring to the notion of schooling. Some specific questions about assumptions may come to you from Part One of the book.

---

An orchestra is a mixed body of instrumentalists. In general, the term is applied to those who play some type of formal arrangement of music, as opposed to jazz groups whose music depends on improvisation. Symphony orchestras have a wide range of instruments divided into sections of woodwind, brass, percussion and strings, whereas chamber orchestras are much smaller. Some orchestras limit the range of instruments. You may have a string orchestra, or combinations of wind and percussion instruments playing dance music or military marches.

Music may be composed especially for the orchestra and its lone performance in the concert hall. Symphonies are musical works of a serious nature and substantial size, written in separate movements, each with its own mood. Other compositions include concertos and sonatas, which use the contrast between the full orchestra and individual instruments to produce their effects. The orchestra may concentrate its repertoire on serious classical music, or may adopt a number of popular tunes for occasions like the Proms, or the Boston Pops, or indeed may concentrate solely on a particular type of dance or marching music.

At other times, the orchestra plays as an accompaniment. The sound track of a film depends on an orchestra to create mood and enhance the visual effect. Specialized orchestras accompany ballet, opera, and theatre musicals, and provide the background for individual singers or instrumentalists in concerts. In this role, the primary focus is on the screen, the stage or the individual. The orchestra takes a secondary position 'in the pit' to be acknowledged publicly only at the end of the performance.

The school can be considered as different groups of students and teachers working together in harmony. Schooling is a social process, where classes move together and focus their attention on a particular lesson, where students learn to cooperate with adult teachers and with their peers, to take responsibility for themselves and for younger students. The 'symphony' produced by the school depends on the combination of different ages; single gender or co-ed; the variety and range of curriculum subjects; the extra-curricular offerings; the quality of examinations results; the relationships between teachers and students, among teachers and students, between the school and the local community. All of these elements give a certain tone and climate to the school.

Like classical and popular orchestras, schools have areas of specialization. Some schools have a reputation for an academic concentration, with emphasis on classical humanistic education. Other schools specialize in technological or vocational subjects. The combination of literature, language, science, art and commercial subjects can be compared to different pieces the orchestra plays. It reflects the emphasis on classical and formal music, and can be combined with other offerings which reflect a less formal piece of music, as say in extra-curricular activities such as a school trip or celebration. The repertoire of the school reveals what it considers worthwhile music.

The way the school is organized also resembles the organization of the orchestra. Students are grouped together according to subjects and age, in much the same way as different instruments are grouped in an orchestra. The mood of the school changes to reflect different times of the year, or different phases in the students' development. At examination time, the school may take on an air of seriousness which differs from the regular mood of the school. Similarly, the 'music' played by senior students may be different from that played by junior students.

The work of the school may be seen as an end in itself. Increasingly, however, it is seen as part accompaniment. For many students, second-level education is no longer the terminus of their formal education. Therefore, school is seen as part of a bigger picture, and the prospect of a place in university, or a job in a particular sector, seems more important than what is going on in school. This can cause a tension within a school, as teachers see themselves in a symphony orchestra occupying centre stage, whereas for the students, the music of the school is just a background to a wider scene — a film or a musical which they are living out.

The metaphor therefore reveals perspectives on and assumptions about the relationship the school has with the life of students, with the general culture of society and on appropriate levels of human activity. Reflection on the metaphor can point to opportunities to affirm the type of orchestra the school is, and its repertoire. It can also raise questions about the appropriateness of the repertoire for the type of players and their skill level. Indeed, whether the school is properly an orchestra, or more a jazz ensemble, where students have a chance to express themselves, has been a fruitful discussion in a number of schools.

### The Players

Musicians are organized into sections according to the instruments they play, and they have different positions within a section. Thus, the strings are grouped together, and within that grouping, the violins are together, which can be further subdivided to first and second violins, then the violas, the cellos and the double basses. Similarly, the different woodwind instruments may be grouped together. Whereas in the string or woodwind sections, each musician typically specializes in the one instrument, in the percussion section, it is not unusual for one player to play a number of different instruments.

The instruments of the orchestra vary in the pitch, the compass of notes they play, the timbre of the sound. The violin, for example, may play notes covering three-and-a-half octaves, the alto-saxophone two-and-a-half octaves, whereas a bugle or a fanfare trumpet produces one harmonic series only, and a triangle in the percussion section gives a tinkling sound without definite pitch. The make of the instrument also affects the quality of the sound it produces, the tone from a Stradivarius violin being better balanced than that from a mass produced model for a novice student. The advance of modern electronics has opened up new possibilities for some musicians, who can now 'synthesize' different instruments and sounds with the aid of computer technology.

In the orchestra, it is the blend of instruments which creates the quality of the final piece. The way the instruments of different pitch play their individual notes together produces chords which create a quality of sound that no individual instrument can produce. Similarly, the quality of sound from the timbre of different instruments — such as strings and woodwind — playing the same note creates a pleasing harmony and symphony. This level of harmony requires a high level of discipline from the individual musicians. Should one musician start on an individualized interpretation, or decide to play at a different tempo, then the potential symphony quickly turns to chaos and cacophony.

In an objective way also, musicians make a varied contribution to the overall production. For instance, in an orchestral piece, the strings may be playing constantly and the percussion players have long rests built into their contribution. Despite their apparent lack of productivity, they are an essential part of the overall effect. There is the famous case of the time-and-motion expert who studied the score of the Tchaikovsky's 1812 Overture. He calculated the productivity of each instrument as the ratio of bars played to the total number of bars. He then eliminated the instruments which were not achieving a high level of productivity by his standards (e.g. the cannon). He ended up with a very reduced orchestra, and, of course, a piece of music which was unrecognizable.

Students and teachers are the instruments of the school as orchestra. As with musical instruments, their quality varies. The personal experience of students, the culture capital they bring with them from home, is akin to the different quality of instrument. Some students are finely tuned for the world of academia, whereas others are less inclined to participate. Some students blend in very well with the work of the school, whereas others, especially during adolescence, find it difficult to conform and try out their own variations, which may or may not be in harmony with the general 'music' of the school. Teachers, too, vary in quality, depending on the talent they bring to their work — a sense of 'moral purpose'; an ability to relate to, inspire and motivate students; and the ability to communicate and teach creatively, adapting their skills to the needs of the students. Some teachers, like musicians, stand out as being excellent teachers, and play with skill and confidence. They have a feel for what they are doing. Others have less confidence in their own ability, and are dependent on the atmosphere and climate developed by others for the level of their own performance. Put them in a good school, and they perform well. However, they would never be able to create that atmosphere themselves. If they have to show leadership and initiative, they are lost.

Having a good instrument does not make a good musician. A 7-year-old beginning to play the violin can make as disconcerting a sound on a Stradivarius as on a cheap violin. The ability to produce good music comes only with practice, by learning the techniques of placing one's fingers properly, of reading music and understanding the importance of timing and rhythm, and above all, of understanding the piece of music and interpreting it. A student learns how to study in much the same way. In time, a student develops techniques of memorization, of appreciation, of writing creatively or critically or of problem solving. A teacher learns tricks of classroom management, presentation skills and people management. Some exhibit a greater talent than others. Some musicians can listen to a piece of music and immediately play it themselves, and others must have the music in front of them. In the same way, some teachers have a natural talent for teaching and relating to students whereas others are very dependent on the textbook and techniques they learn in preservice or inservice courses.

Students may decide to play different roles in the school. Some want to be involved in everything, and others pick and choose activities for involvement. Some are academically oriented, whereas others are more sporting, more artistic, more practical in their orientation. When facing activities in which they are not too interested, they are prepared to rest. It is as if they have chosen an instrument which suits their willingness to play. Other students seek to excel at their subjects, to gain all the honours they can and pursue the subject to a very deep level. They are like musicians who do not wish to remain in the relative anonymity of the orchestra, but seek to establish themselves as solo players.

Instruments may be students, teachers or subjects and activities within the school. Applying the image of musician to students or teachers reveals perspectives and assumptions about human nature, about the place of talent and how it might be developed. Our reflection on the different instruments may reveal that we have a preference for a narrow range of instruments. Some teachers come to appreciate the role of different instruments in their classroom, and are determined to hear the contribution of these instruments. They may even choose a different piece or arrangement of their orchestra so that these instruments may be heard more. This can be applied at the level of the school as well as the classroom.

### The Score

Music may be defined as 'an arrangement of, or the art of combining or putting together, sounds that please the ear'. A composer sets about creating themes and variations by combinations of sounds, rhythm, tempo and emphasis, and evoking a mood and response in the listener. The original theme may be written for a single instrument, such as the piano, and arrangements later written for other instruments which add to the quality of the piece. Thus, in any musical composition, there is the original inspiration which gives the theme and the mood of the music, and there is the arrangement or orchestration of the music so that it can be played in a different medium from that of the original composition. For instance, a piece originally written for a small chamber orchestra can be arranged to suit the different instruments in a full symphony orchestra. Primacy of place is typically given to the originality of the composer, but the development of an arrangement can be equally creative, in terms of using the talents of the musicians available and at the same time faithfully representing, adapting, interpreting and developing the original insight of the composer.

When an orchestra comes together to play, each of the musicians agrees to play the piece set before them. The alternative is chaos. The piece is something which is composed by someone other than the musicians, and chosen for them by the conductor or orchestral managers. It is the job of the musicians to know and learn to play their part in the overall composition. They have no say in the original composition, which is something external to them. Yet, in their reading of the score, there is some room for interpretation. No two orchestras play a major symphony exactly the same way. The conductor will use variations of emphasis — how quiet is quiet? how fast is fast? — in playing the same notes in the same order, and this creates a nuanced interpretation of the original mood of the piece.

Working in a school can be very much like following an orchestral score. The curriculum is frequently determined outside the school, and is the same for every school. It is devised by an 'expert' in curriculum development, who determines the content and the process to be aimed for. The texts to be studied, the skills to be learned, the amount of time to be given to each subject, or each section of a course is set down outside the school. It is true that when teachers come to teach that course, like conductors of an orchestra, they can add a unique personal flavour to the course. They may stress certain sections of the course over others, may spend more time in one section than in another. In a history class, one teacher may stick rigidly to the technicalities of a textbook, while another takes the students beyond the dates, sequences of events and personalities and engages them in a deep appreciation of other times and cultures. Teachers are often well aware of the need to rearrange a prescribed syllabus for their own class. They bring variations of pace and tempo to different sections of the syllabus, changing the 'pitch' to suit the orchestra. They arrange the activity of the orchestra in terms of the needs and abilities of the different players. A good teacher is frequently a brilliant arranger, rather than an original composer. Occasionally, the teacher has the chance to compose some material themselves, based on the inspiration of someone else's piece. Teachers will also encourage students to become composers and arrangers of the music of the curriculum. The role of students is not simply to become players who reproduce the score in front of them, but also to enter into the mood of the music and adapt it for themselves. Whereas the prescribed score may often appear as a major constraint on the players, there is scope within the understanding of the score to develop a level of personal creativity. Sometimes, if teachers are stuck with prescribed lesson plans, or textbooks, they need to be reminded of the possibility of becoming, or letting their students become, composers and arrangers.

The relationship between the score, the conductor and the orchestra is also of interest. In some orchestras, the role of the conductor is that of tyrant — he or she dictates how the score will be interpreted and played. The conductor can squash the creativity of individual musicians, insisting on a purely technical approach on their part to the piece. The model of participation in such an orchestra is one of submissiveness and compliance. Like conductors, some teachers exercise a tyrannical approach to students' learning, insisting that it be done their way. The teacher interprets the discipline of the subject and demands submissiveness and compliance from the student. Similarly, a school principal may insist on a particular approach to the running of the school which gives no say to the musicians on the staff. Yet discipline is an important aspect of learning and cooperation. It is not a capricious exercise, in which any personal preference goes. Reflection on the role of teacher or principal as conductor can reveal many assumptions behind the practices of classroom management, and point to possible new relationships between the orchestra and the conductor, based on a different understanding of the music to be played.

The score of any orchestral piece can be fascinating. It combines, in ordered form, all the different parts allotted to the various musicians in a piece. One version of the score is that created for the conductor. It shows the music for all the different instruments, arranged on different staves down the page according to instrument so that he or she can see at a glance when a particular instrument is meant to be playing. Each of the musicians, on the other hand, plays from a score which contains the notes for that instrument alone. To read an orchestral score requires a particular skill related to music alone — knowledge of notation. For instance, the pitch of the note is denoted by its position on a stave, and this can be varied by changing the clef sign on the stave. The shape of the note (quavers, crotchets, minims and semibreves) denotes the length for which it is to be played, and the combination of notes which might be played together. The effect of these notes varies depending on the number of beats in a bar of music and the tempo at which the music is to be played. All of this needs to be learned as a particular skill in understanding and playing music. Similarly, the notes which accompany a score have a technical language of their own, reflecting the classical Latin and Italian influence on music — *allegro ma non tanto*, *pianissimo* and *glissando*.

In applying this to education, each of the subjects has its own technical language. Students are introduced to a body of established knowledge and procedures which is shared by other scholars. They begin to appreciate the tension which exists between the particular — their own interests and learning — and the universal — the knowledge that is 'out there' — in learning.

The application of the image of an orchestral score and how it is interpreted can therefore be used to reveal assumptions about the nature of reality and knowledge, about the proper function of students in learning, about their role and relationship to one another and to teachers.

---

**Reflection 4.4**

Now evaluate what you have learnt from the orchestra metaphor. Look back over the three parts of the exercise. Compare your own images with those in the text. Perhaps as you read, new images and applications became obvious. What patterns can you detect — common ground, points of difference? What do these patterns reveal? What are the implications for your own personal development — how do you appreciate your symphony, your orchestra, the different instruments in the orchestra, your role as a musician, conductor or composer? How would you like your orchestra to develop? What can you do to bring about this development?

You might also like to return to Reflection 4.1 at the end of the garden metaphor and integrate what has been learned here. What parallels can you see in both images?

---

In the film *Mr Holland's Opus*, Gertrude Lang gives a testimonial to her music teacher. Referring to all the students he has influenced, she says: 'We are your symphony, Mr Holland. We are the notes and the melodies of your life.' There are many powerful images in the metaphor of orchestra which help reflect on either the ideal or the current realities of a school, or an individual career. It brings teachers in touch with fundamental images, values and perspectives which give rise to choices and behaviours which help understand their own inner world and that of the school. It also gives rise to possible changes within the metaphor which point to interventions leading to new developments and growth for the individual and for the school.

### The School as a Factory

The image of the school as a factory gives rise to images of order and efficiency, of a consistent, controlled and guaranteed process for all who enter the educational system. There is a sense of a known output and a stable process, and each part of the process has a definite part to play in the end product. As such, the image appeals to those who see schools in terms of the efficient production of skills and knowledge, where the end product is well defined, and a step-by-step process can be devised to manufacture the product. The machine works the same way for everything that is input, thus ensuring equality of process. There is also an opportunity of controlling the quality of the output, and adjusting the machine to improve that quality if necessary. However, the images which factories generate vary from the small craft industry involving one or two artists, to large and highly complex automated production lines. The image may involve the Dickensian 'sweatshop' as well as the highly technical and automated electronic laboratory. This gives wide scope for exploring the metaphor in different settings, focusing either on the industrial process or on the machines and tools being used.

---

**Exercise 4.5**

A third image of schooling might be that of a factory. There are many different types of factories, production units or workplaces. They contain different kinds of machinery and the workers are involved in many different ways with their work. Levels of supervision, reward and punishment as well as worker satisfaction are also quite varied. The general form of the exercise is the same as that outlined for the other two metaphors — a general description of factory life, and then the application to education.

When you have completed your own reflections, read the following section and reflect on some of the images that are applied to schools. You can then go back on your own work and again reflect on the significance of any patterns that were revealed to you.

---

A factory is generally seen as embodying an impersonal process which accepts raw material and then works independently, in a programmed manner, through a series of sometimes complex operations to give a final output. The general production line of a motor car industry can be seen as a huge machine, where the raw materials which make up the car body are fed into the system, and are then assembled on the production line (increasingly by robots) to a preprogrammed pattern. The aim of the machine is to increase efficiency, to eliminate waste or mistakes, to guarantee a uniform standard of production. A similar production line is often seen in the food industry, where raw materials are brought into the system, prepared, processed and packaged for production. Each stage of the process is controlled by carefully programmed and regulated machines that check temperatures at which food is processed, and check the quality of ingredients used in terms of size, weight, shape, etc. The end result produces packages, bottles or cans which are uniform with respect to quality, colour and presentation. The human role in the process is reduced to supplying the raw material to the machine, and the occasional check on the quality of the goods at intermediate stages or at the final stage of production.

The factory is organized into workers, supervisors and management. Each has a very clear place, and very clear responsibilities. If a worker is out sick, another person can step into their place without disrupting the process. There are clear lines of reporting and accountability, each person knowing who their supervisor is, and who has the authority to make decisions, and there is no need to be involved in any level other than one's own. Decisions are accepted from above and implemented. Not only are people organized on a hierarchical basis, they are also organized into different departments. Thus, some people work directly on the production line, others work in support services such as maintenance, accounting, marketing and personnel. Within the factory, people are promoted from one grade to the next on the basis of expertise and knowledge.

Schools can be compared to large production lines, where the raw material (the students) is passed along from teacher to teacher, from subject to subject. Each classroom is like a stage on the production line where increments are added to the total process, aiming for a particular end product. Teachers, working mainly in their own classrooms, are assumed to have particular skills. They work on the students, each teacher adding a particular element — mathematics, French, science, history, literature, etc. — to what will eventually be a fully educated person. Each of the classrooms works independently of one another, although there are levels of interdependence between some stages, in the way that students must learn to read before they understand literature, or they learn basic mathematical manipulation before they learn calculus. There are regular inspection checks through examinations, which seek to determine the quality of the process and the product. Students are passed on to further stages at the end of each year, and there are major inspections which allow them to pass from elementary to secondary school. At the end of the process, the student is packaged and labelled. Some are high-class products, some might be termed 'seconds' as they come with slight defects, whereas others are branded rejects. The process of schooling is well programmed — what is to be studied in each year, in each subject. Often, the curriculum determines the broad sequence of learning events, and the school timetable determines the movement of students from one station to the next. The process has a momentum of its own, and the batch processing approach where all students move ahead together and are only labelled at the end of the process is seen as a more economical process than taking corrective action if slight defects are noticed during the production phase. Standards of production are determined externally, by a quality control department which is independent of the production line teachers. The standards are easily recognized and are applied objectively in sophisticated testing procedures.

Not all production systems are assembly lines. When you visit a craft centre, the artists work on individual projects. A potter at the wheel shapes the clay by being sensitive to its texture. She works and reworks it until the pot has the shape and strength that she wants. The woodcarver creates curves and cuts using the natural shapes of the piece of wood, being careful of its grain and texture. The painter blends colours in careful brush strokes capturing both image and mood. The production is quite different from that of a factory worker. These workers are not external supervisors of an objective process, but they are involved in a creative act. They are somehow united with their materials. Each product is individual, a blend of the artist's own concept, their skill at the craft and the material itself.

Dewey's basic concept of education was as 'a way of being with others'[3]. His emphasis on process in education led him to see education more in terms of the relationship between artist and material than in terms of an industrial process. The moulding and forming of character implies relationships of trust and cooperation, rather than relationships of control and compliance. The teacher works with students to draw out and develop talents which are already given to them. From this perspective, the ideal of education is an individualized programme suited to each student. The tools the teacher uses are not blunt instruments which force the student into a predetermined 'mould', but rather are tools which are delicately used to highlight pre-existing talents and abilities, and to develop them to the full.

Teachers or parents often enjoy fantasy exercises which explore the images of potter, woodcarver and artist. They experience what it is like to craft something, to create for themselves. Alternatively, they can imagine themselves as a lump of clay, a piece of wood or a sheet of canvas, and what it is like to be worked on by an artist. They relate the work of the artist to their experience of teaching or being a parent, or they reflect on their own experience of learning and being taught, and the quality of relationship with good teachers.

The craftshop image of an industry places an emphasis on process in education. It focuses on relationships within that process. It ignores the problems of the inertness of the clay or the wood — for students are not inert and passive. It ignores the practical demands of large classes. In practice, there is a balance between the homely image of the craft industry and that of the production-line factory.

---

**Reflection 4.5**

This is an opportunity to capture the patterns within the reflection on school as a factory. How does this metaphor tie in with the other metaphors? What is the common ground between them? What do you find affirming, challenging or disturbing? You might even go back to these aspects and explore them a little further.

---

### Conclusion

The exploration of metaphor helps develop a sensitivity to individual beliefs, images and practices. Three metaphors have been explored here. An interesting exercise is to allow teachers to develop their own metaphors. These, too, can illustrate interesting aspects of their inner world, and the culture of the school. For instance, in Africa, I was struck by the use of pastoral images of shepherd, farmer and the family cook-pot, images seldom found in the urbanized mindset of western teachers. The latter tend to focus on images such as family, sports teams or images which have some productive end. There can be interesting differences between primary and secondary teachers in the focus of the image, and the meaning drawn out of it. Exploring a metaphor is an experience of watching your own behaviour, of standing back and seeing things in a creative new context which challenges perceptions. Values, feelings, attitudes, assumptions and behaviours are highlighted in a dramatic way. The metaphor becomes the play which catches the conscience of the school staff, the teacher, or the parent, and leads them to a creative understanding of the culture of the school and their own classroom.

The exercise does not stop with description and application. It can also move to judging the appropriateness of the metaphor for school. Many images of school work — like the image of the prison mentioned at the start of the chapter. This does not mean that the image is appropriate. The metaphor needs to be evaluated for appropriateness. Sometimes, the discovery of the strength and application of the theory-in-use is so strong that it points to the need to change the theory by developing a new metaphor. The beauty of the metaphor is that it allows development. For instance, I can change one corner of my garden, without digging up the whole plot, or I can get my orchestra to play different music. I can develop a new language where I ask colleagues 'How is your garden growing?', or 'How is your symphony coming along this year?' This approach values the present position and allows room for creative development.

### Notes

1   The power of metaphor and story-telling is developed in Kittay (1987); Kosslyn (1980); Lakoff and Johnson (1980); and Ricoeur (1978).
2   The use of metaphors for organizational analysis is well established by Morgan (1980, 1983, 1986); Marshak (1993); Oswick and Grant (1996); Peters (1978); Pondy (1983); Sackmann (1989). As well as Grady's (1993) inventory, specific applications to schools have been made by Schlechty and Joslin (1986); Steinhoff and Owens (1989); and Bredeson (1988). Starratt (1990) has applied a specific metaphor of drama to schooling, and Duignan (1997) has applied the metaphor of dance. A critical analysis of education through the metaphor of the shopping mall was published by Powell, Farrar and Cohen in 1985.
3   This is the basic theme of his description of learning in *The Child and the Curriculum* (1902) and later developed in *Democracy and Education* (1916) in the chapter 'Thinking in Education'.

## Chapter 5

# Typologies of Schools

Humankind has constantly sought to simplify its world. The early Greeks reduced the world to four elements; air, fire, water and earth. Hippocrates associated four physiological factors with personality type and behaviour: blood — sanguine, optimistic; phlegm — phlegmatic, lethargic; yellow bile — choleric, angry and assertive; black bile — melancholic, sad. This process of simplification may be taught to children in nursery rhymes which assign different personalities to boys and girls (sugar and spice) or to children born on different days of the week (Monday's child is fair of face). The modern adult classifies individuals using astrological signs. The astrological sign uses external data — date of birth, position of planets, etc. — to depict something about the individual's personality and temperament, and also generates some expectations about the future and fate.

A similar approach can be taken to organizations, seeking some means or traits by which they can be classified and understood better. Whereas a personal type depicts the individual's personality, an organizational type gives information on the social system and internal dynamics of the organization. The metaphors of Chapter 4 focus on the individual. The typologies discussed in this chapter focus on teams and groups within the school. They provide a useful tool for exploring aspects of school life and uncovering some of the hidden assumptions and values behind the artefacts of school structures and behaviours.

## Typologies in General

The concept of typology is derived mainly from psychological studies of personality. It is metaphorical rather than exhaustive or all-inclusive in its analysis. A personal or organizational 'type' describes its subject in terms of a small number of key variables which suggests the presence of one trait and the absence of another trait. For instance, individuals might be described as introvert or extrovert, active or passive, arty or scientific, creative or unimaginative. Using this type of imagery, one is not completely pigeon-holed in a single type — introvert, active, arty or creative. Rather it is a question of degree.

A personal typology influences expectations of attitudes and behaviours. People thought of as extroverts are expected to be vivacious, outgoing, gregarious, adventurous and fun-loving. Introverts are generally expected to be loners — shy, retiring, and serious in their approach to life. Often, typologies are deeply ingrained in the psyche. For instance, mental, and often subconscious, typologies may influence how parents relate to children — how boys and girls are dressed and the toys they are given. They also influence expectations and tolerance of behaviours such as crying, fighting, active participation in sport, etc. Not only do the attitudes and behaviours of adults express their own beliefs about children, they also work to reproduce and reinforce these beliefs in the children themselves. The resulting attitudes can be carried into school, with expectations of subject choice and performance — that boys do mathematics and physics, and girls do language arts and biology. In later life, this may affect employment sought and expectations of promotion. On another level, people can be stereotyped because of group characteristics — ethnic characteristics based on religion, colour or race; and class characteristics based on employment, address and social status. In rare cases, 'typing' can lead to a genuine appreciation and celebration of differences. More generally, it leads to a distortion of perceptions, to a defensiveness in relating to others and a lack of genuine dialogue and communication. It is only when typologies are examined and confronted that genuine growth in communication between individuals or groups can take place.

Typologies are also applied to organizations[1]. In general, they are descriptive rather than analytical, using organizational traits which are qualitative, rather than quantitative. The typologies used set expectations of outputs, structures and internal climate. For instance, organizations may be described as conservative or innovative, competitive and risky as against stable and gilt-edged, bureaucratic or loosely coupled. Each of the types conjures up expectations of how the organization relates to the environment. Expectations of a conservative company may involve the type of building and how people dress. Relationships between the organization and its clients, and even internally between members of the organization, may be very formal. The image portrayed is one of continuity. On the other hand, an innovative company may project an image of newness, of change and adaptability. The offices are modern. Within the company, there is a low emphasis on status, and hence a lack of formality in relationships. Organizations cultivate image. An advertising agency creates a different image from that of a firm of family solicitors. A supermarket cultivates a different image to that of an art studio. The image communicates something distinctive about the organization. It defines and enhances the work of the organization and also attracts clients and customers. Sensitively used, it focuses attention on the essence of the organization and captures its main thrust and focus. Insensitively used, the type distorts the importance of some variables and leads to unrealistic and over-simplistic analysis of key elements in the organization.

In general personal typologies do not investigate why or how the traits developed — they do not take into account the context in which a person grew up which might have affected their development. As such, a typology is ahistorical and present tense. The trait is taken as a given. Similarly organizational typologies do not take into account the historical context in which the organization has evolved. However, the strength of the image is often deeply rooted in history. Thus, expectations of the traditional professions of lawyers, priests, doctors, bankers persist over time. There is a consistent typing of people in uniform, such as policemen, soldiers,

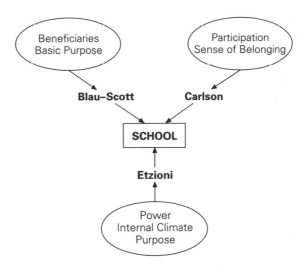

*Figure 5.1  The structure of Chapter 5: areas of underlying assumptions about schools revealed in three typologies of organizations applied to schools*

nurses, traffic wardens, airline pilots and even the standardized dress of those who work in fast-food chains.

Typologies do not evoke the same response from everyone. For instance, the sight of a policeman in uniform walking the beat may evoke a sense of security and serenity in some. For others, it may evoke feelings of guilt or a sense of constraint. The existence of a 'type', communicated by the policeman's uniform, may evoke responses which say as much about the values of the perceiver, as they do about the perceived.

Schools can also be classified according to typologies. As organizations, people have expectations of their output: the effect they will have on students, how that effect will be brought about, and the type of relationships and loyalties which develop within the school. As new teachers and students join a school, part of their induction is to know 'how things are done here'. Usually they spend time getting used to their new environment. Their concerns are mainly those of doing their job well, and of being accepted by others. There is a pressure to adapt to what already works, rather than to upset an already established system. As they develop the habit of certain procedures, they begin to adopt the attitudes associated with these procedures. Thus, they integrate the existing culture into their own thinking and, in turn, they become part of that culture.

In the rest of this chapter, we explore three typologies and apply them to schools (see Figure 5.1). Each of the typologies takes a different perspective on school. Blau and Scott (1962) looked at the beneficiaries of an organization; Carlson (1964) took the perspective of belonging and participation; and Etzioni (1961, 1964) clarified the use of power within an organization and the climate which the response to power can induce. The exploration is presented as exercises which are best carried out in a group of people who share some experience of the same

| BENEFICIARY | TYPE OF ORGANIZATION | CHARACTERISTIC STRUCTURE |
|---|---|---|
| Members | Club | Participative Democracy |
| Owners | Businesses-for-profit | Streamlined 'Lean and mean' |
| Private Clients | Not-for-profit / expert service | One-to-one professional based on expertise |
| General Public | Social/government service | Bureaucracy |

*Figure 5.2   The Blau–Scott Typology of Organizations applied to schools (After Blau and Scott, 1962)*

school. Frequently, different perspectives on the same artefacts are revealed, adding a richness to the understanding of the school culture. The aim of the exercises is to identify the assumptions held about schools. In particular, the aim is to become aware of areas where there is a difference between the way we talk about schools 'in theory', and the way we act 'in practice'. A group can also come to understand the context in which assumptions have developed, and the perspectives which reinforce these assumptions. Members can decide on the appropriateness of these assumptions for the way in which they see their work. This gives individuals or teams an opportunity to explore possible alternatives, and to have a sense how such alternatives might affect the culture of the school. This allows them to develop new desires and make new choices in their work as teachers, parents or administrators in schools.

## The Blau–Scott Typology

Blau and Scott (1962) classified organizations on the basis of their role in society and who they served[2]. Four types were identified (see Figure 5.2) on this basis. Blau and Scott claimed that each type gave rise to distinctive structures within the organization. These structures served a productive function in promoting the goals of the organization, and also worked to socialize the expectations and attitudes of individuals within the organization.

### The Four Different Types

*Social clubs* are founded and run by the members for their own benefit. For instance, I might join a book club, a bridge club, a credit union or a sports club. I have a particular benefit in mind — leisure activity, meeting people, pursuing some hobby or interest. I join the club so that the benefit may be more easily obtained. There are certain rules of affiliation and membership to which I must adhere. I apply for membership and the other members agree to accept me or not — for instance, I may have to be recommended by another member. I undertake certain obligations — to pay a subscription fee, to attend meetings and functions, to adhere to rules and procedures, to promote the aims of the club. As a member, I effectively become a shareholder in the club. I receive certain rights to vote on how the club is run. I elect officers to act on my behalf, and I have an opportunity to evaluate their work periodically. The main function of administration in such an organization is to maintain the levels of democracy upon which the organization was founded, to ensure that members are aware of factors which influence the implementation of their policies, and to carry out these policies as efficiently as possible. Officers of the club report regularly to the general membership and have limited power of personal initiative. Indeed, in many clubs, the central coordinating role of President, Captain or Chairman is rotated among the members on a regular basis.

*Businesses-for-profit* are set up by entrepreneurial individuals, by groups of investors or by large corporations wishing to expand their activities. These individuals or groups have capital to invest in a new enterprise, and the intention of investment is to increase that capital for their own use. The success of the venture undertaken is judged by the profit margin. Therefore the organization is geared to be cost effective and streamlined, open and responsive to market forces, competitive in acquiring raw material and disposing of products and services. Its administration is concerned with efficiency — the minimization of cost and the maximization of profit. Businesses need to be responsive to changes in the environment — the availability of resources, the needs of customers and changing fashions. In general, a profit-seeking company tries to be proactive in both anticipating and influencing developments in the environment, in such a way as to suit itself. Key areas of administration are the procurement of resources (input), the efficient organization of production methods, procedures and personnel (throughput) and the marketing and use of products (output). Dealings with clients are initiated and transacted on the basis of making profits. The company seeks suppliers of resources on the basis of paying the least amount for the raw material. It deals with workers on the basis of lowering employment costs, while balancing the need to promote productivity, motivate the workforce and maintain loyalties. It deals with customers on the basis of securing a competitive advantage by balancing volume and profit margin.

*Not-for-profit organizations* deal with the perceived needs of clients who cannot meet their own needs. This can range from the service given by philanthropic organizations who wish to share their wealth with others, to the highly specialized expertise given by professionals such as doctors, lawyers and nurses. These people have acquired a specialized knowledge, and it is this knowledge that benefits the client. In the relationship between the professional and the client, the client is the main beneficiary of the service. Although the professional gains a livelihood from providing the service, and some services are highly valued and come at a high cost, the relationship established between giver and receiver is based on expertise rather than on profit. Thus, I seek out an engineer, an architect, a lawyer, a doctor, a counsellor, based on their expertise. I come to him or her with a specific need, and he or she attempts to address that need. The relationship is termed professional, in that the expert applies an abstract knowledge to an individual problem or situation. Typically, the relationship is formed on a one-to-one basis, and focuses on problem-solving.

The general public benefits from *social/government services* such as the army, the courts, the police force and government departments such as health and social welfare. At the heart of these organizations is the common good of society. The main benefit is to the general welfare of the state and the organizations are set up to oversee its smooth running. Whereas individuals may have dealings with the government, or with the police on the basis of their own personal needs, the over-riding concern of the agency is the preservation of community order and the fair distribution of entitlements and social welfare. The organization, therefore, is not involved in a personalized relationship with clients, but develops its operation in terms of well-defined procedures and functions, seeking transparency, consistency and fairness.

---

**Exercise 5.1**

Before you go any further, you might like to reflect on where schools fit into this typology. A good exercise is to take four large sheets of paper, one for each type of organization. Ask yourself what elements of a school are examples of the different types. For instance, you may now find it useful to return to your reflections in Chapter 1, where you identified some of the artefacts, values and assumptions which are part of the school culture for material which might be classified.

As in Chapter 4, I will now share some of the insights which have come from workshops with teachers. These might help you add material to your own sheets, and stimulate discussion on how different artefacts in the school take on a meaning related to the ultimate purpose of the school.

---

*Applying the Typology to Schools*

The Blau–Scott typology has proved useful in focusing attention on the goals and aims of organizations. The difficulty in categorizing some organizations, especially schools, has focused the debate on the purpose of schooling, and brought into sharper focus relevant elements in the complex school–client relationship. How do you define the beneficiaries of the school? Students, for instance, can be regarded as both the raw material and the product in an industrial typology. They may also be seen as clients seeking a professional service from the school, and they may also be seen as the infrastructure for the state's economic development. Yet the student is not the only focus of the educational system. School can be said to have a variety of clients, and there is no single beneficiary. Among these client constituencies are: the parents, who theoretically are the principal educators and who finance the operation either directly in fees or donations or indirectly through taxation; the teachers, whose careers and livelihood are tied up in schools; in private and inde-pendent schools, the management group and their goals; the state, with its heavy financial investment and its dependence on educational output for both economic and cultural quality; employers, who benefit from a pool of trained and educated workers from which they can choose. In coming to appreciate the intermeshing of the four types in a school, there has been a heightening of awareness of the complex system involved in the provision and maintenance of schools. Once understanding grows in this area, it helps improve the quality of debate leading to decision-making and the implementation of new programmes in education.

## The school as a club type

In some ways, schools can be considered as clubs[3]. They are formed for the mutual benefit of the members — students become part of the school to develop themselves, and make demands on the school for particular types of activities — a wide range of subjects on the formal curriculum, and demands for the extra-curricular programme. These activities may be seen as a response to membership needs, and the school adapts to changing needs of members. Parents may see themselves as members who are entitled to information about the progress of their children, in much the same way as members of a club hear reports from the officers at the annual general meeting. The parents may be given some say in the direction of the school through votes at the Parent Association, and they may be 'levied' for extra funds to support the school. Teachers can also regard the school as their club, and some staff lounges resemble a club setting. Frequently a teachers' meeting makes decisions on organizational matters in the school using very democratic processes within the meeting, but with a very limited view of who belongs to that democracy. The only people who have a vote are the teachers, and there is little reference to external criteria. This is a club culture.

In some schools there is considerable emphasis on developing a sense of belonging for students, and this has consequences for classroom management and climate development. Students may be given a say in the running of certain aspects of the school through the Students' Council and through democratic procedures within the classroom. The pastoral care system of the school may be designed to ensure that individual students may get maximum benefit from their membership. Parents may also be invited to participate in parent–teacher committees, finance committees, etc., and to be part of the governance of the school on Boards of Management or as school governors. In some schools, parents are involved in instructional activities, sometimes as aides in the classroom. There is a growing awareness of positive benefits which can accrue from involving other adults besides the teachers in schools. It communicates a sense of community belonging — the school belongs to the community, and the community is part of the school.

## The school as a business-for-profit type

Exploring schools as businesses examines the rationale for involvement in the provision and maintenance of schools, and the way owners make a profit. Ownership in education can be judged on:

1 Capital provision in setting up the educational system.
2 Control of allocating current expenditure in the system.
3 Decision-making within the system — leadership, vision and goals, the control of access and process.
4 Psychological ownership of the goals of the school, and levels of participation in their determination.

Private groups, especially religious groups, have a historical tradition resulting from their initial investment of capital and personnel in founding and maintaining schools. Their aims coexist with those derived from a national curriculum and other external sources. They control conditions of work within their own schools, and manage the selection of staff to promote their own ethos and aims. They use a variety of criteria to judge their profit margins: attitudes and values communicated; successful examination results; placement of students in higher education or in work; or maybe profits from fees. Similarly, government also has a major ownership function, with its provision of capital and current funding, its influence on curriculum development, examination and inspection. Government may seek cost saving within the system by rationalizing provision, by amalgamating schools or by preferential funding to some schools for cost-intensive technological courses, or in the provision of resources on a regional basis. It may judge success in terms of unit costing, high retention rates, or levels of certification at examinations. Although profit is not seen in the same terms as in the conventional business concern, the images associated with success are similar. These place demands on individual school activities where the curriculum is influenced more by budgeting procedures than by educational values. The rituals of some schools celebrate success in much the same way as a company reports to shareholders at the end of the year. What is chosen for celebration reveals choices about what is important in the culture of the school.

### The school as a not-for-profit service type

Schools may also be seen as service organizations, with the teachers providing an expert professional service. The most common image of the professional relationship is that between student and teacher. The student is regarded as a client, who comes to the teacher as an expert in the art of learning–teaching in the hope that the student may benefit from the relationship. The school also has a professional relationship with parents, who are charged with responsibility for educating their children, and who engage in a professional cooperative relationship with the school to fulfil this responsibility. Parents are increasingly operating out of this client relationship in demanding a particular quality of product in terms of their child's performance. Similarly, schools can also be seen in a professional relationship with government. In western society, educational policy is increasingly set at a political level, albeit with some participation of educators. The function of the educational system is to deliver that policy in a professional manner.

Teachers frequently develop a very professional, caring relationship with their students. Some teachers have a capacity for noticing and helping individuals within the context of a large classroom. Schools also provide a wide range of services outside formal academic learning. These are all aimed at creating a positive atmosphere for learning, in much the same way as medical personnel are professionally concerned with health, rather than simply curing disease. The term professional can be wide ranging in its application to school activities.

### *The school as a social service*

The relationship of education to economic welfare of the state is well established, both in terms of providing human capital for economic development, and also in the link between the amount of education people have and their level of subsequent employment. However, the benefits of education go deeper than mere economic gain. In any society, two types of wealth can be distinguished, material and immaterial. Material wealth is finite and limited. Redistribution of material wealth works on a Robin Hood principle; that you take from the rich and give to the poor. Some people end up with more and others with less than they have now. Immaterial wealth does not work in the same way. For instance, if education is regarded as wealth, to share my learning with another person does not require me to give up any knowledge so that the other person can gain from it. The process of sharing immaterial wealth actually increases the total wealth. In this sense, education is a central aspect of the cultural and economic infrastructure of the state. A key element in understanding this dimension of school is the way in which the goods of education are distributed. The school may be organized to give special attention to people who are disadvantaged or have special needs, or it may be organized in a way which gives benefits to those who already have talent and educational riches (as in, say, a rigid streaming policy). The debate on school organization can resemble the way people analyse a national budget for the effect it has on the common good — whether it promotes a sense of community, or whether it promotes sectional interests.

This sense of promoting the common good can be an important part of a school's sense of mission. Although there are clear links between the material benefits which can accrue from having the immaterial wealth of a good education, the distinction is important in the debate on educational provision and the purpose of education. In the complexity of today's society, where much of the knowledge that is needed to survive and progress is part of the formal rather than the informal learning process, to be denied an education is to be denied a basic initiation into the structures of society, thus allowing individuals to participate fully in the wealth and progress of that society. This can give ground for social resentment and division. School structures which mirror this aspect of the common good can be seen in the entrance policy of schools, in the way students are allocated to programmes and classes within the school, and also in the way the discipline and reward structures of the school operate.

## The Interaction of the Four Types

Schools do not fit easily into any one of the Blau–Scott types. Each school will have elements of all four types operating at the same time. However, individual schools differ on the profile and emphasis on each type. Some run very democratic processes (club) while others are quite authoritarian (business-for-profit). One school may place great emphasis on the individual learner (professional service) whereas another specializes in a particular type of curriculum (social service). The type may be used at a school level or at a classroom level. Here is where we find a lot of variation within an individual school. One teacher may run a classroom which is high on atmosphere, but low on productivity (a club). Another may have a highly individualized programme (professional service) and yet another may insist on high standards of academic achievement (business). Students can experience all types in the one day.

A feature of the Blau–Scott typology is the way in which the structures of the organization emerge as a natural and logical consequence of its goals. School structures are influenced by the goals, assumptions and expectations of administrators and teachers within the school. These assumptions condition personal attitudes to colleagues, students and parents. They influence teaching methods, classroom management and student assessment. These attitudes become part of a regular behaviour pattern in the school, and thus ingrained in organizational structures. In a similar way, parents and students have levels of expectations with regard to schools. The congruence between their expectations and experience gives rises to levels of satisfaction with the school. This in turn becomes a factor in their perception of and cooperation with further developments within the school.

Frequently the stated aims of the school (theory) and the structures (practice) are in conflict. For instance, a school may aim to produce citizens who will act responsibly in a democratic state, yet the system is organized so that students have no voice in the school. The aim is to develop some element of the club, whereby students take responsibility for their own development, yet the energy of the school is focused on producing highly qualified individuals (business) and the original aim is left to chance. Sometimes the professional service which teachers offer in order to promote learning can create a sense of dependency between the learner and the teacher which is more akin to a social welfare system than a professional–client relationship. Yet, teachers may believe that they are still acting out of a professional relationship, and fail to see how circumstances have changed the nature of their relationship with students.

Practices and attitudes reinforce one another as part of the total system. By examining some of the key practices and structures in the school, and evaluating their contribution to different school 'types', we can get an overall view of the balance within the school. The aim of such an examination is to stimulate reflection on the effects and hidden assumptions behind school practices, and then to either affirm or change these practices.

**Exercise 5.2**

Return now to the four sheets which described aspects of the school which contributed to each of the different types. You may find that the same artefact or value appears on more than one sheet. This is an indication of the interdependence of the four types in a school, and the way a different meaning can be given to the same artefact by different people. The aim of this reflection is to discover the overall balance of types within the school.

Make a list of the different artefacts that appear on all the lists. Prioritize the top 10 of those for the influence they have on the school — those that affect high numbers of students, or that persist over most of the school year. Each person should write these 10 artefacts in the left hand column in the table below.

The next part of the exercise is done individually. In each of the 4 columns which represent the different types, give points out of 10, where a high score indicates that this artefact makes a very significant contribution to promoting this type within the school, and a low score that it has little effect. There is a maximum of 40 points on each line.

When you have completed your own table, share your scores with others in your group. You will invariably find that others in the group see things in the school in a different way than you do. You may even try to come up with a consensus picture of what your school is like.

| SCHOOL STRUCTURE OR ACTIVITY | Club | Business-for-profit | Professional Service | Social Service |
|---|---|---|---|---|
| 1 | | | | |
| 2 | | | | |
| 3 | | | | |
| 4 | | | | |
| 5 | | | | |
| 6 | | | | |
| 7 | | | | |
| 8 | | | | |
| 9 | | | | |
| 10 | | | | |
| OVERALL SCHOOL ORIENTATION | | | | |

*Reflection*

It is important to evaluate what this typology teaches. This exercise has elicited a high level of sharing about the purpose of school activities, in which the actual score agreed became secondary to the value of the sharing. One outcome was that individuals simply became more tolerant of the different types being promoted by their colleagues in the school. This acceptance of pluralism may be deemed the desirable outcome. Frequently the discussion on where the school is at present gave rise to a debate on where the school should be or might be. Teachers began to realize that perhaps one profile was more appropriate than another. This had implications for the school and so they began to ask how the current profile might be adapted. The discussion helped them see the way in which artefacts were given meaning. They could then focus on that meaning, and hence influence a shift in the balance of types for the school. Similarly, some individual teachers found they over-concentrated on one type and they then sought to redress that balance by developing new skills. Schools differ in their willingness and ability to face assumptions and work at the implications. However, if a group has taken this exercise seriously, it usually generates a high level of commitment and energy in changing the focus and quality of activity in the school.

## The Carlson Typology

Carlson (1964) developed a two-dimensional typology for service organizations based on selectivity in the client–organization relationship, and he outlined how clients and organizations adapt to one another in situations where there is a lack of control over participation[4]. The typology is based on control over participation and can be illustrated on a graph (see Figure 5.3)

One axis illustrates the control of the client over their own participation, and the other axis illustrates the control the organization has over admission. When simple yes/no categories are given, and drawn on a grid, this gives rise to four organizational types.

|  |  | Client has control over own participation in organization | |
|---|---|---|---|
|  |  | YES | NO |
| Organization has control over admission | YES | Competitive Market Driven | Conscript |
|  | NO | Service | Fatalistic |

*Figure 5.3  The Carlson Typology of Organizations applied to schools (Adapted from Carlson, 1964)*

*The Four Different Types*

In a competitive and market-driven context, both the client and the organization have full control over participation. A bank may invite me to apply for a credit card. I am free to accept or reject their invitation. If I decide to apply, I fill out the details on the application form, and on the basis of these details, the bank then decides whether to issue the credit card or not. From the organizational perspective, an invitation is offered to selected clients to participate. The invitation may be exclusive or inclusive. Sometimes, exclusive stores, restaurants or clubs try to attract particular clients by offering services and products which are themselves exclusive and therefore very costly. A supermarket on the other hand is inclusive and tries to attract a wide range of customers through promotions of selected products and attractive displays. The client, however, is free to accept or refuse an invitation. As a client, I may decide not to avail myself of certain services being offered to me. I may decide to windowshop or browse through their products, and not buy anything. There is a delicate balance between the organization gearing its invitation to the correct client, making sure that invitation is attractive and suited to the needs of the client, and the client's decision to satisfy his or her needs with the particular product being offered. Organizations must attract the right customers in sufficient numbers to survive, and clients must choose the correct organization or product to suit themselves. If either the organization or the client does not choose wisely, they lose out. A series of poor choices can challenge survival.

In service-oriented organizations the client has a choice about participation, but the organization does not. For instance, you might choose your doctor or solicitor from a list of those in practice. In general, the ethics of the professions do not allow doctors or solicitors to refuse clients on the nature of their problems. In general, there are no preconditions set which a patient or a client must meet before the doctor or solicitor will deal with them. The nature of the service offered is based on the need of the client, and the organization serves anyone who has that need.

In a conscript situation, the organization exercises a choice over who participates, but the client has no choice. For instance, in a time of war, the government may issue a conscription order to enlist people in the army. If my number comes up in the lottery, I have no choice but to present myself. However, the army may in fact refuse to take me. The medical examination may reveal that I am cross-eyed, have a shake and cannot distinguish uniforms. This makes me more a danger to my allies than the enemy!

A fourth type of organization exists in which neither the organization nor the client has a choice over participation. For instance, if I am sentenced to a term in prison, then I have no choice but to serve the sentence of the court. Also, the prison has no choice but to accept me. Their clientele is also determined by the judicial system. Carlson termed such organizations 'domesticated', in that there is no element of competition on the part of client or organization. The existence of the organization is guaranteed and whereas it must compete with other institutions for funds, allocation is not based on quality. The institution is wanted by society and supported by it.

*Applying the Typology to Schools*

Carlson's typology can be applied to many different relationships within the school system. We will look at four such relationships: the student and the education system; the student and the school; the student and the classroom; teachers and teaching. The focus of the application is on the artefacts of choice which exist for both partners in the relationship. We will later look at the effect of the different levels of choice on the organizational culture of the school.

### Students and the education system

This relationship shares elements of all four types. At one level schools exist in a competitive, market-driven environment. Choices exist for the student. Within the system there are choices of the local state school, residential or private schools. In areas where there are a number of schools, the student can choose where to apply and schools may in fact have to compete for students in order to maintain numbers. The student, once he has reached a certain age, can choose to leave the school if it does not satisfy his needs. Schools try to attract students by the types of courses they offer and by an extra-curricular programme in sport or drama. However, schools need not accept all students. Some schools have to limit their size because of lack of facilities, or to maintain a good student–teacher ratio in the classroom. They use a quota system of entry, or perhaps select students based on the results of an entrance examination. In certain cases, schools can dismiss students who do not meet particular standards.

At another level, the relationship between schools and students can appear as fatalistic. A student is legally bound to attend school up to a certain age. As already seen in Chapter 4, school may appear as a prison sentence for some students. In many areas, the financial resources of the home mean that there is no real choice of schools. There is only one school within a reasonable distance from home, and if the student is to be educated, it must be there. Even if a school is selected from a number of alternatives, the selection may be made by parents, and the student may develop a fatalistic relationship with the school. In state education systems, the school is legally obliged to provide for all students within its catchment area. Between these two positions, a number of factors may impinge on the level of choice open to either the student or the school, giving rise to a service-oriented or a conscript situation. We shall discuss how students and schools respond to their situation later in this chapter.

### The student within the school

This typology can also be applied within the school, to categorize the way that school administration exercises control over participation in different aspects of school life, and the level of choice offered to students. One area of school life is the way students are assigned to class groups or to subject options within the curriculum. The allocation may be determined by the school, using a system of its own devising (e.g. academic merit). Alternatively, students may be given some element of choice as to the subjects they take, or whether they are with friends. At junior levels in the school, the school may determine a core curriculum, with few options. As student interests mature, the curriculum may develop a higher proportion of elective subjects, allowing for individual specialization. The extent of the common core curriculum determines a level of choice for students and the school. In the extra-curricular programme, students may have a greater degree of choice. In some schools, however, students are obliged to participate in games, despite having little interest or aptitude. This typology can also be applied to the relationship between teachers and the school, and the choice given to teachers as to what classes they teach, and the degree of freedom to include or exclude certain students.

### The student and the classroom

Within the classroom, choices with regard to participation are also operative. In some cases, students may choose where they sit, what type of learning activities they engage in and with whom. For instance, if a teacher is using a group project as a learning activity, students may choose their companions, or they may be assigned to a particular group. A teacher can give students different forms of assessment — project, essay, oral. The student is allowed choose which suits them best, or builds up a portfolio of different types of assessment. Alternatively, the assessment procedure is set by the teacher or some external body. In some classrooms, the content and pace of work is determined by the teacher. However, some teachers allow students to choose topics, or perhaps the sequence of topics. They develop structures, which allow students to choose the pace of work, for instance through a series of graded worksheets.

### Teachers and teaching

The typology can also be applied to the career of teaching. A good teacher, or a teacher with a particular subject range, may find themselves very marketable. They may seek a transfer to another school, or a promotion to a position of Department Head or Principal. They find themselves in a competitive, market-driven situation where their talents will be appreciated. However, there is also a way in which a fatalistic relationship may develop. A person may enter the teaching profession from a wide range of careers open to them. For the first number of years, they make reasonable progress and find satisfaction in their work. However, in the course of their careers they become disillusioned with teaching but find that time has passed them by, and they have no choice but to stay in teaching. They may have developed new interests, but are unable to risk an uncertain employment situation because of family commitments. Some teachers have a series of poor teaching experiences which sap their confidence, or they are adversely affected by a lack of promotion. For some, personal problems or ill health affect their ability to enjoy teaching, yet their family commitments prevent them from making a mid-career change.

From the school perspective, a new teacher is employed on the basis of their interview and probationary period. Through all these phases, the school has full choice over inviting participation from the teacher, or of terminating their participation. However, if the teachers come through their probationary period in a satisfactory way, they are given tenure. If, at a later stage, they prove to be unsuitable, and do not develop with the needs of the school, the administration may find that their choices of dealing with the teacher are limited. Security of tenure makes it very hard to fire the teacher, and efforts at staff development may prove fruitless.

---

**Exercise 5.3**

Look back over the four applications of the typology above, and add your own examples of how choices exist for both partners in the relationship. What are the artefacts that apply to your school in each of these situations?

Look at some other relationships within the school system (e.g. student and teacher, teacher and colleague, parent and school, etc.) and explore the way that each partner has a choice in their participation in the relationship. How might Carlson's typology be applied here?

---

### *Carlson Developed: Adaptive Behaviours in Schools*

Carlson developed this typology by reflecting on the way clients and organizations adapt to a lack of control over participation. He claimed that there is usually some degree of adaptation, some adjustment to cope with one's lack of control. At school level, this takes the form of segregation, goal displacement or preferential treatment. Students adapt by situational retirement, rebellious adjustment or side-payment adjustment.

### *School adaptation*

*(a) Segregation* of students can exist at a system level, as students of different talents are assigned to different schools, such as academic or vocational schools, grammar or state schools. In some countries, the distribution of students in such schools follows a distinctly social class bias, and allows for a developing ghetto mentality. In other cases, particular schools may become a 'dumping ground' for students who do not perform well elsewhere.

Within a school, students may be segregated into different tracks or streams on academic grounds. The segregation involves not only a physical placement, but also segregation in terms of the curriculum. Teachers also feel a sense of segregation in some schools, depending on the status that is given their subject. The art teacher may be given a room in the basement, and have many of the low achievers assigned to the class, whereas a science or mathematics teacher has a higher status within the staff. The remedial teacher becomes responsible for all students with learning difficulties, and the pastoral care or guidance teachers become responsible for all students with problems, rather than these functions being integrated into the role of every teacher.

*(b) Goal displacement* is an adaptation in which a side issue becomes the main goal of the organization. In some schools, teachers may value discipline and control over student learning. In more than one school I have formed an impression that bright students get an education, middle-of-the-road students get teaching and weaker students get discipline. What happens is that training may replace formation. Custody replaces personal development. Public performance and examination results take precedence over personal learning and growth. There have been cases of schools luring students on the basis of their athletic or sporting prowess, where the school's reputation at games becomes more important than its function in promoting learning. Similarly, the school curriculum may be 'provider driven' and suit the talents of the teachers rather than respond to the needs of the students. This may be particularly true if a school is faced with an ageing, non-mobile staff.

*(c) Preferential treatment* of those who behave according to the norms of the organization. This generally takes the form of rewards or recognition. Students may be singled out in school assemblies for their achievement in academia, in sports, or in some service to the school. Sometimes they are appointed to visible positions in the school such as class leaders, prefects or student representative bodies. The important point here is that they are appointed by the school administration. This is quite distinct from their sociometric position with their peers, although it may also enhance or reinforce that position. The criteria used by individual schools for such reward and recognition is revealing of its culture. In some schools, there are few rewards and these are confined to very limited areas. As a result, these may be keenly sought after, causing a high degree of competitiveness among some students, and a sense of disinterest among others. In other schools, rewards are freely distributed in a large variety of categories and many students have an opportunity of receiving the awards without having to compete too strongly or perhaps even of valuing the awards too highly. Teachers may be rewarded with particular classes, or with their choice of classrooms, and some may even be given timetabling considerations with regard to teaching or non-teaching duties.

*Student adaptation*

Although students may reluctantly enter the school, they sometimes become receptive to the goals and atmosphere of the organization, and are quite productive. On the other hand, they may reject the organization altogether, and drop out. In schools, the problem of truancy or of students dropping out before they have gained qualifications, can give rise to social problems. There is a major challenge to schools or training institutions to find a curriculum or style of learning suitable for these students. Teachers also drop out of the system, taking early retirement or opting for some other career after 5–10 years' teaching.

There are also a number of intermediate adaptive behaviours within the school. Students who find themselves unwillingly participating in school, or teachers who find that they have no choice but to remain in teaching, find ways of coping with their situation to make life bearable.

*(a) Situational retirement* is an adaptive behaviour where the student or teacher goes through the motions, with no real enthusiasm or involvement. Students may adapt to their situation by trying to get lost in the crowd. They do not attract attention either positively or negatively. They work to a reasonable standard without stretching themselves to learn or being stretched by the teaching process. They do just enough to get by without becoming the focus of the teacher's attention as students who merit special promotion or the attention of remediation. Neither do they attract attention by participating in extra-curricular activities in the school, or by asking questions or volunteering answers in class. They do not misbehave either, as this also might attract attention. In some classrooms students experience a high level of boredom. Their underachievement frequently goes undetected, because they have retired from the situation, and are not noticed. Teachers can also go into situational retirement. Teaching becomes a chore in which they no longer invest. They teach in a highly mechanical manner. Their classes are competent, but rather dull and uninteresting. They repeat the same classes, give the same notes year after year. There is little interest in the subject matter, or in the learning process for students.

*(b) Rebellious adjustment* occurs where the client participates in a manner calculated to disrupt the main thrust of the organization. On an academic level, students may refuse to complete homework assignments, answer questions in class or participate in classroom activities. They may constantly disrupt a class by asking questions designed to side-track the flow of the lesson, or by seeking attention or attempting to dominate. On a social level, some students are constantly in trouble for rule infraction. Others may engage in bullying and aggressive behaviour towards peers or towards teachers. A student who is uninterested in PE or in the sports programme will constantly forget to bring their gear or develop illness and injuries to avoid participation. For a teacher, rebellious adjustment might be seen in a constant negative pattern of communication at staff meetings or in a staffroom. This might manifest itself as an aggressive adherence to procedural details at meetings, in personality clashes with other teachers or with administrators, or by generating a general atmosphere of complaining, non-cooperation and negativity.

*(c) Side-payment adjustment* occurs when the client decides to participate in the main processes of the organization in order to be able to benefit from some other aspect of the organization. Examples of this kind of adaptation are students who are not interested in academic work in class, but enjoy taking part in the extra-curricular programme in school. They do their class work so as not to endanger their participation and enjoyment of the other activities. Other students enjoy the camaraderie of being with their friends, and so they stay on in school and perform to a reasonable standard. Teachers may remain in a school because of some side-payment attractions — location, finished at 4 p.m., length of holidays, camaraderie of staffroom, extra-curricular activities and profile.

**Exercise 5.4**

Apply this exercise to your own situation. Consider one relationship within the school where a degree of choice exists for the partners. Individually, make a list of ways in which evidence of segregation, goal displacement, preferential treatment, situational retirement, rebellious and side-payment adjustment shows itself. Compare your notes with those of your companions.

From the lists you have developed, list the different activities — the artefacts of the school. Now, assign points out of 10 for the degree of choice that is involved for each partner (Low is 0 and High is 10). Each activity gets two scores.

| Sample list of activities within a school | School control | Student control |
|---|---|---|
| 1  Amount of homework | | |
| 2  Quality of homework | | |
| 3  Assessment during the year | | |
| 4  Project work in class | | |
| 5  Discipline structures | | |
| 6  Subject choices | | |
| 7  Who their teacher will be | | |
| 8  Extra-curricular activities | | |
| 9  Participation in school activities | | |
| 10  Who they sit beside in class | | |
| 11 | | |
| 12 | | |
| 13 | | |
| 14 | | |
| 15 | | |
| 16 | | |

Each of these activities can now be placed on a Post-It, or a piece of paper. These can then be transferred to a grid (Figure 5.4), to illustrate its position, and its strength. For instance, activities that scored (6,6) and (10,10) would both be in the top right hand quadrant, although there is a qualitative difference to the degrees of choice available. When all the activities have been placed, you have a collage which gives you a picture of how school activities are perceived.

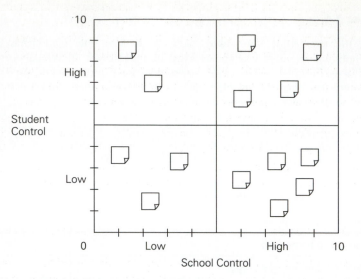

*Figure 5.4   Sample grid for application of Carlson's typology of levels of control over school artefacts for students and school*

Now, evaluate the lessons of this activity. What is the distribution of activities like? Are you happy with the balance of the distribution? Does your perception of activities differ from your colleagues? From that of students? What might be the lesson from this activity?

*Reflection*

The importance of Carlson's typology is its focus on control and choice, and the subsequent adaptation between individuals and the school. Schools adapt to the individual's willingness to participate and the individual adapts to the school's goals and expectations. The challenge facing school culture is the integration of these elements in a way that goes beyond peaceful coexistence to a dynamic cooperation in the development of shared goals and visions. The typology gives a conceptual framework for understanding aspects of the culture within the school. Understanding the dynamics of interaction between the two sides of the relationship gives a deeper insight into the dynamics of culture, and perhaps points the way for interventions into key areas of the relationship, so that participation is more fruitful and enriching for both partners in the relationship.

## The Etzioni Typology

In the Blau–Scott typology the focus was on the organization's goals and its beneficiaries. Carlson's typology focused on the relationship between the organization and the client. In clarifying this relationship, it was seen how client and organization adapt by using coping mechanisms and strategies which define a climate and culture of participation and cooperation. Etzioni (1961, 1964) elaborated on the notion of relationships in an organization. He proposed a typology which focused on the organization as a social system characterized by the use of power, styles of participation and the ultimate goals of the organization. The focus on the use of power and participation recognizes that goals are not simply 'givens' in organizations, but are decided on and mediated by people — leaders and administrators. The implementation of these goals is carried out by individuals, and adaptation results from decisions and actions of individuals. How decisions are made, as well as the content of these decisions, has a major impact on the adaptive processes within an organization, and this is the focus of Etzioni's typology.

### Types of Power

At the centre of Etzioni's analysis of organizations is the use of power. For Etzioni, power is defined as 'An actor's ability to induce or influence another actor to carry out the directives or any other norms he or she supports'[5]. The source of an organization's power, or indeed the power held by an individual within an organization varies. French and Raven (1968) identified the following five sources of power[6].

*(a) Legitimate power* is due to position or rank in an organization. It is the authority that an individual has to make decisions and the influence that these decisions have on organizational outcomes. In schools, principals have legitimate power because of their position. Similarly, teachers exercise legitimate power in the classroom. Legitimate power may be conferred on others such as heads of departments, deans of discipline and student prefects. Thus, legitimate power resides in an official and formal office.

*(b) Reward power* is the influence an individual has as a result of controlling the allocation of resources to others. A principal can allocate financial and other resources to teachers and to departments within the school. A teacher allocates recognition in the classroom, especially in marks and grades, and reports home to parents. However, this power may not always be associated with a formal position. In the informal power struggles of the staffroom, cliques form which sometimes exercise great control over decision-making. By voting en bloc for certain projects, they in fact have the power of rewarding others with approval and recognition or ignoring them.

*(c) Punishment power* is the influence which results from control over the exercise of sanctions. The type of power used here is often coercive, where an individual is threatened with a variety of sanctions — physical or psychological — unless they comply with a particular behaviour. This power can be used in conjunction with a formal position, for instance by a principal allocating work to teachers or by teachers in the way they relate to students in the classroom. It can also be associated with the informal social system where teachers are aggressive in their approach to administrators or to colleagues, or when a student bullies another student.

*(d) Referent power* exists as a result of a relationship between actors. It is fundamentally a charismatic power, based on an affinity of personality or ideals. Influence operates on the basis of maintaining the relationship. A principal may exert this type of power in a school because of the ability to communicate a sense of vision and purpose. Some teachers gain a reputation over time as being excellent teachers, which helps them create a positive learning environment in the classroom and thus influence student learning. Some students stand out as leaders among their peers, and their popularity as athletes or their academic success gives them great social influence. Often this type of power is not associated with a formal position within the organization, but is part of the informal power base within the school.

*(e) Expert power* derives from specialized skill or knowledge. Others refer, and defer, to individuals with special expertise. The specialization can arise from experience, as say a senior teacher in a department. Or it may arise as a result of a relevant skill such as Information Technology, accounting, sports or drama within the school. The individual can choose to use their power in a benevolent way, by placing their expertise at the service of the school. Or they may choose to manipulate, by making demands as to how and when the expertise will be used. For instance, a person skilled at devising a school timetable may dictate the terms of the timetable.

---

**Exercise 5.5**

Review the five sources of power and identify them in your own school. Who are the people who hold power from each of the different sources? In what way do they exercise their power and influence? Describe an event in which each type of power is exercised. What is the typical response to the use of each type of power?

---

### Classifying the Use of Power and Its Effect

Each of these different types of power exists in schools. Also, each type of power can be exercised in a functional or a dysfunctional way. For instance, legitimate power in the school gives rise to structures to ensure that the school runs smoothly, and designates areas of responsibility and the people who carry that responsibility. However, the resulting structures may be dysfunctional and lead to lack of motivation if there is a conflict between seniority and ability in filling these positions, or if holders become fossilized in their positions. The healthy use of power depends on the relationship which exists between people in the organization — those who use power and those who must respond to its use. Etzioni identified three ways in which power is exercised, and three typical responses to that use.

One use of power is *coercive*, whereby people are forced under threat of penalty to behave in a particular way. The typical response to such a use of power is *alienation*, where the participant is negatively or, at best, neutrally involved with the school. The climate developed in such a school is typically coercive, and is characterized by frequent conflict, dissatisfaction and strife.

A second use of power is *remunerative*, where power holders reward parti-cipants according to a particular scale for performing their functions. The typical response to such a use of power is that the participants become *calculative* and adapt their involvement to the reward. The climate generated is utilitarian, in that market forces determine the rewards to be offered, and they must be tailored to meet the needs of the individuals involved.

A third use of power is termed *symbolic*, which strives to place a moral imperative to behave in a particular way by appealing to the value inherent in the behaviour. Participants adapt by becoming *committed* to the behaviour and become wholeheartedly and positively involved in the goals of the school. The climate gen-erated is termed normative, in that people are acting out of a conviction of value.

According to Etzioni, the three combinations outlined above can be regarded as compliance types. Other combinations of the use of power and the adaptation of participants may exist, but only on a temporary basis. They gradually give way to the congruent compliance types. For instance, a new principal may act in a coercive way in a school which has a well-established normative culture. One of two things is likely to happen: either the principal will accept the norms of the school and stop trying to coerce teachers to be different, or else the staff will become alienated and abandon their norms. It can also happen that an individual who is alienated and who enters a utilitarian culture may be drawn into a calculative approach if the rewards or sanctions are strong enough. If teachers find students are alienated and unresponsive to normative or remunerative approaches, they may resort to a more coercive style to get the work done and get students through exams. It can also happen that a teacher approaches a class with negative expectations and a coercive style but finds a class of highly motivated students who ask challenging questions and have created a normat-ive culture of work among themselves. The teacher must adapt to this new culture.

Etzioni further postulated that a particular compliance relationship was more likely with certain organizational goals. One organizational goal is that of *order*, and is typical of organizations such as the army, prison and government. Order goals also exist in schools, in that a large number of people must be coordinated and live in some form of harmony. According to Etzioni, a typical compliance type in these situations is a coercive type, in which authority is used to enforce these goals, bringing different degrees of alienation among the participants. Organizations may also have *economic* goals, typical of businesses and profit-making. In looking at the Blau–Scott typology, we saw how schools too can have economic type goals. These typically give rise to a utilitarian climate, where rewards and sanctions are clearly related to performance. However, if an organization has *cultural* goals, such as those centred on personal values, art and religion, the transactional use of power through coercion or remuneration is unlikely to be effective. What is required here is a climate of shared norms and commitment. Just as there are congruent types between the use of power and the response to that use, so also approaches to power in organizations must be congruent with the goals of the organization. Of course, organizations may try to implement cultural goals through coercive means. This may succeed in some behaviour modification, but the change is likely to regress once the threat of sanction is lifted because values are not internalized.

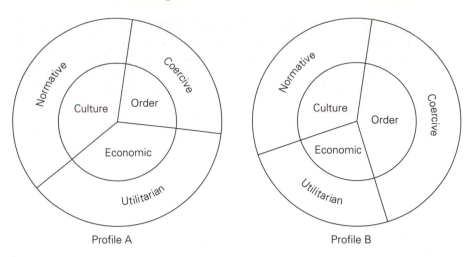

Profile A                                              Profile B

*Figure 5.5   Profiles of schools based on Etzioni's compliance types and goals*

The Etzioni typology raises important questions about the goals and internal socialization processes of schools. Schools are charged with culture goals, passing on the value systems of society through the study of language, art, history, literature, music and religion. Culture goals can be identified in the content of the curriculum, the approaches of teachers to their subjects, as well as the status given to particular subjects and activities. Many culture goals are also enhanced through extra-curricular activities such as drama and school tours. Schools also adopt economic goals, preparing students to participate in the economic life of the country through training in specific subjects such as commerce, science, technology. These goals can be identified in the emphasis placed on particular subjects and also in the reward and recognition system within the school for academic, co-curricular and extra-curricular activity. Schools also have order goals in that they are involved in the process of sorting and ranking students, as well as the orderly occupation and organization of large numbers of people. Order goals are achieved through expectations and regulations for student behaviour in classroom performance, production and behaviour, through emphasis on rules and directives and the formality and use of sanctions in disciplinary structures and through an emphasis on status in relationships.

This mixture of goals in a school setting brings with it a mixture of compliance and involvement styles. Thus, Etzioni's typology represents a perception of the school as the context for the working out of organizational dynamics. The varied responses to and emphasis on the different types of goals determine the climate of the school. This is presented as an image in Figure 5.5. At the core of the school is the value system related to order, economic and cultural goals. The balance of these goals hints at the assumptions schools have about their purpose. These assumptions give rise to organizational systems and climates — the artefacts of the culture. Figure 5.5 illustrates two types of school profile. Profile A represents a school with a strong cultural sense, which seeks to bring students to an appreciation of their cultural heritage, and to develop a sense of personal commitment among students. Profile B on the other hand is very focused on order goals. Emphasis is placed on student discipline, and the school sees this as the ultimate benefit for its students. These profiles may represent different schools, or they may stand for the same school, where Profile A represents the aspirations of the school for students (the theory), but Profile B represents the school as experienced by students (the practice).

Schools come to appreciate the distribution of core values either from an outside–in, or from an inside–out approach. The following exercises may be helpful in helping to clarify the balance that exists in that core dimension.

---

### Exercise 5.6

For the following relationships, can you outline a scenario of behaviours, attitudes and outcomes which would be typical of a relationship in each of the three compliance types?

| Relationships | Coercive | Utilitarian | Normative |
|---|---|---|---|
| Student with Student | | | |
| Student with Teacher | | | |
| Student with Counsellor | | | |
| Student with Form Teacher | | | |
| Teacher with Teachers | | | |
| Teacher with Principal | | | |
| Teacher with Parent | | | |

What types of behaviour on the part of *each side* of the relationship might help move the relationship, positively or negatively?

Make a list of some of the goals of education which are aspired to in your school. Classify these goals as order, economic or culture goals. What are the artefacts in the school which are symptomatic of each of the three compliance styles in implementing these goals?

| Goals of Education | Coercive | Utilitarian | Normative |
|---|---|---|---|
| | | | |
| | | | |
| | | | |
| | | | |

What type of behaviours and attitudes help to keep people in these boxes? Are there artefacts or behaviours which should be changed in order to promote school goals? What might help bring about this development?

If you wish, you can now try to draw a picture which illustrates the balance of these goals in your school, and which identifies the dominant compliant types of behaviour (see Figure 5.5).

### Conclusion

The three typologies presented in this chapter can be used to give both a qualitative and a quantitative measure of the school's personality. In using them, it must be remembered that measures are no substitute for judgements, and that the key to understanding the culture of the school is the wisdom and quality of insight that is brought to discussing these typologies. Development and profit lies as much, if not more, in the process of discussion as in the product.

### Notes

1   Corwin (1974) reviews the development of organizational typologies and models.
2   Blau and Scott (1962) developed a general typology of organizations, rather than one specific to schools.
3   An interesting comparison here is Hargreaves' (1994) typology of school culture as fragmented individualism, Balkanized, contrived collegiality and collaborative.
4   Carlson developed a specific application of this model to American public schools. He focused on two elements of the typology, which he termed 'wild' and 'domesticated'.
5   Etzioni developed his theory in *Modern Organizations* (1964) and also in *The Semi-professions and Their Organizations* (1969).
6   For an application of the notion of power in culture, see Westoby (1988) and Blase and Anderson (1995).

*Chapter 6*

# System Models in Education

In Antoine de Saint-Exupery's story *The Little Prince*, the hero leaves his home planet to visit neighbouring asteroids in order to add to his knowledge. The only inhabitant of the asteroid is its king, who has all the trappings of royalty — purple and ermine dress and seated on a throne. The Little Prince is immediately recognized as a subject, which puzzles him, as the king has never seen him before. He failed to realize 'that the world is simplified for kings. To them, all men as subjects'.

Like the king in the story, we all work with simplified models of the world. The creation of working models is often an egocentric activity in which our experience of the world is organized and explained from our own perspective. Typically, students judge a good teacher by the subjective standards of their own relationship with the teacher rather than by a set of objective criteria. Teachers may also judge classes by their academic performance, or by how much trouble they cause in handing up assignments, punctuality and classroom discipline. In general, our judgements are coloured by our needs and experiences, rather than a schematic understanding of their place in a larger system. Like the king, we have simplified views of how the world is structured, and how it relates to us.

In this chapter, the aim is to move beyond the personal constructs of education and teaching we explored in the metaphors of Chapter 4, and the structures and climate we create in schools, which we looked at in Chapter 5. Here, we explore three different models of educational purpose (see Figure 6.1). The assumptions and values we hold about education itself form the context and perspectives in which the previous two chapters are worked out. The first model looks at the relationship of schooling and curriculum to the social system in which learning takes place. The second model looks at the cultural dimension of values transmission and the third looks at the economic value system related to the return on economic investment and the distribution of rewards in society.

## Schools in the Environment

Identity is defined by some form of boundary. One way to look at the relationship of an organization to its environment is to see how the organization defines its boundaries, what is included inside the boundary and how the organization allows influences to flow across that boundary. In exploring the identity of the school, we

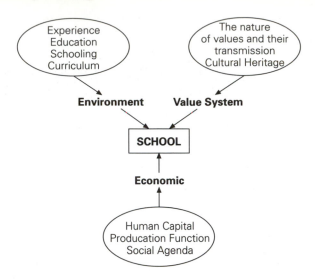

*Figure 6.1   The structure of Chapter 6: areas of underlying assumptions about schools revealed through three models*

examine the boundaries which distinguish all human experience, general educational experience, the formal demands of the schooling system and its curriculum. These four elements of experience, education, schooling and curriculum have common ground, but can also be distinguished from one another. Assumptions about the boundaries between these elements determine in large part the organizational culture of the school. These assumptions influence the values and artefacts which are included in each of the four elements and the relationship that develops between them.

### Experience and Education

Experience is the stimulus of our own existence. Let us think of it as including all the different events that impinge on our consciousness. We classify experiences as good or bad, pleasant or unpleasant, educational or non-educational[1]. Educational experiences are generally positive. They are associated with growth, personal maturity and a deeper sense of purpose in life. We value and seek out such experiences as part of what makes life meaningful. We also realize that not all experience is educational. This is illustrated in Figure 6.2. At times life seems to pass us by. We seem to live in a dream world of our own, unaware of important things going on around us. Also, we sometimes act in a mindless and thoughtless way, when we do not reflect on experience and learn from it. There may be physical, physiological and psychological reasons why an individual does not learn. There may be dysfunction in perception, where an individual does not see or hear. An individual may suffer from a lack of ability to process data and make connections. Perhaps the most common explanation for our lack of learning is a lack of motivation,

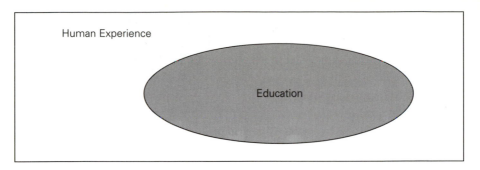

*Figure 6.2   Education as part of human experience*

where we are not interested in what is going on around us, and thus we block out the stimulus.

Teachers attempt to manage the boundary between educational and non-educational experiences, and to help individuals and groups expand the area designated as meaningful experience — the shaded area of Figure 6.2. The larger the shaded area of educational experience, the richer the life of that individual. One aspect of developing educational experience is in the way we define the content of that experience — the experiences we value as teaching us about life. Assumptions about educational experiences can be seen in what teachers call the parity of esteem between subjects — the way that some subjects are valued more highly than others. In the classical tradition, knowledge was seen as having a hierarchical structure, based on levels of abstraction and universality. Thus, practical knowledge and skill were seen at the bottom of the pyramid. On top of this was built academic subjects such as English and history. Mathematics and philosophy dealt with higher levels of abstraction and so were regarded as being higher on the pyramid. In the development of medieval thought, the acme of the pyramid was held by theology dealing not just with the reality of present time and space, but also that of eternity. This hierarchy of value can still be detected in the status of particular subjects in the school curriculum, and the way students are tracked into particular subjects. This transfers into the notion of the educated person, where education is somehow equated with success in key subjects such as mathematics and classical literature. Students may be valued and celebrated in the school in the degree to which they have acquired certain types of knowledge, and, by contrast, somehow devalued if they have not acquired such knowledge.

A second area in which assumptions about education come to the fore is in the way we think of learning and the learner. The boundary between learning and non-learning has both a personal and a social dimension to it. One debate in education centres on how porous that boundary is.

Reflect for a moment on what you think is happening when you test students, and on how you image intelligence. Some common assumptions are illustrated in Figure 6.3. Testing movements in education have claimed to measure the capacity students have for acquiring knowledge, how much knowledge they had been filled

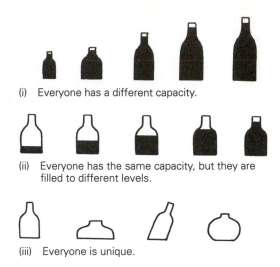

(i)   Everyone has a different capacity.

(ii)  Everyone has the same capacity, but they are
      filled to different levels.

(iii) Everyone is unique.

*Figure 6.3   An illustration of different assumptions about the nature of intelligence*

with, and the quality (or brand) of that knowledge. These tests were commonly used to select students in particular schools and to place them in vocational and academic tracks, and later for career placements. This approach has fallen into some disrepute. The influence of social factors on individuals' test performance, and indeed the cultural bias of the tests themselves have been well demonstrated (see Gould, 1981; Kamin, 1974). The quality of prior experience and the environmental support for learning and development has a major effect on students' attitudes to learning, and on their capacity for self-discipline and focused academic work. More recent research, particularly that popularized by Howard Gardner, has focused on wider concepts of intelligence itself, and the unique profile an individual may have with different intelligences (see Gardner, 1983).

The contrast here is between essentialist and constructivist assumptions about learning. The essentialist sees the individual as a closed system. A fixed characteristic of the individual — termed intelligence — is what determines the boundary between learning and non-learning. The capacity for learning and growth is inherent in the individual. The process of education is to draw out what is innate in the individual (the drawing out which is often characterized as the classical model of Socratic questioning and classical education). How much learning takes place depends on the student, who may be classified as bright or dull, as naturally gifted or stupid, as responsive and ready to learn, or as unresponsive and unteachable. The best that a student can do is to realize their own potential — a potential that is predetermined.

The constructivist on the other hand, sees learning in a social context with a porous boundary between personal learning and the student's environment. The process of learning is seen more as the individual creating their own meaning from their social context. The capacity of each individual for learning is unlimited, and

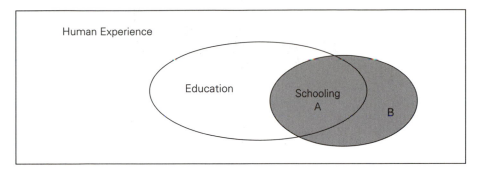

*Figure 6.4    The place of school in the learning experience*

in the process of education students develop their potential, with the school providing the stimulus for drawing in and constructing knowledge.

Thus, the concept of education involves a number of key assumptions about
the nature of knowledge, learning and the learner. When teachers talk about the
purpose of testing, they reveal assumptions and expectations they have about
learning. Some teachers believe that test results reflect innate qualities in the
student, and this allows students to be sorted and ranked on the basis of academic
tests. Others think it merely reflects achievement in a particular social context.
Some schools insist on grading according to a normal curve, whereas others are
more criterion-referenced in their approach. Comments made on report cards such
as 'could do better' and 'underachieving' reveal perceptions of the learner based
on assumptions about the nature of learning. Some teachers distinguish between
'good' students and 'successful' students — those who work to their capacity, and
those who achieve highly on tests.

How we define learning, and the criteria we use to distinguish the uneducated
from the educated person, has implications for the way we value and validate
artefacts in the culture of the school. It gives rise to formal school structures and
classroom management techniques, which are the subject of the next section.


### Education and Schooling

A further development of this model can be envisaged by considering the link
between education and schooling. Education is potentially a lifelong experience. It
is not confined to the school-going years. Even within the experience of the school-
going individual, it is not confined to school. Students learn at home, from their
family and friends, from adults and from peers, from television, books and a myriad
of other experiences available to them. Schooling can be distinguished from education as a formal means of allocating resources to institutional experiences which are
intended to promote certain kinds of valued learning.

The link between education and schooling is illustrated in Figure 6.4. In fact,
only a small part of an individual's education takes place in the formal schooling

system (Section A). It can also be argued that many of the experiences of the schooling system are not truly educational (Section B). Just as an individual some-time does not learn or profit from experience, so, also, schools sometimes fail to provide learning situations and stimuli for some individuals.

Schooling therefore refers to the formal provision of resources and structured experiences for students. It is organized to help produce a certain kind of learning, and has in mind a particular concept of the educated person. The boundary that surrounds formal schooling is highly influenced by the social context of the school. In developed countries, a level of formal schooling is mandated, with legal obliga-tion on parents and guardians to provide a quantity and quality of schooling for their children. The benefits of this provision are in helping the student establish a social identity. As the student participates in further education at second and third level, the focus may change from a social to a productive emphasis. The political system allocates resources to schooling to provide citizens with the means to acquire skills which help them participate in the economic system. As part of the political agenda, choices are made between different needs within the system — social welfare, health, educational provision and economic investment in job promo-tion — and these needs are balanced with other demands of the taxation system. Thus, educational funding is dependent on other factors within the economy. For instance, a declining birth rate and a high proportion of a national population in unemployment or retirement means a diminished tax-base and an increased demand on social welfare programmes and health services (Murgatroyd and Morgan, 1992, Chapter 1). This puts pressure on the funding available for education, particularly new developments in education.

Developments in society have also changed the profile of educational provi-sion, with more students now progressing to third-level education of some form. This changes the nature of second-level education, which, prior to today, would have been terminal for most students. Student performance at second level is increasingly used as criteria for selection to higher level studies. The function of post-primary schools in the eyes of students and parents is changing, and this is posing challenges for schools.

The social context of schooling is also changing. Schools are being charged with new responsibilities for promoting and developing citizenship. Programmes involving civic, social and political education, life-skills, sex and health education are being added to the core curriculum, indicating the changing climate between family responsibilities and formal institutional responsibilities. Demands on schools to provide a wide range of both academic and social experiences characterizes educational policy in many countries. These changing contexts and demands are external challenges to schools, which must be integrated into the organizational culture.

Some schools set up a fairly rigid boundary between themselves and their environment. They run as closed systems, separate and distinct from other edu-cational experiences in the total life of the student. They cater for well-defined experiences through the choice of curriculum, discipline structures and other rituals involved in the relationships between students and teachers, between parents and

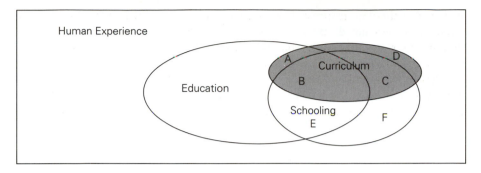

*Figure 6.5   The place of the curriculum in the learning experience*

the school. Working from essentialist principles, they have a fixed curriculum which is given to all students. It is up to the students to benefit as best they can from what the school offers. This internal focus places a strong value on tradition and the continuity of that tradition over time. This may be symbolized in the wearing of uniforms, a classical emphasis in the curriculum, emphasis on extra-curricular activities such as sport and debating. The relationship between administrators, teachers and students aims at developing a negotiated comfortable social system, which is both pleasant and productive.

Other schools have a strong external focus. Working from constructivist assumptions, they set up strong relationships with outside groups to generate a rich and changing environment for students. Links are developed with the local community and industry which give rise to valuable work experiences for students, and are seen as an essential part of a good vocational curriculum. The schools seek a balance between a core curriculum and the interests of the individual student, offering as wide and comprehensive a programme as possible.

Assumptions about the boundary between education and schooling influences how the schools considers outsiders — who it classifies as outsiders and how it deals with them. Parents, the local community, other schools and universities, industry, government may all be considered as outsiders. Of particular importance here is how schools regard parents, and the subsequent organization of the school to promote and encourage the interest and concern of the parent for their individual child. The management of the boundary between schooling and education is guided by assumptions of what type of valuable experiences should be provided in the school, and who can provide such experiences. This leads to a consideration of the curriculum within the school.

### Schooling and the Curriculum

The model can further be extended by examining the place of the formal curriculum within the school (Figure 6.5). For the most part, the curriculum is taught within the schooling process. However, it is now well established that the formal curriculum does not define the whole process of schooling — that there exists within each school a 'hidden curriculum' (Sections E and F). This hidden curriculum, sometimes unconscious and unexamined, is part of the socializing process which communicates powerful messages to students, parents and teachers alike (Lynch, 1989). Some of hidden curriculum can be regarded as positive and supportive of educational aims (Section E), whereas at times the hidden curriculum obstructs the process (Section F).

The formal curriculum is not confined to schooling (Section A and D). A considerable amount of educational material related to the formal curriculum is produced for television or as computer software. Also, students avail themselves of private tutorial systems to supplement school tuition. Parts of the curriculum, whether studied in school (Section C) or outside of school (Section D), may be regarded as non-educational, at least at the level of the individual student. For instance, television may provide stimuli which expose students to new experiences and give them a chance to observe things impossible in the ordinary classroom, but this may leave the student unmoved and unmotivated to go beyond observation and to process the information into real learning. Advances in computer technology promote some level of interaction between the user and the computer program, but this is limited to the possibilities and menu options provided by the computer programmers. This type of learning may be a sophisticated structured experience which may have no result other than satisfying the manipulative curiosity of the user as to 'What happens if I do this?', instead of engaging them with the material to be learned. Learning through technology can be very beneficial for the knowledge base of the student, but it can also lead to social isolation (Lynch, 1989).

Developments in technology, particularly information technology, have also created a major paradigm shift in the world-view of students. The growth of what is termed the Information Super-Highway has created a new industry centred on the gathering and dissemination of information. In a changing pattern of industrialization, with a movement away from high-density employment in production, information has become a key to development. This has meant a refocusing of skills and energies into providing information which keeps people abreast of the rapid developments in all fields. The rapidity of technological advances which make discoveries obsolete in two to five years impinge on the value system where age (and presumably wisdom) held pride of place. In the new scenario, youth and adaptability are the key values. The increasing speed of communications especially through television, and the relative ease of travel, develops an international dimension to people's consciousness which affects the mindset of the students in the classroom. Developments in technology, and the exposure of students to technological wizardry, has implications for the process of teaching and learning. Integrating technology into the classroom, and attracting the attention of students used to being bombarded by a heavily resourced professional media, has become a particular challenge to present-day teachers.

**Exercise 6.1**

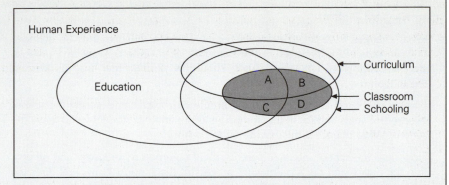

Figure 6.6   *Integrating the classroom into the model*

To finish this section, the reader might like to add a dimension to our model — the classroom itself. Classroom activities all take place within the context of formal schooling. What are the classroom artefacts and values in:
A — the formal curriculum that promotes student learning?
B — the formal curriculum that does not promote student learning?
C — other activities that are of benefit to student learning?
D — other activities that are not of benefit to student learning?

The underlying pattern of societal experience affects both the role of schooling and, at a fundamental level, the content and the processes that develop within the school curriculum. The school may develop a proactive and integrating stance to these developments, changing its curriculum in response to the needs of students and of society. Alternatively, it may be reactive in the face of these challenges and resistant to change and integration. The response is determined by underlying assumptions and values about the process of schooling, and the curriculum as an implement of that process. When teachers discuss these issues in a positive and supportive environment, they come in touch with the larger issues of educational provision and their role as teachers. By sharing with others, they see opportunities of reconfiguring their own belief systems, and of developing attitudes and organizational strategies which better promote their own educational platforms.

**Reflection 6.1**

What use is made of testing in your school? What basic assumptions about the nature of intelligence might be revealed in this?

In the minds of students, do some subjects have a higher status than others? What is the evidence for this? What are the things that influence students in the way they view students? Is it any different for teachers? For parents?

What are the characteristics of good students in your school? What are students rewarded for? Looking over your recent graduates, which students do you term successful? What are the criteria that are used? What are the working models for an educated student?

What changes have taken place in recent years in the demands on schools. Do you notice any changes in the demands of government, society, parents, students, with regard to what schools should be doing? How has this affected the school?

Have you noticed any changes in the profile of (a) students entering the school over recent years and (b) in the immediate destination of students who leave the school? What impact is this having on the school?

How does the school integrate parents, local community, industry (and others), into the policy and decision-making process of the school? How well does the school cooperate with other schools in the area? What structures facilitate this process?

What changes have taken place in the formal curriculum of the school over the past 10 years. Where has the initiative for these changes come from? What has been the reaction of the teachers, the students and the parents to the changes?

What are the criteria for a well-balanced curriculum (Section B of Figure 6.5)? Try to answer this question from a number of different perspectives — student, parent, industry, etc.

How has teaching changed over the past 10 years? Can you observe different responses in teachers in the school? For different subject areas?

What patterns of boundary management can be detected from the reflections above?

### The School as a System of Values

Education has been defined as the passing on of cultural heritage, the initiation of the young into worthwhile ways of thinking and doing, and the fostering of individual growth. The concept of what this means changes over time in any society. Philosophical and literary movements are indicators of paradigm shifts in the understanding of human nature and also interrelationships between people in the way society is organized. These intellectual movements also have their reflections in the changing political structure of society as nations and groups try to find concrete expression for their beliefs and enshrine their assumptions in a meaningful way of life. An understanding of the role of schools in this development requires some understanding of major shifts in value systems in society, the nature of values and how they are determined by individuals and groups, and also a framework for strategies which aim at transmitting these values to others.

The traditional perceptions of cultural heritage have focused on language and history. Formal education has sought to introduce students to the history of thought and culture through language, and to master linguistic competencies in order to achieve this aim. Education was seen as a preparation for participation in the unfolding cultural process. This section explores the underlying models behind the value systems which inform such goals in education, and also the models of value transmission which inform the organization of schools and school systems in carrying out their role.

### The General Context of Values

Historically, the provision of education in western societies has been linked to religion[2]. The tradition of Church involvement in formal education goes back to the early centuries and the apologetic debates between Christians and the Greek philosophers. The main interest in education was the initiation of adults into the Church, the development of an understanding of the faith, and safeguarding the truths of the new religion against heresies. With the establishment of the Catholic Church as the dominant state religion in the Roman Empire, the emphasis changed from the proselytizing, initiating role to a more maintenance role in the training of priests and monks in scripture, and later in philosophy and theology. Much of organized Church education, until the fifteenth or sixteenth centuries, centred around the cathedral canons and the monastic religious orders, which were usually cloistered and enclosed. This reflected a value system which was largely suspicious and distrustful of 'the world', and saw sanctity and salvation in the rejection of the world and its values for the sanctuary of the monastery and cloister.

The sixteenth-century Renaissance period is typified by the development of a more anthropocentric world view which gave a positive and central place to the human person. Individuals were viewed as caring, willing, creating their own beauty and their own worldly destiny. There was a revolution against the reign of religion and authority and a growing interest in civic society and nature. The positive spirit was buoyed by the discovery of new worlds and a missionary zeal to bring western civilization to these worlds. The spread of new attitudes was enhanced by the printing press and the educational revolution in the growth of literacy. The increased involvement of the Christian churches in education for the masses was linked with a desire to control the imagery and loyalty of the laity.

The Enlightenment movement of the seventeenth and eighteenth centuries was convinced that right reason alone could discover useful knowledge and help humankind find freedom and happiness. This approach advocated a completely rational approach to knowledge, devaluing and rejecting the role of intuition, imagination and emotions. In particular, the ideas of a revealed truth in religion were rejected. The progress of science and its application to economic and industrial processes promised efficiency, productivity and prosperity in the Industrial Revolution, and the revolutions against monarchies and colonialism heralded new states based on ideologies of freedom, economic growth and opportunity for all.

The developments were not always as benign as the assumptions behind the self-congratulatory and positive titles — Reformation, Renaissance, Enlightenment — might suggest. The romantic movements in literature and philosophy revolted against the dominance of reason. Darwin's theory of evolution and Marxist social analysis pointed to developments as guided by irrational rather than rational forces. The social conditions which prevailed during the industrial revolution gave rise to high levels of poverty and exploitation and led to a disillusion with capitalism, calls for social reform and eventually the development of the social welfare state.

Different stages in history can be regarded as two-edged swords. From one perspective, each development freed up the human spirit to explore new dimensions of human expression. From another perspective, the same development enslaved the human person in other areas of their lives, waiting for the pendulum of change to swing again. As societies developed, they faced problems generated by new thoughts and movements. Schools as institutions also have had to adapt to the external demands which society placed on them, and also to the demands of internal integration of prevalent values within the school. However, the values of the different ages are persistent and resilient. Integration of new values does not imply the expulsion of old ones, rather a reconfiguration. Thus, schools today simultaneously exhibit religious values similar to the certainties of the Middle Ages; the Renaissance values of self-discovery and positive self-projection; the Enlightenment commitment to reason, objective knowledge and scientific method; the modern values of economic pursuits of productivity and efficiency; and the postmodern values which extol personal experience and the lack of trust in metanarratives[3]. The school exists in a dynamic tension between the contradictions inherent in some of these values and also tries to confront the contemporary critiques and developments in society as these show themselves in the subculture of student life and the lives of teachers and parents. Understanding the inner world of teaching involves some reflection on the way values are understood, and also the methods used to transmit these values from one group to another.

### The Nature of Values

The organization of education has been based in part on assumptions about the nature of the human person and about the nature of values and morals. In one tradition, the philosophical understanding of morality has been embedded in the natural law approach proposed by Plato and Aristotle, and developed by Christian philosophers. Morality was seen in terms of a vision of what constituted a good life — an ordered relationship revealed in the unfolding experience of nature. Living the good life consisted of both a subjective and objective element. The subjective element consisted of a commitment to discovering the good pattern, and then living according to that discovery. The objective element consisted of the values which emerged from reflection. Values existed at a level of abstraction, and had a universal application.

From this perspective, value is *a priori* to the knower, as, for instance, sound is to hearing. It exists whether the individual adverts to it or not, just as sound exists whether one hears it or not. The role of the individual is to come to rational self-consciousness of objective values and, in choosing them, bring their life into harmony with the natural order, and thus, in Christian terms, come to perfection.

The political implications of this understanding of values is for society to structure its laws and institutions according to the vision of the good life, and its promotion[4].

A new view of morality developed with the rationalist philosophers of the seventeenth and eighteenth centuries[5]. Basically, these philosophers focused on the person (subject) rather than the content (object) in judging the moral standard of right and wrong, good and evil. They focused on the interest of the individual and emphasized moral standards as relative rather than absolute, and knowledge of these standards as subjective rather than objective. For these philosophers, values and valuing were one. Value arises from the interest of the knower in an object or action. Individuals vary in their interests, and an individual can change his interests from time to time. Given the relativity of values to each individual, the political implications are for a system of tolerance and accommodation of each individual viewpoint, rather than for a system which demands conformity to *a priori* standards.

The objective and subjective understandings of value outlined above give rise to different assumptions about the process of education. Objective values can be studied in an abstract way, with a view to the future, as something apart from the knower. Education requires exposure, and the assumption is that knowing and seeing rationally is the first stage in coming to adopt a value. A second stage is in developing the will to conform to the perceived value. Since the value is objective, it can be recognized by the authorities (government or educator), and situations devised so that others can be induced to practise the value, if they cannot conceptualize it. Thus, the educational process trains students in good habits, preparing them for the future.

Subjective values, on the other hand, cannot be studied in the same way. From this perspective, education requires immersion in experience and there is a strong emphasis on process over content. The educational endeavour focuses on the present rather than on the future, helping students to recognize the elements which make up their present desires and to choose between them.

A tension in educational provision exists between the role of an objective value-laden curriculum which is *a priori* to the learner, and the need for relevant, immediate and subjective satisfaction in learning. This tension is the underlying context in which the political decisions on the nature of education are worked out. In the pluralist society of today, much effort is needed to agree on common values which can be the focus of education. Where there is disagreement about values, major questions arise about how values issues can be treated in schools, or whether these areas are ignored and simply not dealt with in the schooling process, and left therefore to home, church or other institution.

Problems with values can be seen in the popular reaction to new programmes in schools dealing with value-laden topics such as religion, sex education and life-skills. There is a disproportionate level of controversy attached to these subjects, as opposed to biology, economics and English literature, which are almost assumed to be value-free. In asserting value, primacy is given to the knower and to her personal right of assessing value. One can analyse the controversy in terms of a tension between the rights of the individual to subjectively interpret their own experience and the demand for an acceptance of a particular 'objective' interpretation of the value.

*The Transmission of Values*

Even when values are agreed on, a process is needed for teaching these values and passing them on to a succeeding generation. 'Are values taught, or caught?' is a catchphrase which sums up one of the main problems in the transmission of values, and its application can be seen in facets of educational provision, particularly in relation to integrated religious education, and social and ethnic integration in schools. If education is proposed as a means of overcoming political, social or religious divisions, the means of achieving these aims are important. For example, supporters of separate education maintain the importance of individuals understanding their own traditions, and in addition to promoting that knowledge, they organize curriculum and cultural initiatives designed to promote social contact, discussion and understanding between different traditions. Supporters of integrated education, on the other hand, claim that the problem is deeper than lack of information and that one cannot instruct people to show tolerance and understanding. To bring about changes in attitude, students must live in a mini-society (integrated school) in which values not present in the larger society are lived and promoted. This rationale can be applied to such varied areas as separate religious schools, multicultural education, the integration of special needs students into mainstream schools and the single-sex/co-ed debate.

In choosing ways to pass on values, six strategies have been identified[6]. Each of the strategies copes in a different way with the objective/subjective tension.

1  **Model**: whereby the student is exposed to a role model who exemplifies the required value or value system. The assumption is that the values are objective, and easily recognized. The role model not only reflects the value but inspires the student to the value. This works well in a stable system, where values and value symbols are widely shared and understood. However, in a system more open to change, there is a major problem of conflicting value systems, and deciding which values should be modelled.

2  **Values clarification**: students are trained to search for alternatives, to consider the consequences of each, and in an awareness of their own personal preferences and valuations, to make the choice, affirm it publicly and act consistently with it. The search for alternatives is an effort to objectify the value. The examination of consequences works on an assumption that some values are more appropriate than others in a particular situation, and recognizes that there is some element of subjective choice in this process.

3  **Reward and punishment**: the student's behaviour is modified by the reinforcing action of reward and punishment. In this situation, the value is determined by authority, and transactions are set up which induce students to act according to the values, in the hope that the value will be internalized. The danger is that the values tend to remain external to the student, and do not shape feelings and thought processes.

4   **Explaining consequences**: students are trained to discover and evaluate the logical consequences of their behaviour. They are trained to reflect on the past experience and to deliberate about the future consequences of an action. The focus here is on evaluation of a particular action, rather than on choosing from among alternatives. The choice is whether one wants to act or not, and the consequences are judged in a subjective way.

5   **Nagging**: values emerge from authority, and the student is kept in a constant state of subservience and compliance. There is no sense of reward or celebration for good behaviour, but a sense of constantly being driven to conform to an external set of demands.

6   **Manipulation**: the experiences of the student are manipulated to favour certain externally derived value outcomes. This is done by withholding knowledge of alternatives from students and restricting their world-view or, more sinisterly, by distorting the consequences of certain actions.

Often, a school may have examples of all six approaches. Teachers can discover much about their own assumptions by reflecting on the discipline system in the school, and the way in which values are promoted. One interesting contrast is the different way in which rules operate for teachers and for students. The relative balance between academic, social, sporting and spiritual rewards communicates a strong message about the school's value system. A teacher's approach to academic achievement and pastoral care of students reflects the values of the human person which are inculcated through classroom practice. A teacher who reflects on the distribution of time for teacher talk, student questions and individual work with students in their own classroom can discover the values they actually work from. Similarly, they can reflect on the distribution of their time to particular students. The 80–20 rule in management, whereby 80 per cent of the time is spent with 20 per cent of the students is often very revealing to a teacher. Some teachers are taken up with the 20 per cent of highly motivated students who constantly ask questions, and they miss a large portion of students who are bored or alienated. Other teachers spend 80 per cent of their time dealing with minor discipline problems among 20 per cent of the students which distracts from the main body of work in the classroom. In a school discipline system, the method used to implement values sometimes becomes more important than the original value.

The profile of the school on its approaches to values illustrates some basic assumptions about human nature and the nature of truth. The predominance of one particular model sets a tone to the culture and atmosphere of a school, and gives rise to characteristic artefacts in the school system. An 'objective' approach to values may lead to the promotion of values in either a normative or coercive manner, depending on the use of power. The approach is often based on highly rationalist and bureaucratic assumptions, taking its reference point for values from a closed internal system and from tradition. A 'subjective' approach to value is more likely to give rise to utilitarian and calculative relationships in a school and result in a highly politicized organizational climate which is constantly being challenged by new developments in the immediate environment.

---

**Exercise 6.2**

Over the past year, have you noticed differences in the way students express their values? What is positive about that? What do you regard as negative? What perspectives are obvious in the concerns of young people with regard to work, relationships, the environment, money, music, commitment? How has this differed from when you were young? What does this tell you about the changing context of values?

What techniques does your school use for the promotion of values? Take each of the six methods outlined above. What artefacts of the school can be associated with the different approaches to values transmission? How does the balance of the school develop with regard to these approaches?

How does the school resolve differences in value systems? What structures and procedures are in place which allow students, parents and teachers to express their values and have them incorporated into the school programme?

---

### Economic Models in Education

The growth of participation in second-level education, and the increased role of the state in funding that growth and maintaining the system, adds an economic and a social perspective to the complexity of the educational environment. The history of economic development in western societies and state involvement in the provision of mass education are closely interrelated. Whereas commentators dispute the mechanism of how education affects economic growth, there seems to be little doubt that there is some interaction and positive correlation. As a result, schools have become dependent on the national economy for a level of support funding and they are increasingly being charged with goals related to developing and fuelling that economy.

Economic development is concerned with the accumulation, production and distribution of wealth. When education is regarded as wealth, and economic categories applied to its development, the educational system can be viewed from three perspectives. *Human Capital Formation* is a perspective which looks to the development of technical knowledge and the acquisition of skills as a necessary part of economic growth. Education is seen as the additive effects of individual outcomes, the building up of an infrastructure, a pool of skilled resources for the economic system. The *Production Function* perspective looks to the efficiency of the use of resources within a system, and seeks to establish an optimum cost–benefit ratio in the running of schools. A third perspective can be termed a *Social Agenda*, and deals with the distribution of knowledge in groups in society, with a focus on who benefits from the educational production of skills. The provision of equal educational opportunities to all members of society, and also, the lessening of divisions that exist between social groups and classes, are among the items on a social agenda. An appreciation of the pervasiveness of economic models in educational provision, policy model and even school organization is an important perspective on organizational culture.

## Human Capital Formation

Everyone appreciates the benefits of investment. If we receive a large sum of money, through an inheritance, a lottery win or the sale of property, we invest that money so that it earns interest and adds to the capital amount we have. Personal wealth is measured in terms of available capital assets. In economic systems, growth is measured in terms of accumulated physical and human capital. A particular connection between the economic system and education is the development of human capital. The underlying assumption is that investment in human beings and their skills increases their capacity for productive work. This productivity, in turn, gives rise to greater earnings at a personal level, and to increased economic growth at the system level. To a large extent, credentials in education have replaced property as an indicator of wealth in today's society.

Educational involvement in human capital formation can be measured by the skills being produced — their quantity and their quality. One indicator of this investment is the funding given to primary, secondary and third-level education. Investment at primary level ensures a basic standard of education which allows all citizens to participate in the economic life of the country, in return for which certain welfare rights are guaranteed by the state. Investment at this level is a relatively cheap way to prepare individuals for participation in work and identify them for further education. Investment at post-primary level and particularly third-level focuses on the production of skills which are immediately pertinent to a particular economy. Of particular interest is the focus of that investment, especially in the technological and vocational aspects of higher education. In western countries in particular, there has been a movement away from a general humanities and liberal arts education, to an education which aims at integrating vocational, scientific and technological skills. In some countries, the focus of such programmes has led to quite separate 'tracks' in education systems, an approach which reflects social and political value systems. The strength of these different systems, the expansion of the formal curriculum to include scientific and technological subjects, the numbers of students taking these subjects, the grants given to schools to include these subjects in their curricula and also the incentives to attract students to study these subjects, are all indicators and products of a human capital approach to educational policy making.

The benefits of human capital formation have an individual and a systems dimension to them. On the individual level, the student develops skills which are saleable in the market place. Depending on the skills and the market forces of supply and demand, they may have an advantage over other students in acquiring employment. However, the main advantage seems to be at a systems level — the economic or labour infrastructure. Part of the appraisal of investing in the production of particular human skills is the balance between the cost of producing a general pool of skilled talent through centralized systems such as schools, technical colleges, and universities as opposed to developing the skills in the workplace through human resource management. The principal beneficiaries of the production of human skills are the employers, who now have a large pool of fully or partially skilled people to choose from, thus cutting down their training costs. In an economy where the workforce is mobile and where employment is found in short- and medium-term contracts rather than in long-term permanent positions, this is a major benefit to the employer. Thus, a comprehensive human capital formation programme is typically viewed from a systems perspective. Investment results in the existence of a comprehensive number of high-quality and desirable skills within the system, for the system to use. This investment may result in schools providing a comprehensive range of subjects in their curriculum. The individual student, on the other hand, does not become more comprehensively educated. Because of the conservatism of the system and the way that subjects are packaged in the total curriculum, individuals who invest the same time in education come out with the same amount of education. The content profile may be different, but within the profile, individuals simply choose one skill over another, swap one area of interest for another. The success of personal investment for the student depends on the area in which they invest, on the demands for their particular skills profile, on the level of supply they must compete with, and on the durability of their skills in a technological age where some skills have a short shelf-life and early obsolescence. Unfortunately, in seeking to maximize short- or medium-term saleable skills, areas of the curriculum which might develop capacity for learning in later career — such as the humanities — are frequently neglected.

According to the human capital formation model, individuals stay in school as long as the value of the projected gains they hope to obtain from increased qualifications exceeds the cost of education and the income forgone by staying in education. International statistics show a positive correlation between educational qualifications and employment income. Schools play a major and a vital role in the process of certifying knowledge. Given the role of credentials in the environment, this role of sorting and ranking students in terms of their skills has a profound effect on the organizational culture of the school and its link with the environment. Assessment in schools is no longer simply part of the process of learning, a formative experience of feedback leading to continued and further learning. On the contrary, assessment is regarded as a summative activity, a contest the result of which becomes part of the public record of the student, fixing their social or skill level in relation to others. The role of school assessment in the life of the student poses a challenge to the school to prepare a student to perform well in such a system. In schools which set their own curricula and assessments, there is a need to adapt their curricula to the demands of those who use assessment records — universities, other third-level colleges and employers. In schools where some form of standardized testing is performed by outside agencies, there is a tension of adapting teaching to the tests, and having the agenda for education being determined by those outside the school.

All schools produce students with skills. The problem schools face is the demand for particular types of skills, and the value which is placed on them. The problem is faced in curriculum development projects, in the training versus formation debate, in issues of emphasis on content or process, and in the demand for immediate short-term relevance versus possible long-term value. Schools have to make choices about what courses to run, how students are allocated to or allowed to choose programmes. They have to face demands from parents who are justifiably concerned for the future prospects of their children, and may view schooling in a short-term perspective of a passport to third-level education, rather than a wider perspective contained in a school mission statement. The creative tension which these problems generate, and their solutions, define in part the organizational culture of the school.

### Production Function

No one likes to be cheated out of money. It can be very annoying to buy something in a store, and within an hour to find the exact same product on sale at a much cheaper rate in another store. Political and economic systems are no different. Whereas education is seen as an investment, it is also part-consumption. For most developed countries, it forms a major part of the national budget. There is a demand that moneys are used wisely and that returns on invested capital are high. In an economic system which has to meet competing demands from other areas, there are increasing demands for and a need to justify programmes and the use of these resources.

At a system level, the use of demographic information — population, birth statistics, and regional migration patterns — to plan for provision of new schools or the amalgamation of existing schools in the case of a declining population is an important example of production-function planning. This approach extends to the design of school buildings in multi-purpose units, which allows for easy adaptability to future non-educational usage, and particularly the designation of schools as 'community schools', where the physical plant resources are seen as a multifaceted community resource rather than as an exclusive educational resource. Similar types of calculations are used to determine optimum school sizes, based on profiles of student numbers, the number of subjects to be offered in the curriculum and having a profile of uptake which gives low unit cost in providing options for students.

Production-function modelling can operate in the way that schools organize their internal dynamics. For instance, in order to increase their return on teaching time, some schools exercise stringent quality control on the input into their system — they select incoming students very deliberately with the output in mind. Within the school, students are organized into class groups for more effective results. This is based on the notion of getting a high rate of return on teacher time. Frequent quality control checks are put in place by testing and reporting. Remedial action is taken with students who do not conform to standards — and they may even be advised to leave the school.

Classrooms can also operate a production-function approach to learning. The course is broken down into units very much like a production line. Students move through the process at different stages of the year, adding a little more of the process in each class. Progress is seen in linear and relentless terms, and is frequently achieved by regular, repetitious and predictable methods. The relationship between teacher and student is one of supervision and quality assurance.

Accountability structures in schools also reveal concerns for productivity and effectiveness. Sometimes, this accountability goes beyond that associated with the use of physical resources and exists in covert and dysfunctional ways with regard to people. Teachers keep unofficial tallies of student examination successes, in much the same way as students compare marks when projects are returned. This results in a competitive table which informally determines teacher status. It can also happen that accountability becomes an end in itself, rather than being related to any wider vision. For instance, adhering to discipline structures and certain rituals in the school may become values in themselves, rather than being related to the support of student learning. Production-function modelling is a vital part of any organization which requires coordination and allocation of resources in a complex but systematic way. When it is used as a means to an end, then the choice of ends is very important. Both the vision and the artefacts used to implement that vision become powerful elements of the organizational culture.

### Social Agenda

The major influx of students into second-level institutions and the increased financial investment on the part of governments attests to the efforts made on the quantitative aspect of provision. To a large extent, there is a uniform provision of educational opportunity in that all students have the opportunity to avail themselves of post-primary education. However, on the qualitative level, which refers to the consumption of education, major differences still exist between groups in society. Whereas one may say that the playing field has been levelled, history has dictated that not everyone is equipped to play the game in the same way. The present system allows for a differential use of the system by social groups, depending on their starting point in the system. The role of schools as agents of change in society is based on assumptions and economic perspectives about the distribution of wealth in society.

One aspect of providing equal educational opportunity to all is to give everyone access to the rewards of education — entry into prestigious professions and high-salaried work. The effort to ensure that access to these rewards is based on ability rather than on social influence is termed a meritocratic ideal, where ability is measured in terms of the individual's earned educational qualifications. The increasing availability of education beyond the mandatory gives rise to high expectations among those who remain in education. These expectations focus on the status and nature of jobs. Young people and parents are aware of the decisive role the amount of education has in determining future social role and status, and this often leads people to remain in an educational setting while being negative to the content of the course. Credentials then become a means of placing a person along a line, rather than a certification of what his or her talents are — and the idealistic notion of a student leaving school having been guided to discover and develop their real talents contrasts with the reality of having to choose between alternatives none of which is attractive.

Credentialism can be viewed as one of the strategies within a society of maintaining a social equilibrium and relative distance between groups. With the increase of second-level credentials in the system, the aspirations of students turn to third level. This has the effect of gradually devaluing current credentials. Thus, if a degree was the currency which allowed entry to and promotion within the teaching profession 20 years ago, we now have a situation where a large number of teachers are returning to universities and inservice courses for further certification. A primary degree no longer has the same value as it had 20 years ago. A similar system of changing values of credentials exists in the workplace, where second-level certification is no longer an adequate currency in the competition for work. This forces people to stay in education longer. In a system where reasonably well-paid work is readily available, people leave education and move into the workforce. However, if such work is not available, even for those who stay longer in education, there is the danger of social unrest and disillusion, as students ask: 'I did what you asked. I stayed on in school and trained myself in new skills. Now, where is the work you promised me?'

A dysfunctional aspect of credentialism is that it bases judgement on quantity, rather than quality. It assumes the validity of the relationship between the quantitative aspects of the credential (grades, marks) and the quality of the individual who has these credentials. The main assumption underlying this credentialist approach is that the school system, which gives a general education in a relatively narrow range of skills, adequately prepares and judges people for a wide range of specific careers equally. It probably can be argued that general academic ability is predictive of success in other areas, although the mechanism of ability transfer is not clear. In the competition for entry to prestigious positions based on a general education, some social groups have a distinct advantage in being able to devote more resources (extra tuition, etc.) to acquiring credentials. Wealthier social groups will always have an advantage in acquiring quantities of credentials, and this has a conservative and reproducing effect if quantity is not linked in some way to quality issues. A second assumption is that entry into and enlargement of an educational elite is the answer to equality of opportunity, whereas a reassessment of attitudes to the status given certain types of work might be more equitable.

Evidence of this approach to education is the effort to develop success at school, and a re-examination of the nature of school failure. The focus is slowly shifting from the people who were failing at education — a 'blame the victim' mentality — to the education at which people were failing. Curriculum development therefore increasingly looks to find an appropriate education for different groups. The social agenda in education is slowly shifting from trying to prepare everyone for a single curriculum towards developing curricular initiatives to suit different groups of students. In this scenario, one of the challenges facing schools is the integration of groups with very different identities into their community. Identity may be mediated by special or remedial needs, by language or ethnicity, or by religious affiliation. It is not that the school is asked to choose between these groups in an exclusive either/or way. Rather, how the school values the contribution of these subgroups is indicative of the place an economic perspective on the distribution of wealth has in its organizational culture. Consequently, the way these groups are integrated into the school will have a profound effect on the quality and on the development of that culture.

---

**Exercise 6.3**

Take the three perspectives of the economic model in turn. What artefacts exist in your school that represent each of these perspectives? Do any of the artefacts belong to more than one list? What are the contexts that give these artefacts their particular meaning?

What perspective does your school have on human capital production? How broadly does it conceive that capital — in its range of subjects and in the range of extra-curricular activities? What does it pride itself on in terms of production? How does this link with the assumptions about human activity and human nature discussed in Chapter 1?

What demands are there in the school for uniformity and efficiency in production? How is this experienced by students, and by teachers? How does it apply to physical resources? To human resources? Are the systems of accountability different for teachers and students? How does this reflect on the assumptions about human nature and relationships raised in Chapter 1.

How does the school address issues of distribution? How are resources distributed among junior and senior classes, between 'bright' and 'less bright' students? What mechanisms does the school have in place to monitor the efficient use of resources in terms of producing results? In terms of the equitable distribution of these resources?

Where is the balance of the economic model? How might that balance be changed?

---

## Summary

In this chapter models have been used to examine the relationship which schools have with the environment. Particular emphasis has been placed on the management of the boundaries between the school and the environment. This boundary management determines what constitutes or is valued as educational experience, the learning that is appropriate to schooling, and the choice of learning experiences in the curriculum. Schools are experiencing increased demands on the range of activities which should be included in the process of schooling, and this reflects social challenges being faced by society, changing personal value systems and a greater interdependence between the education and economic systems.

In examining this latter link, we find a microcosm of the questions being asked of education: 'What should we teach students, and why?', 'What value should be put on different skills and knowledge in society?', 'How should people be treated and valued within the system so that there is equality of opportunity?'. The assumptions which inform a school's response to these issues, be they grounded in economic, social reconstruction or classical humanist philosophy, underpin the organizational culture of the school. The more these assumptions can be brought into consciousness and examined, the more the school will be empowered to exercise a vibrant role in choosing its own future.

### Notes

1　'The belief that all genuine education comes about through experience does not mean that all experiences are genuinely or equally educative. Experience and education cannot be directly related to each other. For some experiences are mis-educative,' Dewey (1938) *Experience and Education*. For further critique in the education–experience debate see Friere (1972, 1985); Illich (1971); Kozol (1967).
2　Hogan (1995) traces the effect of institutionalization on a pure concept of learning, with particular reference to the role of the Church in education.
3　The general title given to this experience is postmodernism (cf. Hargreaves, 1994).
4　Riordan (1996) discusses the notion of the common good in policy formation.
5　These philosophers focused more on aspects of the subject in moral decision-making, e.g. Perry (interest); Scheler (direct insight and intuition); Hume (psychological constitution); Kant (reason); and Bentham and Mill (consequences of pain and pleasure).
6　This analysis relies on the Values Clarification models in Raths, Harmin and Simon (1971); and Kirschenbaum (1975).

*Part Three*

# *Roles in Schools*

# Chapter 7

# Assumptions about Students

Imagine a student coming home with a school report which says that they got five 'A's (top mark) and one 'F' (failure). How do you think the parents of this student will react? We can envisage three reactions[1]:

1  A first set of parents take the report and immediately focus on the one failure. They berate the student for a lack of application to work and point out the opportunities provided for the student. The student is blamed for a poor performance in this one subject, and the success of the five 'A's is missed, passed over and forgotten in the light of this failure.

2  A second set of parents will notice the five 'A's and congratulate the student. 'I see you have five As. Well done, we're very proud of you. However, we also notice that you have a bad failure. We really must do something about this, help you to work harder and improve in this subject.' This approach notes and records the successes, but the main focus is on improving the less successful areas. The approach exhibits a perfectionism and competitiveness towards study and results.

3  The third set of parents look at the report and immediately congratulate the student. 'I see you have five As. We're very proud of you. Well done, you really deserve these marks the way you worked. I also see you got one F. Well done, we're very proud of you for this too. You found something that you weren't very good at, and didn't waste any time studying it!' This set of parents see beyond the objective quantitative criteria of the marks and relate the results to the student's interests and development, and judge success on that basis.

These three sets of parents provide very different contexts for their children, and it is likely that these contexts will give rise to different perspectives on success and learning. The way in which self-esteem and locus of control will develop in each of these three contexts is also likely to be radically different. Children develop their sense of identity against the yardstick of absolute, and seemingly objective, levels of attainment, the more relative criteria of hard work and effort leading to success, or perhaps the discovery and pursuit of their own interests.

Similar contexts can be generated by teachers. Some teachers set high standards of 'objective' achievement, with a heavy emphasis on subject matter and success in examinations. Current success is taken for granted and they constantly pick up on mistakes made in an effort to improve results. Other teachers make constant demands for productivity, which is experienced as a form of perfection-ism. They celebrate success, but may also focus on a form of defensive learning (eliminating mistakes) or a slavish adherence to method and discipline. Other teachers may try to generate a social climate in which students can experience and develop levels of interest where all forms of learning are promoted and rewarded in the classroom. In these classrooms, the emphasis is primarily on the individual student, rather than the subject matter or the achievement (although these last are integrated into the notion of success for the student).

Just as individual parents and teachers have assumptions about learning and teaching, structural and ritual elements of the school reinforce these assumptions. Schools can be tyrannical places where failure is not tolerated and students who 'fail' are made to feel like social outcasts. Whether the focus is on academic achievement, sporting success or excellence in other extra-curricular areas, the pressure is to constantly achieve very high externally imposed standards. Students are segregated by success rate (streamed class, first team, etc.) and resources are allocated to 'achievers' in order to promote their success and 'non-achievers' are ignored. Success is the norm, and is taken for granted. What is noted by the school is lack of success. In schools like this, the criteria for success is often locally based. In one school I worked with, students were selected at entrance from the top 25 per cent of the ability range. Within the school they were further organized according to ability levels, in a way which was quite meaningless given the reliability levels of the entrance tests. The segregation of students, and the form of comparison used, had very negative effects on the achievement levels of some very talented students. In another school, trials were held for sports teams at the beginning of the season. A squad was chosen, but there was no intra-mural programme for those students who were not chosen for the squad. In these schools, success was a norm which dictated the organization of the school.

In other schools, this pressure to succeed exists within a culture which celeb-rates success. The dominant culture is one of doing more and trying harder. The focus is on external criteria and continuous comparison. Displays showing photographs of school events such as plays and musicals are witness to a growing sophistication of expectations. At an academic level, constant testing is used to keep students on their toes. Although achievement is recognized, the dominant experience is that of pressure to emulate past performance.

Schools may also have a dominant culture of care for and promoting indi-vidual students. Pastoral care and guidance systems help students discover interest through reflection on experience. All school events have high levels of participa-tion. The academic and extra-curricular programmes are designed to help as many students as possible achieve their potential.

In previous chapters, we have examined the development of a general school climate. In this chapter, the focus is on assumptions relating particularly to the process of learning. Schools seek to facilitate students in acquiring the learning to which they aspire. They also seek to promote learning which parents and society think is important. A school is judged partly on the number of successful graduates, where success is understood in terms of examination results, reports of subjective satisfaction, or the prestige (social and occupational) they enjoy. Teachers are judged by students as to how easy it is to learn — either in terms of technical skills of explaining concepts, or in the relationship which promotes interest and self-development. The aim of the chapter is not to promote a particular set of assumptions about the nature of learning, but to reflect on the way in which teachers have reported the assumptions they bring to classroom work and their struggle to develop a balance between content demands, effort and student interest.

### Biggs's Model of Learning

The verb 'to learn' has a subject and an object. Some*one learns* some*thing*. Therefore, in considering teacher assumptions about learning, we look at three sets of perspectives — the learner, the content to be learnt and the relationship between the two. Biggs (1985, 1987) has developed a model of learning which I have found very useful in helping teachers reflect on the learning process[2]. He identified three aspects of learning:

- PRODUCT — the way in which learning is defined.
- PROCESS — the motives and strategies used by students to engage in learning. It also refers to the way in which teachers motivate students to learn, and how they teach them about learning.
- PRESAGE — the context of learning, based on the personal dispositions of the learner and the institutional context of how learning is organized and valued.

Of particular interest to the organizational culture of the school is the way in which the presage institutional context affects learning. The next two sections reflect on such an institutional context, relating to the product and process of learning. The personal disposition of students is undoubtedly a key element in student learning. The key focus here is the capacity of the teacher or the school to respond to different personal preferences.

### *The Product of Learning*

Concern for the nature of knowledge and learning goes back to the philosophical reflections of the Greeks. Reflecting about the nature of reality and our participation in it, Heraclitus posed the question whether a person could ever step into the same river twice given the flux of change. The question reflected a concern over the nature of reality and human experience — whether something that seems continuous (the stream) is in fact broken up into discrete units (and therefore cannot be repeated). The same question has been applied to many areas of experience. Science sought the fundamental structure of matter in molecules and atoms and later evidence gave rise to atoms being broken down to discrete units of electrons, neutrons and positrons before modern physics questioned the existence of such fundamental sub-atomic particles. The debate on the nature of light evolved around the discrete particle theory and the continuous wave theory. An electric current can also be considered as a continuous stream of charge or as a flow of discrete charged particles (electrons). Vision can be imagined as a continuous stimulation of the eye which is then interpreted by the individual, or it can be imagined as a series of discrete stimuli in much the same way as a projected film in a cinema is made up of discrete frames which give the semblance of continuity. The history of our understanding of the physical universe illustrates the tension between discretion and continuity.

Similar assumptions can be seen in our understanding of knowledge. Knowledge can be seen as the acquisition of a large number of discrete facts, or it can be seen as the development of some unified structure. For example, consider a student who reads a dictionary cover to cover. When the teacher asked what he thought of it, the student replied: 'I found the book very easy to understand, because every word was explained as I went along. However, the plot was pretty boring.'

Students often have a similar experience of learning in school. The breakdown of knowledge into discrete parts takes the form of organizing the dictionary. The student is asked to read the dictionary and comes to understand each of the different 'words', yet fails to grasp any plot or coherent picture behind the process. Structure and detail are in tension. This approach to knowledge has been very common in teacher training programmes. Emphasis is placed on the structure of content. The role of the teacher is to break it down into components, which are regarded as the building blocks of knowledge, so that students can in turn build it up again. Both teaching and learning strategies are concerned with the organization of this material. Lesson plans are written in terms of aims and objectives. The task is broken down into 'bite size' portions which the student can digest. This allows for a highly technical approach to teaching and develops a high level of dependence on textbooks and a shared approach to teaching across the curriculum. At a system level, it protects students from idiosyncratic teachers and creates a common culture of teaching across a large number of schools which allows for the mobility of students. The disadvantage is that it assumes that the primacy of learning is the structure of the content.

Using the image of the 'explained words' and 'a plot', learning can be described as a structure–fact ratio (see Figure 7.1). According to this image, increased learning involves an increase in the value of the fraction. The more facts a student acquires, the greater the denominator, making the value of the fraction smaller (i.e. one fifth is smaller than one fourth). The only way that the fraction can increase in value is to enlarge the structure imposed on the facts, to increase the level of appreciation of the interconnectedness of the facts (i.e. three fifths is greater than two fifths). The aim here is not to disparage facts, or glorify structure. The balance between them is what is important. This can be illustrated in a simple equation.

In Figure 7.2, each of the fractions has the same value. Applied to learning in a school situation, it could be said that the level of learning has been maintained in each case. However, there is a qualitative difference in each of the numbers

$$\text{LEARNING} = \frac{\text{STRUCTURE}}{\text{FACT}}$$

*Figure 7.1   The product of learning as a structure–fact ratio*

$$\frac{3}{4} = \frac{30}{40} = \frac{75}{100} = \frac{7500}{10,000}$$

*Figure 7.2   Developmentally appropriate learning — perspectives on the structure–fact ratio*

because of the size of the denominator and numerator. Central to the involvement of students in learning is the amount of facts that they have to deal with — that there be enough to engage them and focus their attention in a way which stretches them to find a structure. The facts gathered will reflect the developmental stage of the student and the acquired wisdom of the society and/or the discipline being studied. If there are too many facts, then the task becomes too complex and the student gives up and disengages. If the task is too easy, then the structure can be put together very easily and without much engagement, and learning becomes a trivial exercise.

This introduces a second perspective on learning — the affective engagement of the learner in imposing structures on facts. Learning in this model is not just an impersonal, technical process. The acquisition of facts by themselves is very much like Dickens's image of the empty vessels waiting to be filled full of facts[3]. The student is unengaged. However, taking facts and putting structure on them requires involvement and absorption. It gives rise to Archimedes' Eureka factor, and can be seen in the way students sometimes become absorbed in a task, or the way their eyes light up when they work out a problem.

In learning, meaning must be developed from the relevant facts. The challenge facing a school curriculum is to ensure a balance: first, that sufficient facts are gathered; and secondly, that enough time is given so that a structure emerges for the student. It is easy to overload the system with facts, in the hope that structure will emerge over time. Alternatively, teachers may try to short-circuit the process by imposing a structure on the learner, by giving him or her some predetermined structure and have everyone reproduce that same structure.

Motivating students to an engagement and search for structure, and helping them develop strategies to implement the search, is one of the functions of the teacher–learner relationship. Teachers vary in their approach to the definition of knowledge. Some teachers put high value on their own subject area as a collection of objective facts or predetermined structures which they want students to acquire and appreciate. Others accept the idea of a structure–fact ratio but value the way students develop that structure for themselves more than the structure itself. Teachers may change their emphasis depending on the task at hand — using a developmental approach when introducing students to a topic and a more structured approach closer to exam time. Teacher assumptions and habits sometimes lead to an imbalance in the learning process. For instance, teachers may begin a learning programme with an emphasis on facts so that students develop the tools for later work on structure. Unfortunately, the early emphasis on teaching for factual knowledge creates a habitual way of teaching and the pressure of examinations sometimes means that structuring does not occur for many students. In the next section, we examine in more detail how assumptions about the nature of knowledge influence the motivation and classroom strategies used by teachers.

---

**Exercise 7.1**

Reflect on the subject you are teaching. How do you see the syllabus promoting the structure–fact ratio? Where does the balance lie? How does the balance appear in the classroom? What opportunities exist for changing this balance? How much is the balance determined by your approach to the subject? By the interest and ability of the students? How does it change throughout the term, and the school year? If you discuss your course with another teacher, you may find that there are different ways in which the syllabus can be read, and that you do, in fact, bring assumptions about the nature of knowledge, to your subject.

---

### The Process of Learning

Experiments on students' approaches to learning have revealed assumptions about the nature of knowledge which reflect the problem posed by Heraclitus in Ancient Greece. These experiments revealed two basic approaches to study (see Marton and Säljö, 1976). The first of these involves surface or atomistic processing, and the second deep or holistic processing. Surface processors concentrate on the sign, reproducing the material itself. Deep processors, on the other hand, concentrate on what is signified, the intentional dimensions of what the material is about. In the experiments, it was found that students had a consistent approach to material based on their own personal preferences, but that they also picked up cues from the external environment — what was expected of them by teachers and researchers. To these two approaches, therefore, a third was added which reflects the social context in which learning takes place. This latter approach is the desire to compete with others, to do better than them by scoring higher on tests. The focus of achievement is social and the satisfaction and engagement of the student is determined by social factors rather than the material to be learned.

The approach to study can be examined in two ways — the underlying motives a student brings to learning and the strategies that are used to implement those motives.

The *surface approach* operates from a motive which seeks to be successful with minimum effort or is driven by a fear of failure rather than a desire for success. The main strategy is to see learning as a defensive reproduction of facts. Engagement with the content is low, and the reproduction of facts ensures that the structure–fact ratio remains low.

| Approach | Characteristics | Pathologies |
|----------|----------------|-------------|
| *Surface* | Atomizing, focus on sign, reproducing | Improvidence, focus on the present, lacks big picture |
| *Deep* | Holistic, focus on intention, connecting | Globe-trotting, jumps to conclusions with inadequate grasp of detail |
| *Achieving* | Self-promotion, focus on context, competing | Disengagement from learning itself for sake of personal gain |

*Figure 7.3   Characteristics and pathologies of the three different approaches to learning*

The *achieving approach* has as its main thrust the desire to manifest one's excellence publicly by achieving success. The motive behind it lies in competition and self-enhancement, scoring well even if the material is not interesting. The main strategies used involve the organization of the time and space in which the task must be carried out, and also the organization of the material itself. Students check out past papers, eliminate areas of study not likely to be asked, and focus on key elements of the course. There is a moderate level of engagement with the material and the very process of organizing the material gives rise to a moderate level of structure.

The *deep approach* is motivated by the desire to actualize one's own interest, competence and talent. It is linked with the search for meaning and for underlying structure and pattern. Typical strategies used include wide reading and efforts to interrelate old and new knowledge. A student may well ask questions and take initiatives outside course requirements. This results in high levels of engagement with material, and also with an increasing structure–fact ratio.

This model contends that the three different approaches typically give rise to qualitatively different learning outcomes — surface to retention of factual detail; deep to structurally complex and affectively satisfying outcomes; and the achieving approach somewhere in the centre. The model does not presuppose a value judgement on any of the approaches. In fact, some learning tasks may require a particular approach. For instance, learning vocabulary in a foreign language, to play the piano or the symbols of the Table of Elements in science requires strategies associated with the surface approach. Writing an essay or a poem, on the other hand, involves reflection and interconnections — strategies associated with the deep approach. The key to good learning is a metacognitive skill which recognizes the required approach and then chooses appropriate and congruent strategies.

Each of the three approaches has its advantages and its pathologies (Figure 7.3). Surface processors fail to build up a general picture of what is to be learned, and so miss important general analogies or interrelationships which help relate the topic to other topics and to life itself. This pathology is termed improvidence, as it looks to the present moment only, and stores up nothing for the long term. However, surface processors can produce good results if they work their strategies with skill. Many exams require high levels of reproduction, and students may use the image of a quiz show where random questions are drawn from a category. This type of exam gives rise to success for the surface processor. Frequently, however, reproducing skills are hard to sustain, and the lack of an overall picture makes it difficult to retain large amounts of information. Students depend on luck to get the right questions that fit the information they have.

Deep processors, on the other hand, have a tendency to jump to unsubstantiated conclusions because they do not grasp the details or else they invent links between ideas. This pathology is termed globe-trotting, because their compulsion for the larger picture sometimes causes them to despise the local scene and the need to work through details.

The achieving processors may become very disengaged from their learning. The organization of time and space, and the way in which information is retained, may focus on short-term gains, resulting in a student quickly forgetting any details and retaining only a sketchy outline of the structure. The passage of time develops a cynical view of the content itself, the focus being solely on self-achievement.

The focus when working with teachers is to reflect on the likely outcomes of classroom practice on student motivation and learning. A teacher who is strong on surface techniques may encourage surface processors, but may also be a source of frustration for students who are deep processors, and those who need a higher level of structure to develop their achieving approach. Teachers who have a high expectation of deep motivation, and teach with an expectation that students have developed techniques of self-initiative and wide reading, may generate a great sense of unease in students who struggle with a subject area, and who are dependent on structure in order to develop habits of success. In staff development programmes, teachers can be encouraged to reflect on the assumptions they have which lead them to choose particular classroom strategies. They can also be encouraged to reflect on the balance of strategies used in their classroom, and how student strategies are rewarded. A third form of reflection is to try to see how different strategies affect different types of students, and the consequences of these effects on student motivation and achievement.

---

**Exercise 7.2**

With some colleagues, brainstorm on the type of classroom activities which promote surface, deep and achieving learning strategies in students. Reflect on your classroom practice. What type of strategies do you typically promote? What type of effect does this balance of teaching strategy have on student motives?

Think of different students in your classroom. Do they respond equally well to these strategies? What determines a student's response? How do you cater for different needs simultaneously in the classroom?

What influence does your own preference and the nature of your subject have on your choice of teaching strategies? How common are these teaching strategies in the school? What effect will this have on students — do they have the opportunity to experience a balance of different learning climates?

---

## Developing Student Profiles

*Academic Motives*

The three approaches to study, outlined by Biggs, are not mutually exclusive. There is no inconsistency in learning to reproduce facts accurately (surface) in a highly organized manner (achieving) to give a composite surface–achieving approach. It is also possible for a student involved in understanding the meaning of a subject (deep) to do so in a highly organized way (achieving) to give a deep–achieving composite. This gives rise to another way of using Biggs's three approaches — to give a profile of the individual student based on motive scores. Biggs classified students as high scorers on the three motive scales (top 50 per cent or top 25 per cent depending on the purpose of the exercise) and named the different student types based on their profile. He used these profiles as a means of developing academic counselling programmes for students (see Biggs, 1987).

Biggs's work in Australia gave rise to national normative data on the distribution of motive and strategy scores, and also the distribution of student profiles in the population. This data, when adapted to particular cultures, can be used to help schools reflect on the way in which students develop motives and strategies. In Ireland, I have used data generated at local level with schools in one region of the country (or affiliated through a religious order) to help schools reflect on strengths and weaknesses in their approaches to student learning. The aim is not to set up a comparative league table but to generate discussion on the appropriateness of a particular score. For instance, one school might judge a low score on surface motive as appropriate whereas a different school would view scores from a contingency perspective and deliberately aim for a high score, seeing this as an appropriate reflection on the curriculum, and the response of the school to student maturity.

As well as looking at scores on a general level, it is possible to reflect on the distribution of individual student profiles. For instance, what proportion of students in the school have low scores on each of the motive scores? What proportion have high achieving scores? How do they combine these scores with other motives? How are the different profiles distributed among the classes of the school? Do students with a high achieving motive score well on achieving strategies and do they consequently do well on tests? Are students with a deep motive in higher streamed classes? Do all students have an opportunity to develop deep motive and strategies in at least one subject on the curriculum? These are questions which teachers frequently ask about their own schools. In discussions, we look for concrete evidence to support responses. The presence of figures helps to ground some of the aspirational aspects of the discussion. In my own work, survey feedback from students has helped teachers to focus on gender issues in classroom management where boys and girls in the same classrooms had very different scores. In another school, senior students had significantly lower deep and achieving motive, but significantly higher surface strategy scores than junior students. As students in Ireland sit a public examination at the end of a junior cycle (age 15) in post-primary schools, these data generated a very productive discussion on the effect of examination

success on student motivation, and set in train a new academic pastoral care programme in the transition from junior to senior cycle. In one group of schools, we
have set in place a longitudinal study to see how student motivation changes on
an individual level, rather than making judgements from snapshot pictures of two
different cohorts.

In the schools I have worked with, the teachers have sought to become more
aware of the context which students bring to learning, and of the way the organizational context of the school affects student motives. Profiles of learning approaches
reflect the values and assumptions which operate in the school and which send cues
to students about what is important. Schools tend to judge their academic culture by
the outcomes of student learning as shown in examination results. The assumption
is that if the results are satisfactory, then the process that gives rise to the results is
also satisfactory. With these assumptions, interventions in learning systems are
made only in the case of pathologies — a form of crisis management and remediation.
However, outcomes have a qualitative as well as a quantitative dimension. Examination results as a measure of learning may, or may not, produce in the student a
sense of personal satisfaction and a desire for continued learning. The results may,
in fact, hide serious goal displacement in the value system espoused by the school
and the type of learning it wants to promote. For example, the process of adaptation
to the demands of external examinations and the cues the school consequently gives
to students may well produce a qualitatively different culture than that which is aimed
for. If this is the case, the school will need to develop new strategies which somehow integrate the values of deep learning with the drive for examination success.

The three different approaches to study can also be applied to the teacher's
own approach to teaching. Discussing with teachers how they might be classified as
surface, deep or achieving teachers has led to some fascinating discussions on teacher
attitudes, and responses to organizational aspects of school and family situations.
These discussions are taken up again from a different perspective in the next chapter.
However, it is important to note here that teachers see themselves as continually
learning about their own profession, and that these categories can as easily be
applied to adult career learning as they can in the classroom. It helps teachers to
recognize some of the same traits in themselves that they see in their students!

### *Affiliation and Participation Profiles*

School is not the only element in the life of students competing for their affiliation.
Adolescence is characterized by a search for personal identity. This search involves
an interaction of three dimensions of life: work, leisure and family[4].

During their teenage years individuals make decisions which affect their future
lives. On the work level, they focus their future identity on their talents; where they
can be successful and make a useful contribution; whether they can find a career
orientation that suits their own personality and also their need for status and financial
reward. The school plays an important function in developing that identity. However, teenagers also begin to test themselves in the world of work, with part-time

jobs in vacation period and frequently during the school term. In some schools, a high proportion of students have part-time jobs after school or at night. This gives rise to conflicting values systems with regard to school work, homework and paid work. The immediate rewards of extra money and the consumer lifestyle it enables are often more attractive to teenagers than the long-term rewards of study. The work available to students is often low paid and repetitive. Some commentators have termed the work 'McJobs', where there is a high turnover and low nourishment. This development can give rise to conflicts within the school. Not only is there a clash of lifestyles, but also a socialization of expectations. Many students find excitement in work experience, and forget the contribution being made from living at home and the support of their parents. They fail to reflect on the long-term consequences of not continuing with their education. Monitoring the level of out-of-school work can be an important part of school planning. It clarifies the extent of the challenge of integrating the work experience of students into the culture of the school.

The forging of a personal identity in adolescence is often a very turbulent experience, characterized by extremes of stimulation and boredom, self-confidence and self-doubt. On the family level, adolescents begin to rework their relationship with their parents and family and with contemporaries of both sexes. They become engaged in tensions between dependence and independence. In attempting to forge an identity which is distinct from that of the authority figures who have run their lives, adolescents often develop a strong attachment to their peer group. This group may be strongly affected by a culture of sporting activity, loud music, drink, drugs and sexual activity. On the other hand, some groups of adolescents develop a high sensitivity to the environment and are inspired by their common humanity with less well-off people throughout the world. In their altruism, they are highly critical of adults who seem to them to be insensitive to global problems.

Typically schools try to influence the adolescent through a programme of extra-curricular and co-curricular activities. Extra classes, debating, discussion groups, sporting activities involving aggression and skill, non-contact sports, drama, social action, films and dances are all examples of activities run by schools for their students. These activities embrace intellectual pursuits, physical skill development, leisure activities, social development and self-presentation and may be run on an intra-mural basis within the school, or in cooperation or competition with other schools. These events are valuable opportunities for students to test their developing identities and personalities. The high concentration of students in school gives them easy access to these activities. When some of the activities are also introduced as part of the school curriculum, the student has a chance to experiment with the activity. In this way, induction and initiation are easier than if they had to seek out such activities in their local community. The school plays a vital role in the social development of students by providing such opportunities. Keeping a profile record of the students' participation in extra-curricular activities, and the quality and intensity of such participation, can give vital clues to the affiliation of the student to the school and can often be used in a helpful way to motivate and guide the student in the more academic learning which takes place in the formal curriculum.

Drawing up profiles of student participation in a school is a way of understanding the culture. The content of participation — extra-curricular activities, option subjects offered in the curriculum — is the artefacts of the school. The analysis of motivation and the meaning students give to their participation reveals the values that they are in fact picking up. It is a worthwhile exercise comparing the profile of student values with the school mission statement and making some judgement on the result. This comparison can lead a school to question the assumptions it has about how it organizes the artefacts of the school. The process can lead the school, through affirmation or challenge, to a deeper sense of identity and purpose, to embrace in a more meaningful way its own organizational culture.

---

**Exercise 7.3**

Draw up a profile of student motivation to study in your school. Copies of the instruments developed by Biggs in Australia, or by Ramsden in the UK are easy to obtain. A shortened version of the scales has been published by Newstead (1992).

Draw up a profile of student types based on the combination of scales. Are you happy with the profile that is being revealed? Does the profile surprise, please or challenge you? What are the artefacts and values which might be giving rise to this profile? What artefacts and values might be blocking the improvement of this profile?

Apply the profile of learning motives to your own work as a teacher. How might you change the questions asked to correspond to the concerns of teachers? What factors of teaching and the school might turn you into, or confirm you as, a surface, a deep or an achieving teacher?

Search for other short instruments related to student affiliation, e.g. Richmond (1985). Draw up a profile of student participation in extra-curricular activities. Can you find connections between participation and student affiliation scores, or with their motive scores for study?

How can you use this information to develop interventions which help students enjoy their learning more than at present?

---

## Notes

1   This is another story which has been adapted from Don Clifton (cf. the opening of Chapter 2).
2   Biggs published his test through the ACER in 1987. The model of learning is outlined in Biggs (1985). This article explores personal factors in developing study approaches. A parallel approach can be found in the work of Ramsden et al. (1989).
3   In *Hard Times*, Dickens presents Mr Gradgrind and Mr Choakumchild as lining students up by number, to fill them full of facts.
4   Head (1997) details this search for identity as a modern application of Erikson. A short measurement scale of affiliation can be found in Richmond (1985).

*Chapter 8*

# Assumptions about Teacher Development

'I see from your *curriculum vitae* that you were once a lot younger that you are now! What ever made you change?'

Judy Arin Krupp frequently used this question to stimulate people on her workshops to think about personal development and growth[1]. At one level there is an ageing process which cannot be halted, as each one of us gets chronologically more gifted every year, and different organs of the body begin to wear down. However, another aspect of our development allows us to remain youthful, to retain energy and enthusiasm for life, to be aware and responsive to the world in which we live. This is a key area of staff development programmes and is an essential ingredient in maintaining and developing the culture of a school. Teachers are constantly faced with new challenges in their professional development. Some of these challenges are externally generated, from changes in society, government policy on education and school policy development. Other challenges are more personal — integrating changing personal needs and relationships with the world of work. The sense of life teachers bring to these issues depends to a large extent on the assumptions and attitudes they have to personal and professional development.

In Chapter 3 we examined different levels of participation in a school and saw how the quality of that participation influenced the culture of the school. The present chapter complements Chapter 3. Here we focus on the images teachers and schools have of personal and professional development, and how subsequent practices may impact on teacher motivation and school culture. Understanding these images gives insights into why different levels of participation exist and why certain initiatives are resisted and fail, and why others are successful. This understanding also helps form strategies for staff development programmes which take account of individual teacher needs. The chapter examines assumptions in three areas of teacher development:

(a)   the appropriate content of staff development programmes;
(b)   teacher career and development; and
(c)   school approaches to development programmes.

### The Content of Professional Development

Films such as *The Prime of Miss Jean Brodie* (*la crème de la crème*) *Dead Poets' Society* (*carpe diem*) and *Mr Holland's Opus* (*we are your symphony*) explore the tension between different views of education and the proper relationship between teacher and subject matter, between teacher and student. Different stages of career have their own unique needs. In *Mr Holland's Opus*, we see Mr Holland as a beginning teacher, relying very heavily on the textbook and insisting on student compliance. We see a change of heart as he faces the crisis of boredom and develops new approaches to the classroom based on student learning and love of music. He develops new strategies and interests in helping individual students. At the end of the film, his political stance on school curriculum shows how he now formulates a wider vision of what students need to learn. In a sense, Mr Holland's growth has moved through three areas of concern — teaching, learning and education. Part of the work of teacher development is to promote this growth — to provide both the context and the opportunity for teachers to grow in these areas. All three areas of concern are addressed simultaneously, although teachers at different career stages will have a different emphasis. Older teachers, for instance, may have integrated teaching techniques and a responsiveness to student learning into their skill repertoire, whereas a beginning teacher is still developing a range of teaching skills which give them a confidence to adapt their methods to student needs. Sometimes, teacher development can be skewed by a lack of attention to one or more of these areas of development. One way of looking at teacher assumptions about development is to examine the balance of issues addressed or needs identified in teacher development programmes. These needs can be seen as:

- extrapersonal — concern for teaching quality;
- interpersonal — concern for relationship and learning;
- intrapersonal — concern for purpose and education.[2]

---

**Exercise 8.1**

Before reading any further, you might like to make a list of recent inservice courses you have attended, or which have been offered to you. Then read the descriptions of what is meant by extrapersonal, interpersonal and intrapersonal. When you have done that, you will be asked to indicate the extent to which the course dealt with these three areas and reflect on the implications of the balance you discover (see p. 150).

---

*Extrapersonal Development*

The extrapersonal area of teaching refers to the technical aspects of knowledge of subject matter and pedagogical skills. Inservice courses which focus on updating the teacher's knowledge of course content, increasing their repertoire of practical pedagogical skills, the psychology of learning, new methods of assessment, fall into this domain. The courses may focus on enhancement — the teacher seeks to develop a deeper knowledge of some aspect of the curriculum and develop new and alternative strategies for teaching; or they may focus on remediation — where the teacher needs to update deficient knowledge or learn an appropriate skill for teaching a subject. Such courses are frequently designed for cohorts of teachers from a variety of schools. The focus is on the individual teacher and generally abstracts from the particular context in which the teacher works. The link with school development lies in the assumption that the more effective the teacher, the more he or she contributes to a positive school culture.

### Interpersonal Development

Much of a teacher's day is taken up in an intensity of relationships. Interpersonal skills refer to the teacher's skills of communication, motivation, understanding, empathy, and forming objective and fair judgements about students. Understanding the changing nature of relationships with young students, the changing context of their lives, and developing appropriate and effective responses to both their personal and academic needs requires constant reflection and adjustment. Inservice courses which focus on classroom management techniques, mentoring, teamwork, democracy and discipline respond to needs in this area of development. These courses usually take place within the teacher's own school, where there is an effort to share the perspectives of a number of teachers on problems of relationship, and then to link the teachers' response to these problems in a supportive context.

### Intrapersonal Development

The intrapersonal skills refer to teachers' sense of personal mission, their ability to invest their personal satisfaction in the growth of students and have definite role models to guide their work. Growth in these areas has a cumulative effect on the quality of interaction within a school as individual teachers grow into a deeper and more meaningful sense of their career and the work of the school. Inservice courses which encompass attitudes to self and career, stress management and time management might be classified under this heading, as these courses help teachers to reflect on their own priorities in life and how to manage them. A whole school approach to strategic planning is another occasion when teachers are asked to reflect on their priorities, and they get in touch with the deeper desires of their own professional work.

---

**Exercise 8.2**

Return now to the list of recent inservice courses you have attended or know of. Distribute 10 points between the three areas to indicate the emphasis that has been given to each of these areas.

---

| Course | Extrapersonal | Interpersonal | Intrapersonal |
|--------|---------------|---------------|---------------|
|  |  |  |  |
|  |  |  |  |
|  |  |  |  |
|  |  |  |  |
|  |  |  |  |

What does the pattern of weighting suggest about the expectations of teacher development? How satisfied are you with this pattern? The next part of the chapter reflects on some implications of this pattern for teacher development. What type of courses do you prefer? How do you see your own development? What value do you put on investing in each of the three skill areas?

### Reflection

An overemphasis on extrapersonal skills results from seeing teaching as a technical operation, where the demand of inservice training is to ensure a uniform pattern of curriculum delivery. This latter approach has its imagery in an industrial technico-rational model of learning as a product, and teaching as a form of quality controlled process. This would deny the complexity of relationships and purpose of teaching. However, no one denies that good technical skills of organization, communication and feedback to students are very important for a teacher, hence this type of inservice is an important part of professional growth.

Recent years have seen an increased emphasis on inservice training for teachers associated with major developments in the curriculum. Many teachers are confronted with a rapidly changing curriculum as the education system adapts to new economic and technological realities. The new curricula reflect a changed emphasis on the content to be assimilated, the understanding of learning and a philosophy of knowledge. The old approach to curriculum was one where the same material was taught to all students in the same way, and students learned in a linear fashion in a way which consisted mainly in repeating the knowledge of experts. This approach is giving way to more constructivist approaches, where materials are adapted to the students' experiences, and learning is seen as dynamic and 'messy', as part of a cooperative process rather than a lone activity. Changes in curriculum therefore have implications for teachers not only in updating content knowledge, but also in developing new pedagogies. External factors in new technology such as multimedia computers and television also impinge on the need for new approaches to teaching. Most teachers have little say in the design of curricular initiatives. They are decided at a central level and handed down to teachers. Information is communicated to teachers in written syllabi or in regional courses given by experts. The balance of time given to knowledge, practical pedagogy and assessment procedures varies considerably with the programmes being introduced. Very little time is given to allowing teachers to discuss new styles of relationship, or the implications of the new rationale for school organization.

In practice, classrooms tend to be neither wholly subject centred nor wholly learner centred. The two approaches exist in dynamic tension, with teachers balancing deductive and inductive approaches in response to student capacity and the demands of completing the curriculum to a standard mediated by assessment requirements. Problems arise when teachers fail to live with the tension, and opt for one approach over the other. Teachers are sometimes caricatured by students and by colleagues into two types:

- the 'soft' teachers who give great process through projects and discussions, but who are weak on challenge and content; and
- the 'real' teachers who grind out examination successes, but whose classes are controlled, predictable and repetitive.

The aim of inservice in extrapersonal skills is not to see the two approaches from an 'either/or', but rather a 'both/and' perspective. Thus, each teacher develops a wide range of skills to draw from and can use the appropriate skill in a particular situation. The alternative can be illustrated by the old saying — 'If the only skill you have is hammering, then you tend to see every problem as a nail.' The variety of skills ensures a professional response to the wide variety of challenges a teacher must face in promoting learning. Teachers can then plan to promote different types of learning experiences at different times in a programme or a school year. For instance, emphasis can be placed on exploratory learning at the beginning of a course, and then move to a very structured process at the end of the course, in preparation for a given assessment procedure. Unfortunately, assessment procedures tend to dominate teaching techniques at all stages of the course, frequently resulting in a lack of variety in learning experiences for students.

Teachers must also develop relationships which are appropriate to the age gap between themselves and their students. It is readily recognized that grandparents have a different nurturing role to parents, and this in turn differs from the big brother or sister relationship with a younger sibling, and teachers learn to develop these relationships in their personal lives. As teachers gain in 'chronological advantage' over their students, they frequently fail to apply the lessons of personal relationships to their professional relationships and expectations of students, and this gives rise to stress. Finding the balance is an important part of teacher interpersonal development, and is a legitimate part of teacher inservice.

The most frequent request for the development of interpersonal skills seems to be in the area of discipline. Teachers frequently demand better discipline procedures of management, or of themselves — so that they can 'get on with the real work of teaching'[3]. Traditionally, teacher leadership and authority has sought compliant responses from students. However, this type of relationship is being challenged by a number of forces. The new curriculum requires skills of students which are far from compliant. They actively pursue their own learning in project work, and this often takes place in groups. Students relate to the teacher as a facilitator rather than as a distant authority. This makes new demands on the type of relationship between teacher and student, both at an individual level, but also in team situations.

The increasing number of students who stay on in education beyond compulsory school means that a large number of older students in schools have personal experiences of travel, work, relationships and independence outside the school which make them less likely to accept a compliant role within the school. This poses a challenge to traditional concepts of discipline, and there is a need to explore new structures of relationships and model more democratic ways of involving students in their own learning.

The growth of mass education also means that a large number of students come from disadvantaged backgrounds, where their academic experience or ambition may not have been nurtured. Often, teachers have little understanding of the stress in the lives of these students. An adequate response to these students requires that pastoral care become an integral part of all subjects, and all classroom work, rather than an optional function somewhere in the school system. This also requires new teacher–student relationships. Adherence to traditional classroom norms in this context is likely to lead to high levels of frustration for both teachers and students, and inevitably to teacher stress. In this context, reflection on and support for good interpersonal relationships is a key element of inservice planning.

At the intrapersonal level, the constant pressures for change can be very wearying on teachers. This pressure is reminiscent of the cartoon depicting two Arabs wandering in the desert. One of them is obviously tired of wandering and, finally, his companion says: 'Stop asking if we are nearly there. We're supposed to be NOMADS!' When this image is applied to teachers, it is natural to yearn for being settlers — where life is more controlled, more predictable. The challenge that exists is the reconceptualization of the profession to take into account the changing demands of teaching and relationships. Teachers perhaps need to redefine themselves as nomads, constantly moving in the desert of change. In taking on this new role, the desert is no longer seen as a threat, and the individual can enjoy the role of nomad. The advantage of the image of the nomad is that you travel light. You do not gather possessions which weigh you down. In the change process in education, schools have tried to mix the roles of settlers and nomads. They have kept all the possessions of the past and also tried to head out for new pastures. The lack of prioritization has meant that teachers have taken on more and more roles and burdens, and shed none of the older ones. The catchphrase must now become: 'Teachers will work smarter, not harder,' and this requires a reimaging of the intrapersonal mission of the teacher.

The trend of teacher inservice provision emphasizes the technical — the development of teaching and discipline techniques. These are certainly needs within a system where both the curriculum is changing rapidly, and the social conditions of the students become more complex. Given the increased mobility of students within the system there is a need to develop some uniformity of content, teaching mcthods and course sequencing. However, in the way that teachers are frequently 'batch-processed' through such inservice courses, there is also a danger that curriculum delivery is seen from a uniform technocratic perspective in order to give the student a guarantee of minimum teacher competence. The stress is on the teacher 'delivering the curriculum' with in-built quality control. The approach does little to develop individual teacher talent.

The lack of focus on the development of teacher as person seems regrettable. Personal life-histories may, or may not, have significant impact on the individual's bonding to the school. As personal concerns change with age, so also does the need to reflect on the balance between teaching, learning and education in one's professional work. It is important that inservice development addresses all three areas for the teacher if it is to promote a holistic development for the teacher.

## Images of Teacher Development

Teacher involvement in personal development depends on the assumptions and images teachers have of that development. In this section, I present three models which explore the relationship between individuals and their careers[4]. I have found these very useful in promoting discussion on personal and professional development. The models are based on qualities of thought patterns with regard to self, teaching and education. The underlying assumptions in each of the descriptions, and their distribution and intensity in a school staff, colours the perspectives and perceptions of the individuals that hold them. The resulting behaviour becomes part of the accepted process of the school, thus defining its organizational culture. To change an individual's view of self as educator requires a radical reinterpretation on the part of the individual of who he or she is and the role they can play in the organization. Each of the three models of teacher development presented in this section gives a different perspective on how teachers see their own development and how this influences the success of development initiatives in a school.

### Schein's Career Anchors

The bureaucratic perspective on organizations typically sees the organization as having two dimensions. The horizontal dimension signifies different functions and areas of expertise. In education, these functions may refer to the primary, post-primary, third level or further education sectors. Within a school, the horizontal level may be described by subject departments or the age level of students. The vertical dimension refers to levels of responsibility and authority. The higher up the ladder, the greater the level of personal responsibility, going from teacher, head of department, deputy principal, principal. In some schools, teachers also take on responsibilities as mentors, form tutors and year heads, and this is seen as a progressive development of responsibility within the school system.

Career development is typically seen in terms of the vertical dimension. However, schools are flat organizations, with few levels and therefore little room for

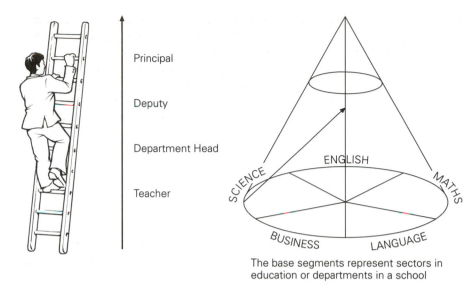

The base segments represent sectors in education or departments in a school

*Figure 8.1   The traditional view of promotion compared with Schein's approach to career development*

promotion according to this model. In general, the same can be said of many professionally oriented organizations — doctors and lawyers frequently work in situations which involve little vertical movement. For them, career advancement is related to different sets of motivators. Schein illustrated this by adding a third dimension to the pyramid which reflected a concept of centrality. This refers to the development of professional expertise and the exercise of influence in an organization through this expertise. Schein described the vertical and inward movement in terms of professional concerns which he termed career anchors, which define this professional development in different ways. He identified eight clusters of concerns, based on personal needs, values and self-perception of talent[5].

- *Technical/functional competence.* This career anchor appears in teachers who organize their work around a particular set of technical skills which they are good at and value. They may organize their classrooms around their skills in lecturing, explaining concepts, giving students feedback on homework assignments, or preparing students for exam success. Others see their skills in terms of guidance and mentoring of students, and build time to use these skills in their classroom management.
- *Managerial competence.* For teachers operating from this anchor, the focus is on promotion. They are not satisfied with influence in their own classroom, but seek influence in the wider school community. They take on responsibility willingly, and like to spend time analysing and solving organizational problems. They hope to be promoted to positions where they can make important decisions.

- *Creativity*. Teachers working from this anchor constantly try to create something new. They take initiatives and develop new projects. They do not like to be bogged down in traditional approaches which everyone else is doing. They set out to be different, and they enjoy the role of finding new and creative approaches to students and learning.
- *Security or stability*. This anchor describes teachers who value the guarantee of a stable future as the most important aspect of their teaching. All other development takes place within that context. They achieve an acceptable standard of living, permanent and pensionable, which gives security to themselves and their family. They are prepared to take a lower standard of pay for that security rather than take risks in a competitive commercial scene.
- *Autonomy*. This anchor describes the teacher whose main source of satisfaction is that they have control over their own lives. Although they are constrained by a fixed curriculum and fixed hours, they get their satisfaction from being able to organize their own teaching style and their own classroom in an autonomous way. They resist efforts at uniformity.
- *Service*. A person who sees teaching as being dedicated to a cause such as helping others and making the world a better place operates from this anchor. This cause is the dominant inspiration of their lives, and they would not give it up. Their main frustration is when others do not seem to want their service.
- *Challenge*. Some people take on work because it is a challenge. They constantly seek greater challenges, in much the same way as the reward for solving a computer game is to move to a higher level with faster action and more aliens. They take on difficult classes, and set very high standards for themselves. They find the easy routine boring.
- *Lifestyle*. This anchor involves people who see work as a necessary part of life, and their priority is to balance work with other personal and family requirements. In choosing teaching, they focus on the convenience of the school day and the annual holidays as a means of achieving this balance.

It is left as an exercise for the reader to discover their own career anchor. The culture of a school caters in different ways for, and promotes these, career anchors. The school may affirm one kind of career anchor over others. For instance, high recognition may be given to technical competence and managerial competence, whereas creativity or autonomy may be marginalized. For teachers other than those operating from a managerial competence anchor, vertical promotion may not be very important, as it takes them out of their main area of competence — the classroom. This is not to say that they might not adapt well to managerial positions, but rather that they may not exhibit strong feelings around applying for promotion. Recognizing career anchors and having a perspective on the centrality of teacher development rather than simply looking at a vertical dimension is an important perspective on the culture of teachers' work, and in understanding the work culture of the school.

### Gouldner's Locals and Cosmopolitans[6]

Gouldner identified two types of teachers based on the reference groups they use to judge their own development and on how they viewed specialized and professional skills. The first of these types he named 'locals', as they are high on loyalty to the school and low on commitment to specialized skills and therefore likely to use internal reference groups and criteria for success. The second type he named 'cosmopolitans', as they are high on commitment to specialized skills but low on loyalty to specific institutions and therefore likely to use external reference groups in setting standards of success for self and their school.

Gouldner further identified four ways in which locals participate in organizations:

> The *dedicated* group are those who are true believers in an ideology. For example, there are teachers who believe implicitly in the worth of their own school, its mission and its tradition and identify strongly with the particular institution. They would find it very difficult to be involved in a different school.
>
> *Bureaucrats* on the other hand are not loyal to the individual school *per se*. These teachers are more dedicated to education and schooling. As long as the school offers support for their concept of education and teaching they will support it. They would easily adapt to a different school with a similar outlook on education. For instance, one teacher would only teach in a private or church school, and another would only teach in a comprehensive school, or an inner city school.
>
> *Homeguards* are loyal to the particular school for various personal reasons. For instance, a teacher may prefer to live in a particular city or place and the teacher's bonding to the school may be in terms of a wider perspective of being in a place where both partners in a family can find work. Alternatively, the institution may provide some side-benefit (extra-curricular involvement) which he or she values.
>
> *Elders* are those whose age, or length of service, makes them immobile and hence negatively committed to the organisation. The commitment is deemed negative as they do not share any of the motivational elements of the other three ways of participating.

Gouldner also identified two types of cosmopolitans:

> *Outsiders* are those who are in, but not of, the organisation. They work efficiently and effectively while they are in the organisation, but they see their skills as being better appreciated outside the organisation. For instance, a young teacher with an ambition to be a principal may be a very efficient teacher, but psychologically is looking for new opportunities of advancement outside the present school.
>
> *Empire builders* use their technical expertise within the organisation to enhance their status in it. The focus of their career development is on their own advancement — literally building an empire of influence — rather than their loyalty to the school itself. However, if the focus of their influence is positive, the school will benefit from their activity and growing expertise.

**Exercise 8.3**

Take each of Gouldner's types — Locals (Dedicated, Bureaucrats, Homeguards and Elders) and Cosmopolitans (Outsiders and Empire Builders) and analyse them as follows:

*1. Personal Perspective*
What are the different aspects of your character that would entice you into each of these categories? For each of the categories, what is the evidence of the past five years that you might operate out of this mentality? How happy are you with this picture of yourself? What mentality would you like to operate from? What does this picture tell you about possible steps for your future development?

*2. About the School (you can answer this as an individual or discuss it in a group)*
What is your ideal teacher orientation, and why? What do you think the balance of types is on the teaching staff in your school? What cultural artefacts help you make this judgement? For each of the different types, what are the features of the school which (a) encourage individuals in that group to stay the way they are and (b) challenge individuals to adopt a different attitude to their own professional development?

*3. Staff Development Initiatives*
For each of the staff development initiatives undertaken in the past five years, try to specify what contribution it made to people in each of the teacher types. Examine the results of your survey for patterns. What do the patterns tell you about the orientation to development? What action might be appropriate?

*4. Planned Initiatives*
What initiatives are planned for the medium-term future? What contribution will they make to people in each of the types? What is the overall balance of planned initiatives? Are you happy with this balance?

*Reflection*

The mixture of 'locals' and 'cosmopolitans' contributes to the climate of the school, to the type of relationships which exist among staff members and acceptability of certain initiatives on the part of management. A predominance of 'locals' gives rise to an emphasis on in-house discussions which reinforce the individuals in their present positions or which seek to re-establish the position of some former 'good old days'. If an outside facilitator is brought in, it is a one-day one-shot effort which generates good feelings among the staff, and the focus is more often on the good feeling of being together rather than the content of the staff day. The assumptions of time are oriented to the past and the general stance is seeking constancy and predictability in the world of the school. The skills of adaptation to environmental pressures are underdeveloped and in fact such pressures give rise to strong resistance.

A staff with a majority of cosmopolitans, on the other hand, will more likely focus on issues which have an external origin, or else will focus on power issues within the school itself. Teachers will seek a greater understanding of policy issues emanating from outside the school and will be interested in gaining information about such issues and developing their own skills and expertise. Such individuals are more likely to seek permission to go on courses being run outside the school itself. Within the school they seek opportunities to influence decision-making processes and to have their own expertise recognized and affirmed.

Initiatives by the school also operate from assumptions about the ideal teacher. Some staff development programmes aim at developing 'locals' within the school through enhanced commitment and loyalty to a school vision. Investment in cosmopolitan teacher skills is seen as a poor investment, as it may lead teachers to seek promotion elsewhere. Yet, there is a delicate balance to be found between programmes which socialize teachers to grow old and become elders together, and developing the skills associated with a cosmopolitan perspective on teacher career. The local perspective on education is often based on a closed system approach with tight links between the individual and the school. The cosmopolitan perspective is outward looking and seeks opportunities for development in the external environment, with loose links between the school and the developing teacher. The 'local' or 'cosmopolitan' orientation of the individual and the general body of the teaching staff determines a culture in the school which gives normative value to what is an acceptable type of development programme for individuals, and also influences the type of programme content which might be acceptable in a school-initiated programme.

Identifying different kinds of cosmopolitans and locals in a school is an interesting exercise. However, it is not always easy to classify someone definitively. We all have some cosmopolitan and some local in us — the desire to have even greater influence and the desire for security and stability coexist in a dynamic tension in each of us.

### *Glickman's Cognitive–Affective Grid*[7]

Building on the concepts of task management and social integration outlined in Chapter 3, teachers can also be classified on the basis of cognitive expertise (the technical side of teaching) and affective engagement (affiliation and commitment) levels. These can be illustrated on two axes, giving rise to four types of teacher (see Figure 8.2).

*The Dropout* is someone who scores low on both the technical and the affective dimensions of teaching. This is a person who, crudely, neither understands nor cares about the issues facing the school. Such a teacher may cynically believe that education is a process of throwing imaginary pearls before real swine. He or she has little regard for the knowledge or skills to be imparted, and relationships with students are impoverished and negative. This may sometimes be a developed position, in which a teacher regresses through burnout.

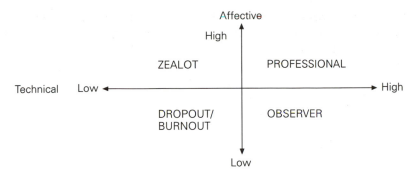

*Figure 8.2  Four types of teacher, based on technical and affective dimensions (Adapted from Glickman, 1981)*

*The Zealot* is highly committed, without really understanding the cause. In fact, zealots are constantly on the look out for causes to champion, and they move easily from one to the other. They are the first to volunteer for committee work and new activities. Their approach to the initial phases of any project is one of unbounded enthusiasm, but this soon wanes and they are distracted by some new idea or goal.

*The Observer* understands the issues involved, but is not committed to their resolution or implementation. Observers sit on the fence and comment. They have seen it all before, have high levels of reflection and analysis and are often very accurate and insightful, but they are sceptical about success and uncommitted to expending energy in creative problem solving. Observers do not volunteer for extra work, but feel free to comment on the efforts of others, particularly if they can 'helpfully' point out mistakes and difficulties.

*The Professional* represents the teacher who is committed to the aims of the school in an informed and practical manner. Projects are evaluated according to accepted criteria and commitment is made in a balanced and purposeful way, integrating personal and organzational needs.

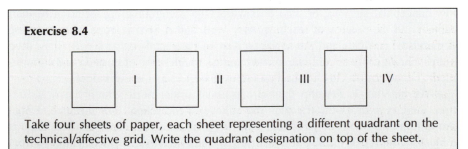

**Exercise 8.4**

Take four sheets of paper, each sheet representing a different quadrant on the technical/affective grid. Write the quadrant designation on top of the sheet.

1   On each sheet, write down the personal factors which would draw a teacher into this quadrant, or which might keep a teacher in the quadrant. (If this exercise is being done with a large group, you might assign a small group to

each sheet, and then ask the groups to rotate and add further ideas to those already on the sheet.)

2   Examine each of the four sheets as part of a gallery.

3   Ask the participants to identify the quadrant which describes themselves best.

4   Are they happy with that quadrant? What activities might help them move along any one of the axes in their preferred direction? If they are already in a preferred quadrant, what activities might help them stay there?

5   Repeat the exercise, this time writing down the institutional factors which might drive a teacher into the relevant quadrant, or which might keep the teacher there.

6   Ask the participants to identify the quadrant which best describes their own school, or their own staff development programme. How might the distribution of different types of teachers on the staff influence the desired content and the success of a staff development programme?

## Reflection

Labelling teachers is a favourite pastime of students, and even of colleagues in the staffroom. Understanding the reasons why individuals may be classified in a particular quadrant is a very important part of staff development programmes. Some teachers have a psychological disposition to see events positively and maintain an even disposition and motivation. Others tend to be more negative, and are easily discouraged, drifting into the observer quadrant. Past events in either the personal or professional life of the teacher may also influence why the teacher has a particular approach to their work and career.

School culture can affect the development of individuals into one of these categories, in much the same way as Etzioni claimed there was a congruence between the exercise of power and participation in an organization (see Chapter 5). For instance, if teachers find their commitment frustrated by lack of opportunity — extra-curricular activities, courses taught, promotion to posts of responsibility — then they may end up as observers or in extreme cases as dropouts. Teachers with low conceptual abilities, or who do not develop a cognitive appreciation of their subject and the process of teaching, may well find it hard to cope with changing demands of curricula and the social context of their students, and will either drop out psychologically or continue to teach out of a high sense of mission and commitment (i.e. as zealots) to an inherited rather than personal set of values.

As individuals develop their professional orientations within the organization, there is a knock-on effect on the culture of the school. For instance, a high proportion of observers on a school staff can produce an atmosphere where there is a plentiful source of ideas, but it is strong on individualism. Teachers choose from ideas on an 'a la carte' basis, and the organization develops in a semi-random pattern. In a school with a high proportion of professionals, teachers are more likely to work together to implement some chosen goal, as they see organizational support as an important factor in success.

The three models outlined above show how the development of individuals can reflect and influence the organizational culture of the school. The focus in the three models outlined above is on the individual's sense of bonding with the school and with teaching. This was outlined as Level 1 activity in Chapter 3 (see pp. 45–7). The school is not always a passive recipient, picking up the crumbs which drop from the table of personal development. The school can influence personal development in how it organizes for and encourages such development. By involving teachers in meaningful teamwork (Level 2) and by providing a coordinated climate for cooperation between teams (Level 3), the school sets up a culture in which personal growth and development is normative. In the next section, some of the underlying assumptions in planning staff development programmes are examined.

## Planning for Development

Teacher growth in terms of self and career is primarily the responsibility of the individual. However, professional development is not simply a private action, tolerated among consenting teachers. As outlined in Chapter 3, teacher growth must be integrated with school development, and this requires the ability to work from team, group and organizational perspectives. There is a system dimension to the reinforcement and establishment of new attitudes and behaviour. Schools play a vital part in promoting and validating personal growth. In this section, I present two ways I ask schools to reflect on their approach to development. The first promotes reflection on their approach to inservice programmes, and the consequences of that approach. The second is helpful in evaluating a proposed programme.

### School Approaches to Inservice

Three approaches to inservice programmes have been identified by Sergiovanni and Starratt (1979):

- *Deficit remediation.* In this approach, the administration identifies deficiencies in the staff and develops programmes to overcome them. The deficiencies may refer to individual's teaching practice, aspects of teamwork at a group level, or it may be the vision the staff has of the school and teaching.
- *Cultural.* In this approach, the school administration provides a rich environment of resources from which the teacher initiates his own development. For instance, the school may make budget provision for teachers to attend inservice courses and subscribe to professional journals or professional associations for subject teachers. The school then leaves it to the individual teacher to avail themselves of that provision.
- *Comprehensive.* Development is not seen as a series of isolated incidents, but as a function of teachers changing as persons — seeing themselves, the school, the curriculum and the students differently. This involves a

cooperative relationship between teachers and administrators. A staff development programme is seen as an evolving and integrated process which must be planned over time. Understanding the individual teacher and his or her needs, and negotiating links between these needs and those of the school is an important element of this type of programme.

Not all negotiation between teachers and the school is founded on principles of mutual trust and understanding. The process of inviting people to participate in development programmes, and how people are treated on them, can also embody assumptions about how adults learn and develop. One set of assumptions is based on *coercion*. The assumption is that change occurs as a result of reaction to the use of power in the organization, either in its formal and legitimate structure, or in the informal subsystem. Programmes devised on the basis of these assumptions are likely to be autocratic, and have little involvement of participants in their planning. The usual focus is on deficit remediation.

A second set of assumptions may be termed *rationality*. The assumption is that teachers will make rational decisions, adopting those innovations which are shown to be in their best interests. Programmes based on these assumptions are informational in content. When there are practical consequences to new information, the implementation depends on the initiative of individuals. Once you have told them about it, and they see the inherent logic, then they go and do it! These assumptions are closely correlated with the cultural approach outlined above.

A third set of assumptions give rise to *re-education*. It is assumed that individuals are heavily influenced by, supportive of and committed to socio-cultural norms. Real change occurs only when attitudes and values which supported the old norms are changed to create a new context for the adopted norms. Programmes developed under these assumptions involve a concentration on process and changing related elements of the system to give support to participants. This gives rise to a comprehensive approach to inservice planning.

The remedial (coercive), cultural (rational) and comprehensive (re-education) approaches to inservice give a model which can be helpful for school authorities to reflect on inservice provision. In line with exercises from Chapter 4, it can help clarify the climate of teacher participation in the school, and give insights into levels of teacher participation in school activities. The same model can be used in helping teachers to reflect on attitudes to student participation and learning.

## *Planning and Evaluating Development Programmes*

Planning for staff development programmes requires a sensitivity to the personal needs of the teachers and those of the school as well as an appreciation of the personal and cultural factors which promote and enhance development. It is sometimes useful to have a checklist of questions about inservice programmes which help reflect on the programme and foresee the strengths and weaknesses of the programme (Waugh and Punch, 1987).

**Exercise 8.5**

Examine the staff development programme for the past five years, or examine the proposed programme for the next two years. Ask yourself the following questions, focusing on the evidence that is available from the content and process of organizing this programme.

1  What assumptions are being made about teachers' basic attitudes to education and teaching?
2  Does the programme deal with the affective aspect of change?
3  Does the programme have a practical pay-back for teachers?
4  Does the programme have any personal cost elements for teachers?
5  What mechanisms are in place to support the outcomes of the programme beyond the inservice itself?
6  How is the support of the school leadership for the programme being communicated?

*Basic attitudes to education*

Basic beliefs and values serve as protective shells preventing outside influences from impinging on the inner world of the individual. Teachers are not likely to be supportive of developments that are at variance with their perception of traditional values or practices in the school or in their own training. Thus, in the design of development programmes and the management of school culture, attention must be paid to the belief systems of teachers and the mechanisms used to maintain and reinforce them. Metaphors and mental models are pervasive forces in teachers' self-concepts and the dominant metaphors are frequently not examined for their appropriateness and their fit with current evidence. It is sometimes important to build into a programme some strategies which look at such basic attitudes. For the most part, the teachers are being affirmed, and the programme builds on current realities. In some cases, beliefs may have to be challenged and reconstructed if the school wants to create a context where new choices can become habitual ways of behaving.

*Affectivity and change*

In a change situation, teachers frequently experience a fear of the future, which is accompanied by self-doubt. Situations of uncertainty result from a lack of knowledge of what the change involves, or an unease with the skills necessary to perform adequately in the new situation. This is linked with a perceived risk to the personal status of the teacher. Thus, a culture which involves a teacher in role confusion or overload, or where individuals are acutely conscious of personal status, is unlikely to be conducive to teachers experimenting with new ideas of self or of teaching. Creating or developing an atmosphere of trust is an essential element in successful staff development programmes. Teachers who see staff development in terms of change and loss rather than development and enrichment may perceive a judgement that there is something inadequate with their present contribution. They become defensive and need to be convinced that development can be positive.

## Practicality

Individuals tend to regard change in terms of practical consequences for their own behaviour. Teachers tend to make decisions about school matters in a very pragmatic way, based on implications for (a) classroom contingencies and (b) their personal situation and style. Teachers frequently complain about the lack of practicality of whole school inservice. They say it takes time away from teaching, deals with management concerns only and produces no obvious benefit for the classroom. It is important that teachers see some practical and personal benefit from the inservice.

## Personal cost appraisal

Individuals also assess the cost of change on a wider perspective than their behaviour within the organization. Effects on personal investment in school affairs include effects on home and social life, personal satisfaction, student response and career opportunities. Thus, the personal context of teachers impinges on their relationship with the school. This affects their sense of participation and belonging, and impacts on school culture. Sensitivity to changes in the personal and work context of the teachers must be part of programme development, especially when planning for implementation.

## Realized expectations

Once a development programme is initiated, and teachers begin to have new experiences, they find that their hopes or fears are either confirmed or challenged. For instance, they make comparisons between assessments, academic standards and discipline in the old and the new systems. They experience changes in work practice such as 'administrivia' and marking systems. New situations evoke responses from students and colleagues which impinge on the teacher's own relationship with them, giving a positive or negative perception of the project. The quality of each individual's experience evokes different responses. Frequently, the consequences of new programmes cannot be fully anticipated. Teachers need the opportunity to interpret new experiences, and of having the aims of the programme reinforced through practical reflection. The general acceptance or rejection of the outcomes of change determines the continued development of the programme. Thus, particular attention must be paid to providing support structures which give feedback to participants during the implementation phase.

## Leadership support

The support and involvement of key administrative personnel is essential for the success of any change process. Individuals take their cues for organizational values and symbols from the behaviour of leaders. Thus, the role of the principal plays an important role in ongoing inservice programmes. It is important that this support be made visible in some way throughout the programme.

These six elements weave a complex tapestry of assumptions, values and established artefacts in the educational system. As well as asking these questions of inservice programmes and their own development, teachers can adapt the questions for classroom planning. The process of learning and change sets off complex reactions and interactions in the learner. The change leader tries to be sensitive to each of these elements and to interpret them for participants. This chapter has presented frameworks by which some of these interactions can be analysed — in terms of the content of development, attitudes to development and the way in which it is planned. In the next chapter, we look more closely at how this leadership is exercised, and assumptions about leadership in schools.

### Notes

1   Krupp (1986) is an example of her work. Much of her focus in workshops was on how people resisting change, but for different reasons at different stages of their careers.
2   The classification of teacher skills in these categories is taken from training courses by Selection Research Inc. in Lincoln, Nebraska.
3   Curwin and Mendler (1988), Riordan (1996), and Ilk (1995) explore different approaches to discipline.
4   Much research is available on the changing concerns of men and women at different stages of the lifecycle (Levinson, 1978; Sugarman, 1992; Sheehy, 1995) and these have been applied to teachers (Krupp, 1981; Ball and Goodson, 1992; Huberman, 1993).
5   Schein originally gave five such anchors in *Organizational Psychology, 3rd edition* published by Prentice Hall in 1980. The other three were added in 1990.
6   Gouldner (1957, 1958).
7   Glickman (1981) developed a similar model in terms of the beginning teacher. His approach has been adapted here for teacher development.

## Chapter 9

---

# Leadership

---

Leadership and leaders have fascinated humankind almost since the beginning of history. Each nation and tribe has its set of gods, its powerful heroes who performed great deeds on its behalf. Leaders are recognized through the success of their actions and their ability to produce results. People are celebrated for leadership in politics, culture, business, sport and academia. In general, leadership is associated with positive growth and development, although it has been associated with evil outcomes and cruel dictatorships[1]. The lives of these leaders have been examined by sociologists, by historians and by psychologists to extract the elusive secrets of leadership. Such research has focused on the personal traits of the individuals, their relationship with their followers and also the content of their achievements.

When we think of leadership in organizations, we generally focus at the top, on the president, the chief executive and the Board of Directors. In schools the focus is on the principal. We look for highly dynamic bosses, and celebrate heroes who make a major killing in the business world, or who single-handedly turn a school or class around from failure to spectacular success. Statements such as those which glorify the role of the principal as 'the single most important factor' in school effectiveness, give credence to that tendency. Defining the role of the principal as vision setter, instructional leader, staff developer, chief executive and occasionally 'all of the above' contributes to the belief that personal leadership is an essential ingredient in organizational success. A high level of expectation is placed on the principal to bring about this success. Both the burden and the mystique of leadership are placed on the single individual who exercises this role.

There is undoubtedly some truth in this belief. Individuals have had great effects in the sphere of politics and of organizations, working with and inspiring others to achieve extraordinary things. Personality, style and luck (being in the right place at the right time) have played a part in the success of such leaders. This is also true for schools. Principals have played key roles in motivating, energizing and developing excellent schools. Teachers do look to the principal for vision and inspiration. Yet, in schools, there is wide scope for leadership outside the formal position of the principal. As we have seen already, individual teachers may exercise an informal leadership function because of their expertise or status. Teachers may also exercise a leadership role for students in their teaching or in extra-curricular activities. Students may be recognized for their leadership potential and afforded opportunities to exercise this as prefects, as captains or leaders of sports teams and as functionaries in school societies. The informal system of the school provides opportunities for individuals to influence and inspire others. In fact, many schools initiate leadership programmes or participate in national projects such as the President's Award or the Duke of Edinburgh awards.

When leadership is considered from the perspective of vision and inspiration, rather than as a 'job' within the school, teachers have an opportunity to reflect on their own leadership function and style and their contribution to the overall vision of the school. They renew or re-evaluate how they choose to exercise that leadership. A consideration of leadership contributes to the development of the organizational culture of the school, as it clarifies the content of that culture, develops a shared value system and elicits commitment to promoting that culture. It also allows for critical self-evaluation, for goal clarification and for recognition, appreciation and celebration of what is important in the school. This chapter examines different approaches to the exercise of leadership, and reports on how principals and teachers reflect on the leadership context and challenge.

## Understanding of Leadership

### Leadership Characteristics

Early studies of leadership focused on the traits of leaders as great people. The general study of the life and work of acknowledged leaders sought to isolate particular traits and characteristics, either behavioural or psychological, which might identify potential leaders in another context. One approach was to examine physical and social traits (e.g. royal families, wealth). Another was to build profiles of one-dimensional personality or behavioural scales which leaders might use with a degree of regularity. One example of this was McGregor's (1960) classification of managerial assumptions about human nature. McGregor used his Theory X — Theory Y model as a dichotomous classification. People could be divided into two groups. Those who fitted into the Theory Y category were regarded as the elite, who should manage those in the other group. The model can also be used as a description of an individual manager's assumptions about others, and can be used to explain managerial behaviour and attitudes. However, individuals have a complex mixture of both sets of assumptions, which allows each set to be seen as bipolar opposites on a one-dimensional scale (see Figure 9.1). The individual's place on the scale indicates their overall tendency to be influenced by one of the poles[2].

The trait approach to leadership shows itself in a number of different ways in school settings. One instance is the seniority–talent debate for promotions. In some school systems, there is an expectation that promotion will be based on seniority. The trait of 'experience' is thought to automatically entitle the possessor to promotion. To clarify issues in this debate, a good question is: 'Are you a person with fifteen years' experience, or a teacher with one year's experience fifteen times?' The debate will usually reveal assumptions about the necessary qualities of leaders — charismatic talent or a particular type of experience. Certainly, there is a link

| **Theory X** | **Theory Y** |
|---|---|
| • People are motivated by self-interest, and unless controlled will act against the organization's goals.<br>• People are inherently lazy and must be motivated by outside incentives.<br>• People have irrational feelings and are incapable of self-discipline and control. | • People are responsible and, if encouraged, will work with commitment and creativity.<br>• People are self-motivated and self-controlled, and react negatively to excessive external control.<br>• People will integrate their own desires with that of the organization. |

Scale  ☹                ☺                ☺

*Figure 9.1   An application of McGregor's Theory X and Theory Y assumptions as a one-dimensional scale*

between age and wisdom. One has to invest time in order to be exposed to a variety of different situations and to learn from them. However, some people pack a lot of living into a short time whereas others have a less varied experience of life.

Another instance of the 'great person' trait syndrome is the development of 'us–them' language. When a teacher is appointed within his or her school to the position of principal, it is not uncommon that the staff develops a very different set of expectations of their colleague, and a new language emerges in their relation-ship. The expectation is that the leader will possess new powers of inspiration and achievement — that he or she will somehow be different. It is as if the new role should transform the individual to allow general leadership traits to appear. Prin-cipals can also develop a language about themselves that emphasizes their different status, talking about 'my school', 'my staff' and 'my vision'. The principal is set up as being apart from the rest of the staff, and the implication of the ego-identification of school and principal sets a moral quality to that difference.

The trait approach to leadership was largely discredited when the focus was on physical traits and accidents of birth, each trait being as often absent as it was present across the spectrum of different leaders (see Burns, 1978; Stogdill and Coons, 1957). However, the approach has come to the fore again in recent years with a renewed emphasis on what might be termed 'inside out' leadership develop-ment, which places a major emphasis on the development of character as the basis of leadership. Kouzes and Posner (1987) described six personal traits of leaders — honesty, forward looking, inspiring, competent, fair-minded and supportive. Block (1993) echoes the early work of Greenleaf on the Servant Leader when he writes of leadership as stewardship, moving away from positions of power and paternalism, with their concerns for consistency and predictability, to a concern for partnership and empowerment. Covey's (1989, 1990) seven habits and his principle-centred leadership focus on personal characteristics of the leader, as well as interpersonal, managerial and organizational abilities. His emphasis on the personal vision of the leader focuses on the need for personal mystique and charisma attached to leader-ship. Bindhi and Duignan (1997) have focused on the notion of authenticity in leadership, stressing self-knowledge and personal values, meaningful quality rela-tionships and congruent organizational structures. The shift in focus in the modern approach to personal trait is to stress the moral dimension of leadership, and the community dimension of that morality. Leadership is not seen as creating a gap or a distance between leader and follower, but rather linking both through a sense of vision and purpose.

---

**Exercise 9.1**

Viewing a short clip of video which demonstrates some leadership qualities can be a good way of helping a group of people talk about leadership qualities and then to apply them to their own situation. For example:

- *Robin Hood, Prince of Thieves* deals with the transformation of the men in the forest as 'outlaws into free men' leading to dramatic action.
- *A Man for All Seasons* deals with the role of personal vision and integrity.
- *Mr Holland's Opus, Dead Poets' Society, Renaissance Man* portray leadership as inspiration and empowerment of followers in an educational setting.

Questions which might be asked:

- Who are your own heroes? What do you admire about them? What are their characteristics?
- When you imagine yourself doing 'heroic things', what behaviours, attitudes and situations do you imagine yourself in?
- If you compare your own dreams of heroism and the actions of your own heroes, what patterns do you see? What does this tell you about your own expectations for leadership?
- How might you try to emulate this approach to leadership in your own work?

---

*Transactional Leadership*

A second approach to leadership studies focused on the leader–follower relationship. The role of the leader was seen mainly in transactional terms, in motivating followers to bring about intended outcomes, and to reward them appropriately. This gave rise to an interest in leadership behaviour and its consequences for follower participation.

> Leadership is not a matter of passive status, or the mere possession of some combination of traits. It appears rather to be a working relationship among members of a group, in which the leader acquires status through active participation and demonstration of his capacity for carrying out cooperative tasks through to completion. (Kerry and Murdoch, 1993, p. 221)

From the 1950s to the 1980s, leadership studies focused on two dimensions — task orientation and relationship orientation. In the Ohio studies, these two dimensions were taken as independent scales, where an individual could have high or low scores on both scales (Figure 9.2). Scores gave rise to typical leadership styles and behaviours.

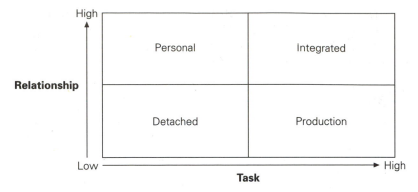

*Figure 9.2   General structure of leadership style based on task and relationship*

- A *detached* style shows little concern for either production or for relation-ships. Followers are left to their own devices, with little feedback on the quality of their work or their performance. The principal does not interfere with the teachers, and does not expect to be troubled by them. Detached teachers come in and lecture their classes, with little relationship between them and the students, and sometimes even with the material they teach.
- A *production* style shows a high concern for task goals and achievements, with low concern for relationships among the people who perform the tasks. In a school, this might be expressed as a high concern for academic performance, with little concern for the emotional development of students or the professional development of the teachers.
- The *personal* style on the other hand shows a high concern for relation-ships with low concern for actual production. This might be true of a teacher in a low ability class who sees his or her job as maintaining a good social atmosphere in order to alleviate a sense of student alienation, with-out challenging the students to progress academically. Similarly, it might refer to a principal who shirks all responsibility of teacher evaluation and challenge, opting instead to promote a sense of bonhomie in the staffroom.
- The *integrated* style shows a high concern for production as well as a concern for good relationships and cooperation. This stems from a belief that people are happy only when they are doing meaningful and productive work. In a classroom or a school this refers to the teacher and principal who integrates academic challenge with an atmosphere of personal growth and development, believing that the two are intertwined.

Blake and Mouton (1964) developed their managerial grid using these two scales to measure the leader's orientation to followers. One can score from one to nine on each of the scales, and they found that people clustered in five areas; (1,1), (9,1), (1,9) and (9,9) corresponding to the four quadrants outlined above, and a middle position (5,5) which showed some commitment to both dimensions. This is some-times termed compromiser because it is prepared to sacrifice a concern for production

| Dysfunctional | **Style** | Functional |
|---|---|---|
| Disinterest — takes no responsibility for role of leader. | **Detached** | Bureaucrat — does not interfere with well-defined roles and structures. |
| Dictator — coerces others to carry out programme with no concern for followers. | **Production** | Benevolent Dictator — presses forward with worthwhile projects for the good of the group. |
| Dependent — demanding a conforming response from followers. | **Personal** | Mentor — a supportive structure whereby colleagues learn from one another. |
| Political — balances concerns for task and people, negotiating them against one another through compromise. | **Integrated** | Professional — integrates high levels of production and high levels of satisfaction. |

Figure 9.3   *Functional and dysfunctional approaches to leadership style*

for good relations, and also will sacrifice good relations for some production. For them, the ideal leader was high on both task and relationship.

Other researchers focused on cultural context in which leadership occurs. For them, leadership effectiveness must take into account the contingent situation. There is no one way of being a leader. Different contexts make different demands on leaders, and require an adaptation of style and behaviour if leadership is to be effective. For example, if your building is on fire, you need someone to become very task oriented — they take charge and get people out rather than organizing a committee to discuss different alternatives. Hersey and Blanchard (1982) analysed situations in terms of follower experience, ability and motivation[3]. For example, when someone is learning a new skill for the first time, then it may be appropriate to be highly directive and less supportive. However, when dealing with experienced professionals, a supportive role with less directive intervention may be more appropriate. They believed that leaders can learn to expand their range of skills and thus by choosing an appropriate style, become more effective. Fiedler (1967) on the other hand believed that leadership style could not be adapted, and leaders should try to find a situation which suited their style.

Thus, when looking at leadership style, the style can be functional or dysfunctional depending on how well it matches the needs of the situation.

The *detached style* has a low concern for production and a low concern for relationships. This can be an appropriate style in a bureaucratic context, where there is a fixed and stable agenda, and roles are clearly defined and people act according to these roles. In adopting this style, the leader assumes that the followers know their job and they get on with it. There is no need to get involved. In education, a particular notion of autonomous professionalism gives rise to this approach. The principal sees each teacher as responsible for their own professionalism and their own classroom and does not interfere by either setting standards or by examining teaching styles. Academic freedom is a strong cultural dimension of the school. Whereas this approach can lead to entrepreneurial creativity with teachers, it can also lead to isolation among teachers. The teachers feel unappreciated, that they are working on their own. Ideas are shared on a haphazard and random basis and there is little teamwork which focuses on developing learning in the classroom, or developing a sense of bonding with other teachers. Burnout, incompetence or a sense of being overwhelmed by problems can create situations where leaders blame followers, and followers blame leaders, where no solution is sought to problems, and relationships and morale deteriorate. This breeds a sense of separation and routine. If no leadership is shown at all, then the school can suffer from a sense of desertion and paralysis in the face of problems.

The *production* style focuses on the end result, on achieving a particular goal. This leadership style flows from a strong conviction about the product, and sells the goals to others. The product is frequently seen in terms of the school itself, rather than the individuals in it. For instance, examination results or extra-curricular successes reflect on the school, rather than the particular students who achieve them or the teachers who mentor these students. The benevolent dictator pushes and cajoles people, who freely accept the goals but perhaps find it hard to achieve them or to maintain momentum. A coach or trainer may exercise their role in this way, setting targets for the athlete and pushing them through pain barriers or through constant repetition to perfect a skill. This style can be transferred to the school, where there is constant reference to targets, examination results, sports wins, etc. These are often made in a semi-joking but fully serious way, reflecting the production style of the leader. An inappropriate use of the production style is to turn into an autocrat and dictator. This approach seeks to suppress all personal relationships and coerce others to the task at hand. Such a leader is manipulative, uses gamesmanship and is economical with information to suit his or her own purposes.

An effective use of the *personal style* is the development of a mentor relationship. A common approach to induction and development of teachers and administrators is a peer coaching programme, where inexperienced and experienced personnel agree to share perspectives on problems, leading to creative and practical solutions. This style can become dysfunctional if a dependency relationship develops between the two parties, or where the leader seeks unquestioning conformity and loyalty from followers. An ineffective use of this style divides the school into cliques and camps identified by slogans or 'proselytizing' leaders.

In the *integrated* style, there is a concern for task and people. The political operator works out of these concerns, but sees development in terms of wins and losses. They try to minimize the effects of losses and have some gain. They sacrifice both relationships and productivity with the result that satisfactory relations are rare, as no one is happy with their lot, and also productivity is lower than it need be, as resources are inadequate. The professional, on the other hand, represents a high level of commitment to both productivity and relationships, and is effective in bringing them about. This behaviour type is what Covey terms 'win–win, or no deal'. The underlying belief is that everyone can be happy with the outcome of any decision, provided they work at it together. In the dialogue which goes on at this level, individuals come to understand their own needs in terms of organizational needs, and learn to cooperate with one another rather than compete. They find a balance between their own personal needs and those of the organization.

The transactional approach to style is consistent with a closed systems approach to organizations, where the task or product of the organization is relatively easy to define, and well-marked boundaries allow for easy measurement of relationships and productivity. It is undoubtedly true that leadership style has much to do with the satisfaction levels of teachers in schools. Working in situations where there is low attention to personnel is very demoralizing. Teachers feel unappreciated and this can have long-term effects on career development and motivation. Similarly, in schools where there is low attention to task or where implementation of regular administrative functions is poor, high levels of frustration develop and teachers feel stress from role overload. However, it is equally clear that style is not everything. Many principals have good relationships with their teaching staff and run efficient schools. There is a general air of contentment in the school, yet there is something missing — a sense of excitement and purpose. The inward-looking contentment of the school lacks the sense of belonging and achievement in the larger environment. Once environmental forces impinge on the school, and the school is forced to adapt in either its internal structures or even its product, one finds that concerns of productivity and relationship are necessary, but not sufficient, for survival. The challenge of change and development looks to the core purpose of the school — the substance of leadership vision becomes more central than the external manifestation of style. This leads to a consideration of transformational leadership.

---

**Exercise 9.2**

There are many instruments which can be used to measure leadership style. Some focus on general managerial style, whereas others focus on style in particular situations (e.g. conflict). Having a leader fill out a self-report questionnaire on their style, and then comparing that to one filled out by followers, can be a very enlightening exercise, giving rise to self-knowledge. Of particular interest to teachers will be feedback on classroom climate[4].

A second approach to clarifying style is to interview a leader, asking them to describe some critical incident in the school, and how they handled it. By exploring alternative ways of handling the same situation, either in projection or role play, the leader can often come to appreciate their own style. Developing alternative scenarios on how to handle situations can help increase the leader's repertoire of skills.

---

*Transformational Leadership*

Hersey (1983) described three types of skills in administration — technical, human relations and conceptual. The first two skills reflect traditional thinking about leadership behaviour. The third skill, conceptual, involves the leader seeing the big picture

— how the parts fit together and contribute to the overall function of the organization. However, the focus on the conceptual level can be deceptive.

> Effective leaders have the vision required to see things differently from others. They collect and arrange the same data we all see in ways that allow them to conceive of new and unseen phenomena. A core characteristic of all effective leaders is the ability to have a vision of where they are trying to go and to articulate it clearly to potential followers so that they know their personal role in achieving that vision[5]. (Wilhelm, 1996, p. 223)

Although working from a transformational rhetoric, this remains a transactional leadership style, where the leader develops and articulates the vision, and offers it to followers as a more rewarding future. The rewards being transacted are now intrinsic rather than extrinsic, but the basis of the leader–follower relationship remains a transaction. Transformation goes deeper than this. Whereas transaction indicates a power over people, transformation discovers power through people. The transformational leader empowers others. Through his or her leadership, followers find new meaning and new purpose in themselves. This new power enables them to transcend the ordinary routines of work and achieve extraordinary results. The follower becomes transformed, goes through a metamorphosis which releases their potential and their own leadership skills, and this in turn has a powerful effect on others.

In reconceptualizing organizations as open systems, more recent studies on leadership have moved beyond the task and human relations dimensions of schools. These studies focus on the vision and meaning dimension leaders bring to schools. Bottery (1988) criticized programmes training school principals which turned out effective administrators, but which failed to address issues of what is appropriate leadership content. Bennis (1989) distinguished administrators as those who 'do the thing right' and leaders as those who 'do the right thing', focusing on the distinction between efficiency and effectiveness in organizational planning and development. Bolman and Deal (1991) have typified the work of the school principal as a balance between logic and artistry, drawing attention to the importance of the symbolic in bringing meaning and energy to the day-to-day technical processes of the school. Duignan and MacPherson (1992) have developed a model of educative leadership which focuses on three areas — things, people and ideas. These three areas echo the three concerns of Hersey, but with a focus now on developing purpose. Starratt (1996) also reflects similar concerns in his three leadership concerns of meaning, community and excellence. Sergiovanni (1992) focuses on the moral dimension of leadership, and the responsibility of the leader to articulate and promote an inclusive vision which represents the community. Sergiovanni uses the religious term 'covenant' to depict that relationship.

Sergiovanni (1984) has outlined five forces or skills which leaders use in schools[6]. The first two of these he terms technical and human. These refer to the transactional skills of task orientation — planning, organizing, coordinating, timetabling, etc; and human relations orientation — encouraging, building morale, using participation, managing conflict and, in general, enabling people to attain satisfaction. The other three skills are conceptual skills. The first of these he termed *educational*, which derives from expert knowledge about learning and schooling. Principals are regarded as instructional leaders within the school, and they exercise their expertise in terms of programme development and teacher supervision. This expert knowledge in schooling helps principals to understand and judge the importance and relevance of different practices, and to promote particular approaches to school development. A second aspect of conceptual skill is *symbolic*. Principals focus attention on matters of importance to the school, and they also model important behaviours and values. Thus, where the principal spends time and energy are powerful symbols of what is important in the school. Symbolic leaders constantly seek rituals and ceremonies which are congruent with the important values and the vision of the school. The third aspect of conceptual skill is what Sergiovanni termed *cultural*. This involves building a unique school culture and includes creating, nurturing and teaching the organizational story of the school. It involves the articulation of the school mission, the induction and socialization of new members to the story, as well as reinforcing the beliefs and traditions within the school. This function builds the unique identity of the school.

For Sergiovanni, all five skills — the technical, human, educational, symbolic and cultural — are essential elements of leadership, and they build on one another. The traditional emphasis on the technical, human and educational aspects of the organization is essential for the development of competent schools. These schools master the predetermined essential fundamentals of education. However, there are schools which go beyond competence and pursue excellence. They develop a love of learning greater than academic performance and achievement. In these schools, great attention is given to symbolic and cultural development, and the presence of a symbolic and cultural leadership force builds on the other three levels and in turn nurtures them.

Starratt (1993) uses the metaphor of drama to illustrate the work of a leader. Drama deals with ordinary events and emotions in the lives of the audience, and puts them together in a more intense experience. This forces the audience to experience these events in a different way, to look at them with different eyes and perhaps to see a new way of responding to them. In a sense, the drama both specifies and reframes the context of the experiences, giving the audience a new perspective and a new perception of what is happening in critical events. So also with the leader. He or she interprets the events of the school in such a way as to clarify their meaning or the drama of the challenge they offer. This helps the individuals enter more deeply into their own experience of these events in a clearer and more empowered manner. However, leadership is more than just a prophetic role which interprets the events of the day. It requires the ability to find ways which structure this vision, which give it some form of permanence, and at the same time allow it to be reviewed and restated periodically. The metaphor of drama involves systems thinking about leadership. The drama of leadership requires a writer, a producer, a director, actors and an audience, and people in the school can play each of these roles at different times.

The function of symbolic and cultural leadership is not the sole reserve of one person in a school. Whereas transactional leadership emphasized the difference between the leader and the followers, with transformational leadership, the gap between leaders and followers tends to be more blurred. Transformational leadership tends to build community. In the daily encounters between teachers and students, there are many opportunities to develop and nurture symbols of meaning — and indeed, by not attending to these symbols, we do in fact communicate a message. The strength of school culture is where the meaning behind these symbols is shared and asserted by all participants. Symbolic and cultural leadership in the school is everyone's domain — the board of governors, the principal, the teachers, parents and students. In as much as everyone participates in the symbols and culture, so also they reinforce or weaken the cultural bonds. The examination of symbolic and cultural forces within the school is a powerful tool for all stakeholders to appreciate the quality of their own participation, and the quality of their contribution to the living culture of the school.

---

**Exercise 9.3**

To reflect on transformational leadership, take each of Sergiovanni's five leadership skills in turn and make a list of how this skill is represented in the life of the school.

Apply the same five skills to your own work in the classroom. How much time to you consciously devote to each of the skill areas? How do you think these areas affect students? What are the implications for your own development as a teacher?

What are the pressures that exist (a) which help you and (b) which hinder you in exercising each of the five skills?

---

### Practice of Leadership

The three perspectives on leadership outlined above — personal, transactional and transformational — interact together in the life of every leader. They are not options from which you choose. Each leader is involved in three sets of drama:

- Their own personal development.
- The development of their followers.
- Their involvement in the development of their followers.

The drive for authentic leadership involves a struggle with all three elements of development. Principals speak about their need not to be constantly generating vision in the school, but to be sustained by the vision of others, in a culture where leadership is shared. In their involvement with others, they seek the time to be inspired by the development taking place, and to renew their own energy and development. In this next section, we explore some responses school leaders have made to the personal struggles they go through in developing an authentic leadership service.

### Context

Leadership in schools takes place in the context of a general crisis about leadership in society. The media sensationally reports heroes as having clay feet. An inordinate amount of time and space is given over to exposing corruption in government or business, and scandals with church leaders, royalty, sports heroes and pop stars. This gives rise to a suspicion of people in positions of trust. It is not surprising that principals and educational leaders suffer from the same distrust and suspicion which is shown to leaders in other areas of society. They feel trapped in a cult of perfection. If they make a mistake, they feel they will be ruthlessly exposed as inadequate. To take on a leadership role is therefore to expose oneself to personal risk.

Within institutions, the demand for democratic processes is part of a general climate which stresses individual empowerment. In support of this development, there is a general climate of critical analysis — a heightened awareness of personal rights to participation, reinforced in most western countries by legislation, and a sensitivity to occasions of exclusion. This has its downside. We are trained to '*criticize the system*' rather than to '*care for it*'. We are reactive to situations and learn to find fault with what is being done. The flip side of this exercise, finding a creative alternative and implementing it, has found much less attention. This creates a lot of pressure on those in leadership roles.

Faced with an increased pluralism in the value system of society, and a relativism in how people understand values, leaders are often reluctant to confront others about standards of behaviour. In an atmosphere where the individual, and individualism, has a central value, confrontation becomes difficult and is often avoided. Teachers, too, are often reluctant to advise a particular value system to their students. They seek a discipline system within the school which absolves them from serious interpersonal relationship with the student so that they can focus on a technical function and 'get on with the job of teaching'. Whereas schools aspire to making a major contribution to the lives of students, the context in which that contribution must take place is often very confusing and may even paralyze those who wish to contribute.

In this context, a real danger exists that talented leaders will lack the desire to take on leadership positions. Some excellent teachers who have developed skills of participative learning in the classroom are reluctant to move into the area of school administration and leadership because of the forces and expectations of the system. Whereas the language is that of participative management, what seems to be valued is a high-profile, personal decisiveness — a Robin Hood or John Wayne heroism which says 'the buck stops here'. Followers look for leaders who will be insightful and make decisions. But the relationship is without commitment or loyalty. Followers participate in an 'a la carte' fashion. In practice, the temptation is for participative leadership to be consigned to the background, to exert influence through informal channels — an influence which ultimately depends on the benevolence of the appointed leader.

There is no shortage of people who wish to be promoted to the status of leadership, but they exercise their roles in a conservative and custodial way rather than in terms of development and empowerment. For them, leadership is defined in purely technical and functional terms — thus ensuring competence rather than excellence. Vision and direction are given to the school from outside, through national or local educational policy, or through the policy of the sponsors of the school, and the leader defines his or her role in a technocratic way, efficiently implementing this vision. The increased focus of the economic power of education and its role in the social future of the student, as well as a willingness of teachers, parents and others to resort to litigation, can have the effect of focusing the energies of the principal on to efficiency concerns, where energy is taken up on routine within the school. Principals busy themselves with technical functions, ensuring that the building is well maintained and that the schedule runs in an efficient way. Teacher leadership is also affected in a similar way. External demands on teachers may also entice them into more technocratic approaches to teaching, especially now that second-level education is increasingly a means of entry to institutions of further learning, with consequent demands from students for guaranteed marks in qualifying examinations. The teacher focuses on product in terms of assessment, and the relationship between teacher and student is built on technocratic delivery rather than personal empowerment.

In order to enjoy the leadership role and grow in it under these contextual pressures, maintaining a personal platform on education becomes a central task. This platform is the inspiration which keeps the leader motivated through the daily routine. The vision sets the criteria by which school events are judged, and how the leader evaluates events. Principals need to give regular personal time to reflection on this vision, and on the forces which are operative in their school. This involves critical reflection on the impact of educational policy on the school and on students, as well as understanding movements in the sensibility of students and teachers to the task of learning and teaching. The task requires reflection on one's personal experience and also stimulation to new experiences by reading and listening to new ideas, being inspired by the stories of other leaders, particularly those in school. Active reflection expands one's horizons as to possibilities, and deepens one's appreciation of the pervasive cultural norms in one's own school. The commitment of the leader is to focused self-development which is both personal and professional. Without this commitment, vision can often be lost and a dysfunctional goal displacement can occur, where the leader is distracted into giving disproportionate energy to less important issues and avoiding the more critical needs of the school. This type of reflection is not just the preserve of principals. Teachers too need to develop a critical awareness of the personal impact of their own work. This goes beyond the effectiveness of their teaching techniques and relationships in the classroom, and incorporates a sense of the overall thrust of education and its impact on their own attitudes and those of the students. Prior commitment to maintaining the platform is necessary, or else the immediate demands of the present erode the vision and lead to burn-out.

### *Relationships*

A central and paradoxical aspect of personal vision is its community dimension. Vision is not developed in seclusion but rather in dialogue with others. It is this sense of connectedness with others that sustains personal vision. There are many aspects of school which constrain this type of dialogue between leaders and followers. One of these is the image of leadership as a paternalistic 'knowing what is best for others', and who gives direction and control to their lives. The consistent portrayal of leadership in terms of leader–follower dynamics places the leader on a plane above the follower, giving him or her added status. Hope, vision and prestige are concentrated in the leader. The present situation of followers is deemed to be inadequate but they have an unarticulated belief in a better future for themselves. The leader is the person who articulates that vision for a better future, has a plan of how to get there, and the means of bringing the group with him or her. Acts of leadership are recognized in creating vision, knowing what is best for the group, deciding the steps to be taken to get there, and coaching or motivating people along the path. All these images imply distance between the leader and the group, with the leader being 'more advanced'. The leader may sell the vision, invite others to enlist, offer inducements of rewards and positive reinforcement along the way, and may clearly demonstrate the positive benefits for followers. Yet, the primary owner of the vision is the leader or the elite group which holds the power. There is still a position of dominance and a position of dependence.

Principals experience this expectation of themselves as school leaders. To some extent they are flattered by it. Most people appointed to a leadership position have a personal vision, a transformation they want to see happen. Being in a leadership position gives a new opportunity to experiment with that vision. However, most leaders quickly come to realize that leadership is not a licence to implement a capricious personal policy. To bring about real transformation requires a high level of shared vision and teamwork. A key to this development is the quality of relationship between team members. In the classroom, teachers often miss out on the challenge of teamwork with equals, and are frequently lured into a paternalistic approach to leadership.

In each of us, there is a tension between a desire to be autonomous and a desire to be nurtured and dependent. We want to be part of the group and yet we want to be free of any ties which hinder our personal development. Some students like to be told what to study and how to answer questions on exams. They feel insecure when left to their own devices, yet they resent the constraints of discipline in the classroom. Among teachers, discussions within a school staff often indicate an attitude that 'management should look after it', whether the problem be a disruptive pupil, the organization of the school schedule or the promotion of the school in the community. Patterns of behaviour are embedded in long-standing arrangements and ways of thinking about leadership. We internalize the patriarchal system which has been our context. This may be particularly true in schools where the relationship between teacher and pupil is often characterized by the dependence of the student on the teacher for information, resources, time, permissions, etc. This style of relating may also transfer to the relationship between teacher and administrators. Teachers expect administrators to provide resources, to maintain discipline, to make decisions much in the same way as they do in their own classrooms. In some cases, teachers may also exhibit the same rebelliousness which they themselves experience from students (Ilk, 1995).

Some management reforms are thinly disguised reinventions of the patriarchy. Forging new relationships is difficult. Individuals and groups have a strong tendency to define territory, to be possessive of power and defensive of their own vision. Efforts to be more democratic go hand in hand with renewed efforts to influence the way the majority think by controlling the information they have about development. The importance of media image in advertising and in political electioneering testifies to this trend. This trend can be seen in school structures as well. Movements to bring about greater participation by teachers and parents in the running of the school can stop short of real influence and empowerment by identifying participation with some peripheral status symbol. Committees are set up to involve others, but they are granted little power or resources. The power to ignore or accept their suggestions still resides within a conservative power structure.

In the complexity of modern organizations, there is a clear need for some centralized decision-making. This requires an element of trust between individuals. This trust brings compliance on the part of the trusting and responsibility for those who are trusted. There is a delicate balance between the trust demanded by the complexity of the task, and a blind trust which cedes control to others. Similarly, there is a delicate balance between accepting the trust of others and acting on their behalf in service, and using their trust to exercise control over them and dominate.

Facing these challenges, leaders and followers have had to develop new skills. When the model of leadership was one of a nurturing parent, people learnt processes and skills which enabled them to deal with decisions being handed down from the top, and authority being exercised in a custodial way. In a genuine partnership, these skills are no longer adequate. In partnership relationships, individuals need to embrace team learning, shared decision-making and dialogue. Individuals also require conflict management skills, on the one hand to confront excessive authoritarianism, and on the other to overcome the reluctance of others to be committed to teamwork. Teamwork skills of dialogue, cooperation, and commitment, where the emphasis is frequently on consensus rather than majority, are quite different from the skills of influence and compliance in a patriarchal system. Leaders face the work of developing responsive attitudes in themselves, and helping followers develop the skills and trust in this new process. When this happens in a school, the distinction between leader and follower blurs. A synergy develops in which leader and follower alike are motivated by a shared vision.

### *Transforming Vision — Property or Process?*

School leaders are very conscious about the development of vision. It is central to the development of effective and total quality schools. Yet, the experience of developing a vision statement and developing a school plan has sometimes turned out to be a sterile exercise. Whereas it caught the mind of the participants, it somehow failed to capture their hearts. Some vital ingredient was missing. Leaders regularly reflect on the tension that exists in strategic planning between 'having a plan' and 'developing capacity'.

A school plan or vision is sometimes regarded as a blueprint for the future, a bible which gives clear focus to future projects and the distribution of resources for the future. The selection and priority of projects is well known, and targets and goals can be assessed regularly. Sometimes, however, the plan is interpreted too rigidly. New projects are resisted 'because they are not in the plan'. Opportunities are missed. Another problem is that the production of a plan somehow brings closure to the process, and it is difficult to have participants involved in the planning process again. There is a feeling of 'Been there, done that, bought the T-shirt'. Participants feel they have played their part, and it is now up to the leader to deliver on the plan.

Everyone has experience of failed vision. Politicians sometimes fail to deliver their election promises and to enact legislation which brings greater social equity or better economic conditions. Education also fails to deliver on its promise. The rhetoric suggests that staying in school longer, getting more education, is a passport to better jobs and a brighter future. Yet, a common experience of those who stay in education is that there seems to be no improvement in their lot. A growing credentialism within society devalues their qualifications and keeps them in relatively the same position as before. This leads to cynicism and a culture of anti-vision — a frustrated idealism which denies any more idealism. This type of cynicism can be seen in schools from teachers who have seen reform movements introduced and fade out, and from students who find a wide gulf between the world of school and the rest of their lives.

Senge (1991) illustrated the tension as a twofold pull, similar to the tension that exists in a piece of elastic. On one level there is a tension between vision (future) and where we are. The vision must be far enough ahead to create some dynamic tension and draw us towards it. If it is too close, there is no attraction, and if it is too far, the elastic loses its pull. There is also a tension between our present and our previous experience (past), which tends to get us to settle down and to stay as we are. Our present therefore is defined by these two forces. The expectation of the leader is to clarify the vision of the future, or else motivate followers to rise above their history. Both these activities tend to be transactional. They promise the individual a reward for responding in a particular way — of being better off by overcoming the past, or by adopting a particular future vision. It is easy to be lured into that role. However, transformational leaders are firmly rooted in the present. They focus on the creative management of the tension between the forces of the past and the future. They help clarify why we should keep struggling with the tension, and how, in the struggle, the future will become clearer and the past can be transcended. This is where real empowerment takes place, when a core meaning evolves for participants and they develop the strength to grasp and enact that meaning for themselves.

School leaders constantly run the risk of regressing to a transactional base, of 'helping' the other, of 'doing what is best'. In a genuine search for a solution to the autonomy–dependence tension, the discovery is one of interdependence. Leadership and followership are seen as part of a systemic whole, a complex series of enabling interactions.

Block (1993) writes of a paradigm shift — to see leadership as stewardship and service rather than as ownership and authority. In this paradigm, the leader focuses on the present-tense *visioning* (active) to which individuals or the organization commit themselves, rather than on the vision to be cared for. Each person relates to the school through vision, and relationships between individuals within the organization are mediated through the vision. Individuals take different roles, some clarifying the vision, others implementing or developing structures which institutionalise the vision, others maybe criticising the vision. These roles are not fixed. Individuals move between them, responding to felt needs within themselves and also to external circumstances which challenge their vision, or their relationship with it. What is constant is a commitment to 'visioning', to move towards a shared vision.

The prime concern of transformational leaders becomes the quality of relationships in the school. The commitment is to dialogue versus debate. In a *debate*, we take sides in the argument before the discussion. Our pre-formed opinions and attitudes act as a kind of outer shell through which all other opinions are filtered. We only half listen to the other person, looking for an opportunity to assert our own point and counter anything which seems contrary. In the process of *dialogue*, common understandings emerge from the sharing, rather than a set of different understandings competing for dominance. There is an assumption and a belief that the common ground to be discovered is more substantial, and more inspiring than any differences which exist. The leader embodies the old saying that we were created with two ears and one mouth, and we use them in proportion. The skill of active listening means suspending one's assumptions and judgements in listening to others. A prerequisite for dialogue is the desire to hear what others are thinking and feeling, a belief that what they say is important and central to the development of the school, and a willingness to be influenced by them. There is also a willingness to share openly one's own vision, and to understand one's own experience in terms of a wider picture. Transformational leaders are committed to serious dialogue with others about what is important in schools. The commitment to dialogue is a celebration of the interconnectedness of people in the school, and builds a sense of shared leadership and teamwork.

The development of transformational leadership involves a radical shift from leader behaviour which focuses on planning, control and predictability, to an ability to live with ambiguity, trust and uncertainty. Central to this development is the integration of the personal, transactional and transformational approaches to leadership. Individuals focus on their personal beliefs, trying to ensure that their beliefs represent a human, ethical and moral stance with regards to others and to the work of education. Leaders who strive for authenticity examine their transactional styles, seeking congruence between their behaviour and their beliefs, and trying to ensure that they are not seeking to dominate others through the types of transactions and power plays that exist in the school. The developing leader is also conscious of transformation. His or her concern is with others, and with their growth and development. The criteria for success is the learning that is taking place in building a sense of shared meaning, of a developing community which strives for excellence in achieving its mission.

### Notes

1   Adolf Hitler and Machiavelli have been studied for leadership qualities, and the power they had to produce negative results. A more light-hearted approach to the study of dictatorship can be seen in Roberts' (1989) *The Leadership Secrets of Attila the Hun*.
2   Another of this type of scale is Fiedler's (1967) Least Preferred Co-worker (LPC) scale which sees task and person concerns as opposite ends of a continuum. Tannenbaum and Schmidt (1958) described leadership behaviour on an autocratic–democratic continuum. This was seen as a zero-sum situation; as one gained, the other lost.
3   Hersey and Blanchard have also published a series called *The One Minute Manager*, which explores different aspects of situational leadership. Cf. also Hersey (1984).
4   Kouzes and Posner (1990) deal specifically with leadership. Ramsden, Martin and Bowden (1989) have a specific application to schools.
5   This focus on the personal vision of the leader in terms of cognitive skills required for executive success dominates the literature. Cf. Gronn (1996).
6   The model is outlined in Sergiovanni (1984). His later development focuses strongly on the symbolic and cultural dimensions of leadership.

# Epilogue

The development of this book has been a journey of discovery. It was conceived primarily as a stimulus for those who work in schools to reflect more deeply on their own experience and their involvement in the enterprise of education. In the introduction, I invited you, the reader, to become a participant in the process, to enter into the exercises and to explore the images and assumptions for yourself. The hope was that you would make connections with your own experience and your own work in school. This is the touchstone for the book — that you have somewhere been inspired to enter into that reflection, and found affirmation or challenge for the future.

As we come to the end of the journey, it is good to look at some of the places we have been. We have been immersed in the inner world of teaching. One danger of this type of cultural exploration is that we think of culture as something 'out there', that can be manipulated and changed in a technico-rational way. Therefore, it is important to think of this book in terms of its parts, and simultaneously, as a whole. The exercises are interrelated and connected. They allow us to stand outside our experience and examine it, and at the same time, they also allow us to enter into it in a deeper way.

The exploration of assumptions can be very revealing and very rewarding. It can also be very frustrating. Our relationship with our culture is a complex phenomenon. Some areas are clearly defined, and we are clear about what we want and value. Other areas, however, are messy. At times we find our values contradictory, and we are challenged to make choices. At other times, we ourselves are inconsistent in how we live our values — we find ourselves doing the very things we detest in others. The exploration may seem like a meandering and eclectic process. But insight into life tends to be like that. None of the exercises presented here ever turned out the same way twice. There are always individual twists and turns, new insights to be gained, new stories to be heard. Teachers bring different contexts to the exercises, and so they see the parts of the exercises in different ways. For some, the exercise will not make sense the first time they go through it. Yet, months later, they will come up and say, 'I know what that exercise was about now. Something happened the other day, and I really began to understand what it was about.' I have had this reaction in schools I have worked with, and also with students on postgraduate courses. We explore these images at the beginning of the year, and at times it is only at the end of the year that connections are made, and new meanings found.

This is an important aspect of doing exercises. They do not always give neat results. The exercises are as much, if not more, about building capacity as they are about producing definitions and measures of organizational culture. Therefore, when you experience frustration or exhilaration, that is normally a sign that the exercise is incomplete. The apparent banality of some exercises often indicates that important issues are being avoided and more work is needed to allow the issues to surface. There may be a need to return to the exercise in a more focused way, looking at it through a new set of binoculars and finding a new perspective as the little girl did in the story in Chapter 2. When the exercise gives rise to levels of euphoria, then equally it should be revisited, and grounded in a practical perspective. The process of development is a constant search for inspiration and the means to make the dream a reality.

Another aspect of working on culture is our expectation. Many approach the process as a problem-solving exercise. Whereas reflection frequently does reveal some areas for improvement, by far the most important aspect of the exploration is the discovery of life and a reason to celebrate. I quoted Seamus Heaney in the 'Introduction' on the role of the poet in revealing our innermost and inarticulate feelings. In the same essay, he compares the technique of the poet to that of the water diviner:

> ... you can't learn the task of dowsing or divining — it is a gift for being in touch with what is there, hidden and real, a gift for mediating between the latent resource and the community that wants it current and released. (1980, pp. 47–8)

The richness of the culture deep inside us, waiting to be discovered, makes the journey worthwhile. Finding the desire in ourselves, and knowing some of the techniques is the key to releasing the water so that it brings a refreshing new life to our work.

Our journey is both a personal and a community task. In my work and in my own life, I have come to appreciate that growth and change is essentially an experience of interrelatedness. The introspection required to examine one's own assumptions is a personal skill, but also needs a trusting context. Isolated, introverted self-examination can lead to a distorted view of self, exaggerating areas of minor importance, in much the same way as the unreflected life fails to address issues of major importance. The 'community' context in which reflection takes place, where feedback grounds the reflection, is an important contribution to personal growth. It is this sharing that frequently allows us to move to deeper levels, to find kindred spirits who share our concerns and who inspire us with new words to speak a new language and explore the depths of our own meaning.

With the increasing and intensifying demands for educational change, it is important that we, as teachers, come to understand our own meaning, and that our commitment to the work of teaching grows out of a deep and authentic core set of values. One of the images I used in the text was that of becoming a nomad through the changing times, rather than settling down and trying to preserve our present, or reinvent our past. Hopefully, along your personal journey, you will find fellow nomads, as I have, who share their story with you, and that their story inspires, affirms and challenges where necessary. My hope is that this book, and especially the stories of the teachers which are reflected in it, can be a companion on that journey, pointing in some way to techniques and exercises which, in Heaney's terms, divine and reveal the hidden sources of life to a community that seeks to grow more deeply into its own culture.

# References

ARGYRIS, C. and SCHON, D. (1974) *Theory in Practice: Increasing Professional Effectiveness*, San Francisco: Jossey-Bass.

ARGYRIS, C. and SCHON, D. (1978) *Organizational Learning: A Theory of Action Perspective*, Reading, MA: Addison-Wesley.

ASHBAUGH, C.R. and KASTEN, K.L. (1984) 'A typology of operant values in school administration,' *Planning and Changing*, **15**, 4, pp. 195–208.

BALL, S.J. and GOODSON, I.F. (Eds) (1992) *Teachers' Lives and Careers*, London: Falmer Press.

BECKHARD, R. and PRITCHARD, W. (1992) *Changing the Essence: The Art of Creating and Leading Fundamental Change in Organizations*, San Francisco: Jossey-Bass.

BEGLEY, P.T. and LEITHWOOD, K.A. (1990) 'The influence of values on school administrator practices,' *Journal of Personnel Evaluation in Education*, **3**, pp. 337–52.

BENNIS, W. (1989) *On Becoming a Leader*, Reading, MA: Addison-Wesley.

BENNIS, W. and NANUS, B. (1985) *Leaders: The Strategies for Taking Charge*, New York: Harper and Row.

BIGGS, J.B. (1985) 'The role of metalearning in study processes,' *British Journal of Educational Psychology*, **55**, pp. 185–212.

BIGGS, J.B. (1987) *Learning Process Questionnaire Manual*, Melbourne: Australian Council for Educational Research.

BINDHI, N. and DUIGNAN, P. (1997) 'Leadership for a new century: Authenticity, intentionality, spirituality and sensibility,' *Educational Management and Administration*, **25**, 2, pp. 117–32.

BLAKE, R. and MOUTON, J. (1964) *The Managerial Grid*, Houston, TX: Gulf.

BLASE, J. and ANDERSON, G. (1995) *The Micropolitics of Educational Leadership: From Control to Empowerment*, New York: Teachers College of Columbia.

BLAU, P.M. and SCOTT, W.R. (1962) *Formal Organizations: A Comparative Approach*, San Francisco: Chandler Publishing Co.

BLOCK, P. (1993) *Stewardship: Choosing Service over Self-Interest*, San Francisco: Berrett-Koehler.

BOLMAN, L.G. and DEAL, T.E. (1991) *Reframing Organizations; Artistry, Choice and Leadership*, San Francisco: Jossey-Bass.

BOTTERY, M.P. (1988) 'Educational management: An ethical critique,' *Oxford Review of Education*, **14**, 3, pp. 341–51.

BOWER, M. (1966) *The Will To Manage: Corporate Success Through Programmed Management*, New York: McGraw-Hill.

BRADFORD, L.P. (1976) *Making Meetings Work: A Guide for Leaders and Group Members*, San Diego: University Associates.

BREDESON, P.V. (1988) 'An analysis of the metaphorical perspectives of school principals,' in BURDIN, J.L. (ed.) *School Leadership: A Contemporary Reader*, Newbury Park: Sage, pp. 297–317.

BROOKS, J.G. and BROOKS, M.G. (1993) *In Search of Understanding: The Case for Constructivist Classrooms*, Washington D.C.: Association for Supervision and Curriculum Development.

BURNS, J. (1978) *Leadership*, New York: Harper and Row.

CARLSON, R.O. (1964) 'Environmental constraints and organizational consequences: The public school and its clients,' in GRIFFITHS, D.E. (ed.) *Behavioral Science and Educational Administration*, N.S.S.E. Yearbook, University of Chicago Press, pp. 262–78.

CARLYLE, T. (1841) *Heroes and Hero-Worship*, London: Routledge Universal Library series.

CHAPMAN, P.D. (1988) *Schools as Sorters. Lewis M. Terman, Applied Psychology and the Intelligence Testing Movement, 1890–1930*, New York: New York University Press.

CORWIN, R.G. (1974) 'Models of educational organizations,' *Review of Research in Education*, **2**, pp. 247–95.

COVEY, S.R. (1989) *The Seven Habits of Highly Effective People*, New York: Simon and Schuster.

COVEY, S.R. (1990) *Principle-centered Leadership*, New York: Simon and Schuster.

CRAWFORD, M., KYDD, L. and RICHES, C. (1997) *Leadership and Teams in Educational Management*, Buckingham: Open University Press.

CURWIN, R.L. and MENDLER, A.N. (1988) *Discipline with Dignity*, Alexandria, Va. Association of Supervision and Curriculum Development.

DEAL, T.E. and PETERSON, K.D. (1994) *The Leadership Paradox: Balancing Logic and Artistry in Schools*, San Francisco: Jossey-Bass.

DEPREE, M. (1992) *Leadership Jazz*, New York: Dell Publishing.

DEWEY, J. (1902) *The Child and the Curriculum*, Chicago: University of Chicago Press.

DEWEY, J. (1916) *Democracy and Education*, New York: Macmillan.

DEWEY, J. (1938) *Experience and Education*, New York: Macmillan.

DREXLER, A.B., SIBBET, D. and FORRESTER, R.H. (1988) 'The team performance model,' in REDDY, W.B. and JAMISON, I. (eds) *Team Building: Blueprints for Productivity and Satisfaction*, San Diego: University Associates.

DUIGNAN, P. (1997) *The Dance of Leadership: At the Still Point of the Turning World*, Melbourne: Australian Council for Educational Administration Monograph.

DUIGNAN, P. and MACPHERSON, R.J.S. (eds) (1992) *Educative Leadership: A Practical Theory for New Administrators and Managers*, London: Falmer Press.

DYER, W.G. (1977) *Team Building*, Reading, Mass.: Addison-Wesley.

ERIKSON, E. (1968) *Identity, Youth and Crisis*, New York: Norton.

ETZIONI, A. (1961) *A Comparative Analysis of Complex Organizations*, New York: Free Press.

ETZIONI, A. (1964) *Modern Organizations*, New Jersey: Prentice Hall.

ETZIONI, A. (ed.) (1969) *The Semi-professions and their Organizations*, New York: Free Press.

FIEDLER, F. (1967) *A Theory of Leadership Effectiveness*, New York: McGraw-Hill.

FRENCH, J.R. and RAVEN, B. (1968) 'The bases of social power,' in CARTWRIGHT, D. and ZANDER, A. (eds) *Group Dynamics*, New York: Harper and Row.

FRIERE, P. (1972) *Pedagogy of the Oppressed*, New York: Herder and Herder.

FRIERE, P. (1985) *The Politics of Education: Culture, Power and Liberation* (Trans. D. Macedo), Basingstoke: Macmillan.

FULLAN, M. (1991) *The New Meaning Of Educational Change*, New York: Teachers College Press.

FULLAN, M. (1993) *Change Forces: Probing the Depths of Educational Reform*, London: Falmer Press.

FULLAN, M. and HARGREAVES, A. (1991) *What's Worth Fighting For: Working Together for Your School*, Toronto, Ontario Public School Teachers' Federation.

FULLAN, M. and HARGREAVES, A. (eds) (1992) *Teacher Development and Educational Change*, London: Falmer Press.

GALLAGHER, M.P. (1997) *Clashing Symbols: An Introduction to Faith and Culture*, London: Darton, Longman and Todd.

GARDNER, H. (1983) *Frames of Mind: The Theory of Multiple Intelligences*, London: Harper Collins. (1993 edition by Fontana)

GLICKMAN, C.D. (1981) *Developmental Supervision: Alternative Practices for Helping Teachers Improve Instruction*, Washington, D.C.: Association for Supervision and Curriculum Development.

GLICKMAN, C.D. (1993) *Renewing America's Schools: A guide for school-based action*, San Francisco: Jossey-Bass.

GOFFMANN, E. (1990) *The Presentation of Self in Everyday Life*, London: Penguin.

GOULD, S. (1981) *The Mismeasure of Man*, London: Penguin.

GOULDNER, A. (1957) 'Cosmopolitans and locals: Toward an analysis of latent social roles I,' *Administrative Science Quarterly*, **2**, pp. 281–306.

GOULDNER, A. (1958) 'Cosmopolitans and locals: Toward an analysis of latent social roles II,' *Administrative Science Quarterly*, **3**, pp. 444–79.

GRADY, N. (1993) 'Examining teachers' images through metaphor,' *Studies in Educational Administration*, **58**, pp. 23–32.

GRAY, A. and McGUIGAN, J. (eds) (1993) *Studying Culture: An Introductory Reader*, London: Edward Arnold.

GRONN, P. (1996) 'From transactions to transformations: A new world order in the study of leadership,' *Educational Management and Administration*, **24**, pp. 7–30.

HANDY, C. (1984) *The Future of Work: A Guide to a Changing Society*, Oxford: Blackwell.

HANDY, C. (1991) *The Age of Unreason (2nd edition)*, London: Century Books.

HANDY, C. (1994) *The Empty Raincoat: Making Sense of the Future*, London: Hutchinson.

HARGREAVES, A. (1994) *Changing Teachers, Changing Times: Teachers' Work and Culture in the Postmodern Age*, London: Cassell.

HARGREAVES, A. (ed.) (1997) *Rethinking Educational Change with Heart and Mind*, Alexandria, VA: Association of Supervision and Curriculum Development.

HARMIN, M. and SIMON, S.B. (1971) *Values: The Teacher's Handbook*, Chicago: Scott, Foresman and Co.

HEAD, J. (1997) *Working with Adolescents: Constructing Identity*, London: Falmer Press.

HEANEY, S. (1980) *Preoccupations: Selected Prose 1968–1978*, London: Faber and Faber.

HERSEY, P. (1983) *An Intensive Experience in the Process of Change: Situational Leadership*, Calif: Leadership Productions, Inc.

HERSEY, P. (1984) *The Situational Leader: The Other 59 Minutes*, New York: Warner Books.

HERSEY, P. and BLANCHARD, K.H. (1982) *Management of Organizational Behavior: Utilizing Human Resources*, Englewood Cliffs, NJ: Prentice Hall.

HERZBERG, F. (1966) *Work and the Nature of Man*, Cleveland: World Publishing.

HESSELBEIN, F., GOLDSMITH, M. and BECKHARD, R. (1996) *The Leader of the Future*, San Francisco: Jossey-Bass.

HODGKINSON, C. (1991) *Educational Leadership: The Moral Art*, Albany, NY: SUNY Press.

HOGAN, P. (1995) *The Custody and Courtship of Experience: Western Education in Philosophical Perspective*, Dublin: Columba Press.

HUBERMAN, M. (1993) *The Lives of Teachers*, London: Cassell.

ILK, J.M. (1995) 'Two worlds: As we might see ourselves,' *Management in Education*, **9**, 1, pp. 28–9.

ILLICH, I. (1971) *Deschooling Society*, New York: Harper and Row.

KAMIN, L. (1974) *The Science and Politics of IQ*, Maryland: Erlbaum.

KERRY, T. and MURDOCH, A. (1993) 'Educating managers as leaders: Some thoughts on the context of the changing nature of schools,' *School Organisation*, **13**, 3, pp. 221–30.

KIRSCHENBAUM, H. (1975) *Beyond Value Clarification*, New York: HEW Publishers.

KITTAY, E.F. (1987) *Metaphor: Its Cognitive Force and Linguistic Structure*, Oxford: Clarendon Press.

KOHN, A. (1996) *Beyond Discipline: From Compliance to Community*, Alexandria, Va: Association of Supervision and Curriculum Development.

KOSSLYN, S.M. (1980) *Image and Mind*, Cambridge Mass: Harvard University Press.

KOTTER, J.P. (1996) *Leading Change*, Boston: Harvard Business School Press.

KOUZES, J.M. and POSNER, B.Z. (1987) *The Leadership Challenge: How to Get Extraordinary Things Done in Organizations*, San Francisco: Jossey-Bass.

KOUZES, J.M. and POSNER, B.Z. (1990) *Leadership Practices Inventory: A Self-assessment and Analysis*, San Diego: Pfeiffer.

KOZOL, J. (1967) *Death at an Early Age: The Destruction of the Hearts and Minds of Negro Children in the Boston Public Schools*, Boston: Houghton Mifflin.

KRUPP, J.A. (1981) *Adult Development: Implications for Staff Development*, Conn: Regional Inservice Education.

KRUPP, J.A. (1986) 'Using the power of the principalship to motivate experienced teachers,' *The Journal of Staff Development*, **7**, 2, pp. 100–11.

LAKOFF, G. and JOHNSON, M. (1980) *Metaphors We Live By*, Chicago: University of Chicago Press.

LEVINSON, D. (1978) *The Seasons of a Man's Life*, New York: Ballantine.

LIEBERMAN, A. (ed.) (1986) *Rethinking School Improvement*, New York: Columbia Teachers College Press.

LOADER, D. (1997) *The Inner Principal*, London: Falmer Press.

LYNCH, K. (1989) *The Hidden Curriculum: Reproduction in Education, an Appraisal*, London: Falmer Press.

MARSHAK, R.J. (1993) 'Managing the metaphors of change,' *Organizational Dynamics*, **22**, 1.

MARTON, F. and SÄLJÖ, R. (1976) 'On qualitative differences in learning,' Series of articles in the *British Journal of Educational Psychology*, **46**, pp. 4–11, 115–27.

McGREGOR, D. (1960) *The Human Side of Enterprise*, New York: McGraw-Hill.

McLAREN, P. (1993) *Schooling as a Ritual Performance: Towards a Political Economy of Educational Symbols and Gestures* (*2nd Edition*), New York: Routledge.

MORGAN, G. (1980) 'Paradigms, metaphors and puzzle solving in organization theory,' *Administrative Science Quarterly*, **25**, pp. 605–22.

MORGAN, G. (1983) 'More on metaphor: Why we cannot control tropes in administrative science,' *Administrative Science Quarterly*, **28**, pp. 601–7.

MORGAN, G. (1986) *Images of Organisations*, London: Sage.

MORGAN, G. (1993) *Imaginization: The Art of Creative Management*, Newbury Park, CA: Sage.

MORTIMORE, P., SAMMONS, P., STOLL, L., LEWIS, D. and ECOB, R. (1988) *School Matters*, California: University of California Press.

MURGATROYD, S. and MORGAN, C. (1992) *Total Quality Management and the School*, Buckingham: Open University Press.

NAISBITT, J. (1982) *Megatrends*, New York: Warner Books.

NEWSTEAD, S.E. (1992) 'A study of two "quick-and-easy" methods of assessing individual differences in student learning,' *British Journal of Educational Psychology*, **62**, pp. 299–312.

OSWICK, C. and GRANT, D. (eds) (1996) *Organisation Development: Metaphorical Explorations*, London: Pitman.

PETERS, T.J. (1978) 'Symbols, patterns and settings: An optimistic case for getting things done,' *Organisational Dynamics*, Autumn 3–23.

PETERS, T.J. and WATERMAN, R.H. (1982) *In Search of Excellence*, New York: Harper and Row.

PONDY, L.R. (1983) 'The role of metaphors and myths in organisation and in the facilitation of change,' in PONDY, L.R., FRONST, P.J., MORGAN, G. and DANDRIDGE, T.C. (eds) *Organisational Symbolism*, Greenwich, Conn: JAI Press.

POWELL, A.G., FARRAR, E. and COHEN, D.K. (1985) *The Shopping Mall High School: Winners and Losers in the Educational Marketplace*, Boston: Houghton Mifflin.

RAMSDEN, P., MARTIN, E. and BOWDEN, J. (1989) 'School environment and sixth form pupils' approaches to learning,' *British Journal of Educational Psychology*, **59**, pp. 129–42.

RASHFORD, N.S. and COGHLAN, D. (1994) *The Dynamics of Organizational Levels: A Framework for Managers and Consultants*, Reading, MA: Addison-Wesley.

RATHS, I., HARMIN, M. and SIMON, S.B. (1971) *Values and Teaching*, Columbus: Merrill Publishing.

RICHMOND, P.G. (1985) 'The relationship of grade, sex, ability and socio-economic status to parent, peer and school affiliation,' *British Journal of Educational Psychology*, **55**, pp. 233–9.

RICOEUR, P. (1978) *The Rule of Metaphor: Multi-Disciplinary Studies in the Creation of Meaning in Language*, London: Routledge and Kegan Paul.

RILEY, K.A. and NUTTALL, D.L. (eds) (1994) *Measuring Quality: Education Indicators, United Kingdom and International Perspectives*, London: Falmer Press.

RIORDAN, P. (1996) *The Politics of the Common Good*, Dublin: IPA.

ROBERTS, W. (1989) *The Leadership Secrets of Attila the Hun*, London: Bantam.

RUTTER, M., MAUGHAM, B., MORTIMORE, P. and OUSTON, J. (1979) *Fifteen Thousand Hours*, London: Open Books.

SACKMANN, S. (1989) 'The role of metaphors in organisation transformation,' *Human Relations*, **42**, 6, 463–85.

SACKMANN, S.A. (1991) *Cultural Knowledge in Organizations: Exploring the Collective Mind*, Newbury Park: Sage.

SARASON, S.B. (1971) *The Culture of the School and the Problem of Change*, Boston: Allyn and Bacon.

SARASON, S.B. (1996) *Revisiting 'The Culture of the School and the Problem of Change'*, New York: Columbia Teachers' College Press.

SCHEIN, E.H. (1980) *Organizational Psychology (3rd Edition)*, Eaglewood Cliffes, NJ: Prentice-Hall.

SCHEIN, E.H. (1985) *Organizational Culture and Leadership*, San Francisco: Jossey-Bass.

SCHEIN, E.H. (1990) *Career Anchors*, San Diego: University Associates.

SCHLECHTY, P.C. and JOSLIN, A.W. (1986) 'Images of schools,' in LIEBERMAN, A. (ed.) *Rethinking School Improvement*, New York: Columbia Teachers' College Press, pp. 141–57.

SCHON, D. (1987) *Educating the Reflective Practitioner: Toward a New Design for Teaching and Learning in the Professions*, London: Jossey-Bass.

SCHON, D. (1991) *The Reflective Practitioner: How Professionals Think in Action*, New York: Basic Books. (Previously published in 1983)

SENGE, P.M. (1991) *The Fifth Discipline: The Art and Practice of the Learning Organization*, London: Century Press.

SERGIOVANNI, T.J. (1984) 'Leadership and excellence in schooling,' *Educational Leadership*, **41**, pp. 4–13.

SERGIOVANNI, T.J. (1992) *Moral Leadership: Getting to the Heart of School Improvement*, San Francisco: Jossey-Bass.

SERGIOVANNI, T.J. and CARVER, F.D. (1980) *The New School Executive: A Theory of Administration* (*2nd Edition*), New York: Harper and Row.

SERGIOVANNI, T.J. and CORBALLY, J.E. (eds) (1986) *Leadership and Organizational Culture: New Perspectives on Administrative Theory and Practice*, Chicago: University of Chicago Press.

SERGIOVANNI, T.J. and STARRATT, R. (1979) *Supervision: Human Perspectives*, New York: McGraw-Hill.

SHEEHY, G. (1997) *New Passages: Mapping Your Life Across Time*, London: HarperCollins.

SHEIVE, L.T. and SCHOENHEIT, M.B. (1987) *Leadership: Examining the Elusive*, Alexandria, Va: Association of Supervision and Curriculum Development.

STARRATT, R.J. (1990) *The Drama Of Schooling and The Schooling Of Drama*, London: Falmer Press.

STARRATT, R.J. (1993) *The Drama of Leadership*, London: Falmer Press.

STARRATT, R.J. (1995) *Leaders with Vision: The Quest for School Renewal*, Thousand Oaks, CA: Corwin.

STARRATT, R.J. (1996) *Transforming Educational Administrators — Meaning, Community and Excellence*, New York: McGraw-Hill.

STEINHOFF, C.R. and OWENS, R.G. (1989) 'The organisational culture assessment inventory: A metaphorical analysis in educational settings,' *Journal of Educational Administration*, **2**, 3, pp. 17–23.

STOGDILL, R. and COONS, A.E. (eds) (1957) *Leader Behavior: Its Description and Measurement*, Ohio: Ohio State University Press.

SUGARMAN, L. (1992) *Life Span Development: Concepts, Theories and Interventions*, London: Routledge.

TANNENBAUM, R.T. and SCHMIDT, W.H. (1958) 'How to choose a leadership pattern,' *Harvard Business Review*, **36**, 2, pp. 95–101.

TETLOW, J. (1989) *Choosing Christ in the World*, St. Louis: Institute of Jesuit Sources.

TOFFLER, A. (1970) *Future Shock*, London: The Bodley Head.

TOFFLER, A. (1981) *The Third Wave*, London: Pan Books.

TUOHY, D. (1995) 'Teacher self-evaluation: Discipline or dyslexia in a learning organisation,' *Irish Educational Studies*, **14**, pp. 64–82.

TUOHY, D. and COGHLAN, D. (1994) 'Integrating teacher and school development through organisational levels,' *Oideas*, **42**, pp. 83–97.

TUOHY, D. and COGHLAN, D. (1997) 'Development in schools: A systems approach based on organisational levels,' *Educational Management and Administration*, **29**, 1, pp. 65–77.

VROOM, V.H. (1964) *Work and Motivation*, New York: John Wiley.

WAUGH, R.F. and PUNCH, K.F. (1987) 'Teacher receptivity to systemwide change in the implementation stage,' *Review of Educational Research*, **57**, 3, pp. 237–54.

WEBER, S. and MITCHELL, C. (1995) *'That's funny, you don't look like a teacher': Interrogating Images and Identity in Popular Culture*, London: Falmer Press.

WESTOBY, A. (ed.) (1988) *Culture and Power in Educational Organizations*, Milton Keynes: Open University Press.

WHEATLEY, M.J. (1992) *Leadership and the New Science: Learning about Organization from an Orderly Universe*, San Francisco: Berrett-Koehler.

WILHELM, W. (1996) 'Learning from past leaders,' in HESSELBEIN, F., GOLDSMITH, M. and BECKHARD, R. (eds) *The Leader of the Future*, San Francisco: Jossey-Bass, 221–6.

ZAIS, R.S. (1976) *Curriculum: Principles and Foundations*, New York: Harper and Row.

# Index

ability 128–9
accountability 128
achievement 123, 140–4
actions, artefacts and 12
adaptation 45, 98–100, 102–3
affectivity and change 163–4
affiliation profiles 144–6
age and learning 143
alienation 104–5
Archimedes 139
Argyris, C. 60
Aristotle 120
artefacts
    cultural 12–14, 16, 19, 22–3, 28,
      33–4, 38
    curriculum and 146
    participation and 43–4
    school and 110, 113, 123
    teacher development and 165
*As You Like It* (Shakespeare) 59
assessment 126, 136, 143–4, 151, 178
assumptions
    culture 26, 28, 32, 38, 41
    exploration of 185
    leadership 167
    participation 43–5, 51–2
    school 109–13, 117–18, 120–1
    school culture 9–24
    systems models 122–3, 131
    teacher development 124–65
    typologies of schools 86, 92, 106
attendance 53
attitudes 20, 83–6, 92, 147, 161–3, 165
authority 43, 103, 122–3, 153
autonomy 155

behaviour 21, 83–4, 123
beliefs 20, 118, 163, 182–3
belonging 9, 44, 46, 85, 89, 164
beneficiaries typology (Blau-Scott)
    85–94, 102
Bennis, W. 52, 174
Biggs, J.B. 137, 143
Bindhi, H. 168
Blake, R. 170
Blanchard, K.H. 171
Blau, P.M. 5, 85, 86–94, 102, 105
Block, P. 168, 182
Bolman, L.G. 174
bonding 45–7
Bottery, M.P. 174
Brooks, J.G. and M.G. 1
bureaucrats, teachers as 156–7
Burns, J. 168
businesses-for-profit 87, 89–90, 92–4

calculative participation 105
calculative values 123
career
    anchors (Schein) 153–5, 161
    development 27, 30, 46–7, 52, 97,
      144, 148–9, 173
    locals and cosmopolitans (Gouldner)
      156–8, 161
Carlson, R.O. 5, 85, 94–102
Carlyle, Thomas 2
*Catcher in the Rye* (Salinger) 20
challenges 27–8, 155
characteristics
    of culture 9
    of leadership 167–76